News Values

News Values

Paul Brighton and Dennis Foy

SAGE Publications
Los Angeles ▪ London ▪ New Delhi ▪ Singapore

First published 2007

SAGE Publications Ltd
1 Oliver's Yard
55 City Road
London EC1Y 1SP

SAGE Publications Inc.
2455 Teller Road
Thousand Oaks, California 91320

SAGE Publications India Pvt Ltd
B 1/I 1 Mohan Cooperative Industrial Area
Mathura Road
New Delhi 110 044

SAGE Publications Asia-Pacific Pte Ltd
33 Pekin Street #02-01
Far East Square
Singapore 048763

Library of Congress Control Number: 2007922104

British Library Cataloguing in Publication data

A catalogue record for this book is available from the
British Library

ISBN 978-1-4129-4599-8
ISBN 978-1-4129-4600-1 (pbk)

Typeset by C&M Digitals (P) Ltd, Chennai, India

To my mother Beryl Brighton, and the memory of my father Doug Brighton
Paul Brighton

For Pat, who is always there for me
Dennis Foy

Contents

Acknowledgements

Alistair Coull of the *Liverpool Daily Post*; Charlotte Gapper of the Press Association; UoW colleagues Alan Apperley, Aidan Byrne, Dorothy Hobson, Steve Jacobs, William B Pawlett, Jackie Pieterick, Marc Scholes, Sarah Williams – and countless students at undergraduate and postgraduate levels whose contributions within seminars and debates have helped inform our choices of topics; colleagues at Han Chiang College Penang and UCSI Kuala Lumpur; various members of the Royal Television Society and the Radio Academy; Katy Johnstone, Louise Denham, Kasel Kundola, and colleagues in several BBC newsrooms; the staff of Kic FM for the use of their studios to record interviews for this book.

Introduction

So what is wrong with Galtung and Ruge's News Value system?

Gay vicar in mercy dash to palace

That allegedly was the ultimate English tabloid newspaper headline; it combines suggestions of sexual deviancy, charity and the Royal Family in one neat banner; as close as the tabloid press can get to a full house, the editorial equivalent of a royal flush in poker. It has been impossible to isolate the source of the 'headline'; some say it was a group of bored sub-editors on the *News of the World*, others attribute it to relaxing *Sun* journalists in the pub nearest the office after finishing a shift. Just as likely is that it is an urban myth. But buried deep inside that apocryphal headline is a certain truth; it is the confluence of several contemporary news values.

It is news values that give journalists and editors a set of rules – often intangible, informal, almost unconscious elements – by which to work, from which to plan and execute the content of a publication or a broadcast. In its purest sense everything that happens in the world is a new event, and somebody, somewhere, will have some level of interest in that occurrence. But what takes it from being new to becoming news? The set of values applied by different media – local, regional, national and international, print, television, radio, internet, bulletin board – are as varied as the media themselves. Some form of matrix system is needed to prioritise those events, to filter them into levels of applicability and relevance to the audience. In an attempt to rationalise and analyse this process, Norwegian social scientists Johan Galtung and Mari Homboe Ruge developed and eventually published a paper on this in the 1965 edition of the *Journal of International Peace Studies*. Entitled *Structuring and Selecting News*, they began by analysing the output of a cluster of newspapers in their native land, and identified a number of common strands – the presence of élite nations or individuals, the cultural proximity of events to the intended audience and so forth – then went on to create a system for prioritising news. This was ground-breaking research, and from its initial publication has become what is in essence the core text for the process; everything that has followed has been built on those initial findings.

But there are substantial problems with the Galtung and Ruge thesis. Firstly comes the matter of their agenda; both Johan Galtung and Mari Homboe Ruge were essentially concerned with the reportage of conflicts within newspapers from the perspective of academics with a specific interest in peace studies. Secondly there is the issue of the narrow range of publications which they studied, and thirdly there is the fact that the research was carried out in Norway. While it appears impossible to argue against some of the findings of this team, there are, we feel, some areas where opportunities exist to develop further some of their key findings with a view to developing a pattern applicable to the media of the 21st century. When Galtung and Ruge were devising their theories broadcast news was still in the first flush of youth, newspapers were still essentially serious publications, and the internet did not exist. There was little trans-national broadcasting (unless one counts Voice of America, which was essentially propagandist, or Radio Luxembourg, which was essentially a popular music station and not one renowned for either the quality or quantity of its news) and most broadcast news stories based on foreign events relied on film shipped physically from the place of event to the home country of the broadcast organisation, where it would be mediated prior to broadcast. Today the live 'to camera' piece is commonplace in television news, and this brings with it both rewards and problems. As John Simpson pointed out: 'Live reporting is the hardest and most rewarding broadcasting you can do, and live reporting from a battlefield is harder than any other kind' (2002: 408). Simpson was referring to a specific report he had made from a war zone – Afghanistan – which had required him to deliver, via a videophone, a live report for broadcast on BBC Television News. The subtext to his comments is that there is rarely time consciously to mediate the news being delivered, and the process of a live transmission means that there is no room for any process of remediation by the editorial staff in London, thousands of miles away from Simpson's vantage point in the Shomali Valley, near Kabul.

A key element of the work of Galtung and Ruge hinges on the audience; the issues of resonance and cultural proximity discussed in *Structuring and Selecting News* relies on an expectation that the audience will fulfil their half of the bargain. But there are huge sub-divisions in audience within a country – and within a region made up of several nations, such as the Pacific Rim that is covered by Star, Europe as covered by Sky and BBC News 24 – and much of the world that is reached by either BBC World Service radio or BBC World television – the likelihoods of confluence and a common cultural proximity are virtually nil.

An often-used (some might say overused) quotation, 'People everywhere confuse what they read in newspapers with news' (A. J. Liebling: *The New Yorker*

1965) leads, in an oblique manner, to another problematic area when it comes to any rigid application of Galtung and Ruge's values, the so-called op-ed (opinion-editorial) column. Opinion and editorial is often a longer view of a news item; sometimes this will be dealing with issues for which there was insufficient space in the original item, in others it draws in other, associated, news items which can be converged into a single column. Often charged with the personality of the writer (hence the opinion element of the nomenclature) these are still news items, but can often be quite some way removed from the core values that were applied to the initial story. When it comes to rolling news items – a storyline which gradually unfolds as more information becomes available – then the problems of applying the Galtung and Ruge values can become more problematic still. This is especially true when the 'citizen journalist' is responsible for propagation of news; another trend that did not exist in Galtung and Ruge's day, but is viewed by industry observers as having an increasing value. Citizen journalists are not usually trained or skilled, but they nevertheless abide by some unconscious adherence to conventions. We will investigate those protocols.

Then there is the matter of those strange, sometimes quirky, stories which emerge on a daily basis; typical of these is an item from Reuters news agency's feed on 4 August 2005: 'A bid by Mexican police to polish their image backfired after youngsters at a police summer camp were filmed chanting that they had killed their dads and tossed their sisters into ditches'. The value of such items can be in direct opposition to one of Galtung and Ruge's core values, that of cultural proximity; it is precisely because such stories are in opposition to the culture of anywhere other than where they originate, in this case Mexico, that they work.

Further problems arise when proactive media story placement agents, the so-called 'spin doctors' and public relations consultancies, have been involved in the news generation process prior to it reaching the publishing or broadcast organisation. In essence The Story has already been through a mediation process and in pure terms is already corrupted; the difficulty is squaring this with 'pure' news values. And so it goes; each new element that has been introduced since that first report was published in 1965 has had an impact on the ultimate value of some of the parameters set by those two Norwegian researchers.

Yet despite these various difficulties, there is still a place for a matrix which sets out the variables and allows them to be applied to news stories as a means of prioritising items. Through the course of this book we will analyse the various branches of the media and its key players, with a view to establishing the values which apply for this great new age of media.

One of the other major changes in the news landscape since Galtung and Ruge is the increasing self-awareness of news, and its growing reliance on considerations of style as well as substance. This manifests itself in differing ways according to which news medium is under discussion. But its effects are profound on the nature of news values in practice. For instance we shall note how, in broadcast news, issues of programme format contend with more traditional news values in determining which stories are selected for mainstream network television news bulletins. We shall look at specific instances where, for example, stories have been included or dropped for reasons more to do with what might be termed 'aesthetic balance' than on purely journalistic criteria. We shall see how this can take a number of forms. For example, on grounds of subject balance: if there is a story about famine in Niger, how likely is it that another, entirely separate famine in, say, Chad will be extensively reported on the same programme? It may be included as an add-on to the main report, but it is highly unlikely to merit a separate package; whereas, on another night, it would be given much more prominence.

Similarly, we shall examine how stories' inclusion and prominence in television bulletins will be shaped by stylistic factors. We shall investigate the role of story treatments in broadcast news – such aspects as the overall 'shape' of the programme package, the live two-way exchange between studio and on-location reporter, live voice-piece. These and other factors affect the editorial decision-making process. We shall then argue that balancing these treatment genres is as important as story selection. This, too, is having a great effect on news values in practice.

We will also consider how far the same issues govern story selection in radio. Here, too, there is an increasingly self-conscious use of these stylistic factors as well as the exercise of more conventional news values judgements. We shall investigate whether these factors play the same prominent role as in television news, and whether their effects are similarly far-reaching.

We shall examine the role of planning in news output and investigate what might be called the growing grip of the news diary – the tendency for news agendas to be set well in advance, and only exceptionally departed from. Do we see further instances of this in the rise of the 'anniversary story'? and in the increasing popularity of themed news? Are these merely a symptom of a desire to fill a blank news diary well in advance, or a demonstration of the rise of what some see as slanted or biased journalism?

This will lead to a review of another of the huge changes in recent journalistic history: the change in the role of the newspaper. Many journalists and academics have remarked upon the evolution from fact to comment in much print journalism – what Andrew Marr describes as 'the growth of an office-based, editorial culture, rather than a reporters' journalism' (2004: 115). There is also a widespread assumption that this has been in response to the rise of the 24-hour broadcast news cycle; and of the change in people's reading expectations, rather than habits. However, the same close attention has not been paid to what this means in practice for the exercise of news values in practice. If we read papers less to find out **what** has happened, and more to find out **why** it happened, and **how** we should think about it, what, then, are the implications for working journalists? Is this simply another version of what used to be regarded as the divide between 'ideological' newspaper coverage, and 'unbiased' broadcast coverage? Is it, further, a recognition that the old, convenient divide between news and comment – frail at the best of times – is now a substantially meaningless concept?

Finally, there is the specific area of news items used in weekly newspapers, periodicals and magazines. These have less immediacy than hourly or daily news items, but must still be news in some form or other. What criteria are adopted in the decision to include or exclude events? This is an area that has been overlooked, unfairly, in most studies; we intend to rectify that situation.

In order to explore our thesis, we shall conduct a detailed analysis of news output in print, broadcast and new media. We shall also – applying the perspectives of working journalists and broadcasters, as well as academics – pay due heed to the compromises and pragmatic considerations which often inform news judgements. As well as reflecting on the continuing relevance of some of Galtung and Ruge's concepts, we shall also examine their shortcomings as guides to the 21st century news landscape. We will also put forward a set of formulae to replace them, a flexible set of rules which are more appropriate for this digital age of converged media forms.

Analysing News Values

The Key Analysis of Galtung and Ruge's Structuring and Selecting News

Many books on journalism and news contain sections which either attempt to define and codify news values, or review previous attempts to do so. It is important to look at some of these previous attempts to set the scene for our own analysis, and to help us see how the authors' own backgrounds tend to determine which kind of news values analysis they conduct.

Broadly, previous accounts of news values tend to be of two kinds. The first examines news stories from the perspective of the working journalist, and tries to isolate the features of an event which make it likely to qualify as newsworthy. The second attempts to take a broader approach – incorporating areas such as ideology, cultural conditioning, technological determinism and others. We will review both of these approaches in detail but will also argue that a *third* approach is needed in conjunction with these two existing schools of thought. This third approach is necessary because of changes within individual media, and because of a shift in the nature of the relationships between providers and consumers of news. (Terms such as 'professional', 'sociological' and 'cultural' are used as convenient and recognisable shorthand in this context.)

In their seminal article on the process of establishing a set of values which turn an event into a news item, Johan Galtung and Mari Ruge drew an analogy with radio broadcasts; in essence, for broadcasts to mean something they need to make a cultural connection with their audiences. If they do not do so, they are simply a form of noise, essentially worthless. The key premise of their argument is that we need to attune to events for them to mean anything, and for them to mean anything they need to have some form of cultural connection.

Galtung and Ruge wrote as social scientists, as people to whom human behaviour and all that it entails is of significance and interest. The magnitude of this perspective cannot be overstated; it sets the core agenda and colours their work. A journalist, reporter or researcher would take a different perspective, one which is determined, at least in part, by the audience at which that publication of broadcast is targeted. As Max Hastings observed when he became editor of the *Daily Telegraph*: 'Readers have no rational idea of what they do or do not want in their newspaper – by proxy they employ editors to decide for them.' (Hastings, 2002: 100).

It is worth beginning with a brief overview of the criteria that Galtung and Ruge decided would best fit their prognosis, in the order in which they were introduced to the readers of 1965:

Relevance   The effect on a likely or potential audience.

Timeliness   Is it a recent occurrence? Is there a good chance the audience will previously have been unaware of this development?

Simplification   Can it be described simply and straightforwardly?

Predictability   Could the event have been foreseen and, if appropriate, planned for?

Unexpectedness   Was it something entirely out of the ordinary, and not capable of being planned for in advance?

Continuity   Is it a new and further development in a sequence already established?

Composition   Is it particularly suitable to the demands of that medium or news outlet?

Élite peoples   Is the subject of the story already famous?

Élite nations   Does it affect our nation, or nations we consider important?

Negativity   Is bad news always likely to be good news to the journalistic community?

Galtung and Ruge applied a further set of qualifiers which affect their core value system:

Frequency   The time span needed for an event to unfold itself and acquire meaning.

Amplitude   Threshold expands beyond the normal, and the unexpected becomes news.

Clarity   the less ambiguity a signal has, the more the event will be noticed

Meaningfulness   Cultural relevance and social consonance or dissonance of an event.

Predictability   Expect and/or desire an event to happen, and it becomes a news item.

Continuum   Once an event has become news it gathers its own momentum.

Composition   Internal relevance of items within a programme or publication, as a system for determining running order.

Naturally, these headings will be considered, along with examples and possible revisions, during the course of this book. Galtung and Ruge's work remains an ideal starting-point for any serious discussion of news values.

From a social scientist's perspective, there is much in favour of their analysis. From an editorial perspective, it is less satisfactory. There is, for instance, no room within these criteria for individual perspective or ambition of a news gatherer, of a publisher, of an editor. No room for the corruption that comes from a publisher's or broadcaster's reliance on advertising revenue – revenue that could be compromised by an adverse piece of editorial work. Nor is there room for the quasi-political manoeuvring that is integral to the pacts between the angels and devils of the public relations and journalistic trades. Such pacts are made on a daily basis – and it is for the reader to decide which of the two types, angels or devils, the two opposite branches of the news generation and reportage industry fall. Not that it is always the case that those people stay on the same side of the fence at all times; they can jump from one side to the other and back again, dependent on the story. Or from one job to the other, as Alastair Campbell proved (whose notoriety in a high-powered public relations role was cemented by a six-year stint as Director of Communications for the Labour government of Tony Blair). Campbell worked his way up from being a junior reporter to becoming Political Editor of the *Daily Mirror*, before resigning to become spokesman for Blair when the latter was still in opposition. Since resigning his government post in 2003 Campbell has returned to writing occasional columns in newspapers. We will examine more closely Campbell and his role in the news processes surrounding the Iraq invasion of 2003 in a subsequent chapter.

Since Galtung and Ruge wrote, other media academics have revisited their conclusions, and suggested amendments. For instance, Denis MacShane (1979: 46) subdivided newsworthy events into the following categories:

Conflict
Hardship and danger to the community
Unusualness (oddity, novelty)
Scandal
Individualism

It is worth noting that MacShane was writing as a practising journalist; though he later became a professional politician and served as a British government minister in the Blair administration. Hartley (1982) attempted to account for differing news agendas as being driven by the following areas: politics, the economy, foreign affairs, domestic stories, one-off stories and sport.

As we can see already, the danger in attempting to codify news values is that we can end up simply listing subject headings of stories – almost like an account of the sections of an extensive broadsheet newspaper.

Harcup and O'Neill's (2001) study of the printed press resulted in their attempt to revise and update Galtung and Ruge. They identified these headings:

Power élite
Celebrity
Entertainment
Surprise
Bad news
Good news

Magnitude
Relevance
Follow-ups
Media agenda

Some of these are more concerned with the subjects of, and actors within, the story (power élite, celebrity), while others are more conceptual (relevance), and yet others are accounts of media practice (follow-ups, media agenda). All three of these areas will be considered in detail later. Harrison, summarising previous authors' conclusions (2006: 137) also lists a number of criteria by which news stories can be judged and listed:

Availability of pictures or film (for TV)
Short, dramatic occurrences (which can be sensationalised)
Novelty value
Capable of simple reporting
Grand scale
Negative (violence, crime, confrontation, catastrophe)
Unexpected
Or expected
Relevance/meaning
Similar events already in the news
Balanced programme
Élite people/nations
Personal or human interest framing

These, too, contain elements of media practice (the creation of what is perceived as a balanced programme) as well as more recognisably journalistic headings.

Sociological and cultural accounts of news values

This is a more contested, varied and complex area. A number of widely different approaches have been taken. Harrison (2006: 18–38) refers to three types of views of news – common sense (broadly from the perspective of the consumer), practitioner (as reviewed above) and academic. Within the academic, she distinguishes between Marxist/political, culturalist, organisational product and new media theory approaches.

In this section, we will look at how previous academic discussions of news values – often within the areas outlined by Harrison – have approached the question of news values.

One of the most influential analysts of news values is Stuart Hall. In 'The determination of news photographs' (Cohen and Young, 1981), Hall specifically distinguishes between what he terms 'formal' news values (broadly the approach analysed in the last section, starting with Galtung and Ruge) and 'ideological' news values. His 'formal' news values are:

Linkage   Is the story linked, or capable of being linked, with a prior event, happening, occurrence?

Recency   Has it happened recently?

Newsworthiness of event/person   This criterion may be thought to pose or beg more questions than it answers!

Crucially, Hall goes on to distinguish between the sort of *formal* news values outlined by Galtung and Ruge (and Ostgaard), and what he terms *ideological* news values. He contrasts the foreground structure of news and the events reported with the hidden 'deep structure'. This involves what he describes as the 'consensus knowledge' of the world, which, he argues, provides a framework within which the news operates.

Within Hall's broad approach, there are several views of the extent to which the operation of news within a broadly manufactured consensus of values is conscious or unconscious. Young (Cohen and Young, 1981: 393–421) refers to a number of theories of news as crisis. As well as the market and the consensus paradigm theories, to which we will return, he also includes the manipulative theory. As its name implies, this infers a conscious manipulation of news agendas and news organisations – with consequent effects on news values – by individual proprietors or the power of market capitalism. This is an area of media activity which has also been explored in some depth by Noam Chomsky and by Robert McChesney, amongst others. The outcome is the perpetuation and reinforcement of market capitalist and social consensus values. While the role of individual journalists may not be a conscious participation, the net effect of their activity is the maintenance of the effects of such manipulation. Young himself, it should be noted, does not subscribe to this view.

Hall also does not see this 'consensus knowledge' as the result of an overt conspiracy by media practitioners and journalists. Writing with Chritcher, Jefferson, Clarke, and Roberts (in Cohen and Young, 1981), Hall attributes the reinforcement of such value systems to:

1. **Time pressures in newsrooms** leading to the increased reliance on 'pre-scheduled events'
2. **Notions of impartiality, balance and objectivity**. This, they argue, leads to extensive reliance on 'accredited sources' which tend to be sources embodying or buttressing existing power structures. This, in turn, they argue, leads to over-representation of existing power élites in news output. This results in yet further perpetuation and strengthening of the existing power élites. These power élites become what Hall *et al.* refer to as Primary Definers of the news discourse and the news agendas. They have the power, consequently, to become framers of the contexts within which problems are addressed and discussed.

Within this context, Hall et al. talk about structural imperatives, rather than an overt conspiracy of the type implied in Young's 'Manipulative theory.' This, they argue, embraces:

Selectivity   Different slants on the reporting of events.

Coding   Use of specific types of language and imagery.

Also influential, but adopting a different starting-point, is the work of Herbert Gans. His 1979 book *Deciding What's News* was reissued on its 25th anniversary in 2004 with a new Preface, taking (brief) account of developments in the intervening years. In his original text, in an important discussion of story selection, Gans (2004:78–79) outlines four theories of the way such selections and decisions are made:

Journalistic judgement

Organisational requirements   Commercial pressures – including circulation/ratings; the structure and hierarchy of the organisation and its effects on story choices

The Event/Mirror Theory   The idea that journalism and the journalist, in Shakespeare's words, are holding a mirror up to nature

External determinism   This involves factors such as Technology; Economy; Ideology; Culture; Audience, and Sources

Equally important is Gans's subsequent categorisation of criteria for story suitability. He enumerates the following:

Importance   Impact (e.g. on numbers of people). Past or future significance.

Interest   People. Role reversals. Human interest. The expose. The Hero. 'Gee-whiz' stories.

Factors of the product   The Medium. The Format.

Novelty   ('Internal' novelty. The news peg. The repetition taboo. Fresh v. Stale news. The avoidance of excessive freshness – e.g. stories no-one else will yet run).

Story quality   (Action. Pace. Completeness. Clarity quickly obtainable. Aesthetic/technical features).

Story balance   (Story mixture. By subject. By geography. By demography. Political).

Competition   (Within the same industry).

Naturally, we shall have cause to revisit many of these in subsequent chapters. They represent an important (and perhaps underappreciated) watershed in the evaluation of news and news judgements because of Gans's concern with formal, stylistic and aesthetic factors, as well as what Hall termed the Formal (or professional) and Ideological approaches to news values. It is also important that, unlike many writers on the subject, he was specifically studying broadcast as well as print media.

Interestingly, Gans (2004) also includes a section on the values that he sees news as upholding or reinforcing. He was writing, of course, in an American context. The values are:

Ethnocentrism

Altruistic democracy

Responsible capitalism

Small-town pastoralism
Individualism
Moderatism

These may be worth assessing in conjunction with Van Ginneken's attempt (quoted in Burton (2005: 282) to review generic values implicitly upheld by much journalistic output:

Economic   free enterprise/ the free market.
Social   individualism/social mobility.
Political   pragmatism/moderation.
Lifestyle   rationalism/autonomy.
Ideological   'we have no ideology'.

Lule (2001) approached from the perspective of "Myths" of News, and felt able to use the following archetypes from within the pantheon of mythologies as staples of news stories:

Victim   death as sacrifice.
Scapegoat   challenge/ignore social beliefs.
Hero   humble birth, a quest, a triumph, the return.
The good mother   a model of goodness.
Trickster   crude, stupid, with animal instincts.
The other world   'Our' way of life as against 'Others'.
Flood   the humbling power of nature.

This last, incidentally, echoes Bourdieu's passage in *On Television* (1998: 7–8) on the procession of random and irrationally-linked natural disasters, famines and other events which he sees as symptomatic of the malaise of television news.

There is another element of the categorisation of news values which we should note; Harrison (2006: 137–48) follows up the enumeration of news values noted above with a consideration of further causes of the evolution of news values. These are:

Socialisation of journalists.
The routinisation of journalistic practice.
Views of impartiality and objectivity.

Overlapping with, and drawing on, Hall, Gans and others, these look at other factors potentially influencing news judgements (and thus news values). **Socialisation** refers to the tendency of newsrooms and news organisations to develop their own distinctive cultures – resulting in shared or common news values, albeit often instinctively acquired rather than consciously articulated. **Routinisation** of practice (extensively studied by Gans and others) takes account of the development of links between sources and news providers on the one hand and journalists on the other. This is particularly likely to occur with 'beat' reporters (covering a particular area or institution), and with subject-based correspondents (health, education, lobby, etc.). (It is also, incidentally, likely to be increasingly common in war reporting with the increase in the practice of 'embedding' journalists with particular military units.) The ideals of impartiality and objectivity also informs developing news values by entrenching the practices of:

Verifying facts.
Adducing supporting evidence.
Considering conflicting possibilities.
Attribution to sources (and others as appropriate).

Allan (2004: 60–62) approaches definitions of newsworthiness from the perspective of the News Net (as outlined by Tuchman, 1978). This is based on the notions of geographic territoriality, organisational specialisation, and topical specialisation. A link is then made to a range of other influential factors: economic and profit pressures on the organisation; daily production schedules; routinising the uncertainty of future happenings to fill story quotas; anticipation or pre-planning of news-as-event; and the role of new technology.

Allan also quotes Bell (1991) on the over-access to news agendas of the 'pre-existing text'. 'A story which is marginal in news terms but written and available may be selected ahead of a much more newsworthy story which has to be written and researched from the ground up' (1991:59). As we note elsewhere, the increasing reliance on planning diaries and early decisions on running orders are a prominent feature of broadcast news as well as the newspapers Bell specifically studied.

Venables, in *Making Headlines* (2005: 7-1 to 7-24), in addition to summarising previous attempts to codify news values, takes a somewhat different approach. Invoking anthropology and evolutionary psychology, he also sees news in terms of 'risk signals'. Within more traditional concepts like 'boundaries of relevance' [I am more likely to be interested in my neighbourhood than in a far-away country with which I have no links], he cites our reactions to the likelihood of personal danger to ourselves or those we know as important constituents of news values. Uncertainty, unexpectedness, negativity and the awareness and perception of risk all feed into a formula for news. News (N) is a function of change (C) and security concern (Sc). Or, more concisely (2005).

$$N = f(C, Sc)$$

As Venables notes, this is similar to the formula outlined by the human ecologist sandman (1993): public perception of risk is a function of hazard and outrage. Or (2005):

$$R = f(H, O)$$

Meanwhile, here, from an altogether simpler age of journalism, is an interesting insight into news values in practice. Reuters, in 1890, codified the list of events that would trigger their 'Special Service'. They were:

> The wreck of an ocean liner or steamship.
> A calamitous railway accident.
> A fire or explosion involving serious loss of life.
> A destructive earthquake, cyclone or inundation.
> Especially startling crimes and outrages. ('Mere brutal murders and domestic tragedies, such as occur almost daily in every part of the world, SHOULD NOT BE NOTICED AT ALL'.)
> Popular disturbances.
> An attempt upon the life of a monarch or statesman, or the discovery of some far-reaching plot. (Storey, Reuters' Century, 1951: 110).

Some of these values tend to be taken as axiomatic and on face value by most working journalists. However, they are the subject of much debate by academic critics of journalism. This will be considered as we examine different media.

As we see, all previous attempts to study and systematise news values have tended to fall mainly or solely into one of the three camps we have identified: the journalistic/professional/formal; the ideological/culturalist; and the aesthetic or medium-driven. Of these, the third has received the least attention. Partly, this is because it is more difficult for media studies academics or sociologists to factor in these demands unless they have worked extensively as news professionals. Even extensive field observation of the kind carried out by Gans and others is not quite able to replace the daily experience of professional work in a newsroom or news environment (and the resulting 'socialisation' that we have noted). Working journalists tend to become uncharacteristically inarticulate when asked for their own philosophy of news values. Answers tend to be like the one quoted by Bourdieu (1998: 26) 'It's obvious' or 'You just *know*'.

Similarly, many journalists tend to be resistant to the approach taken by Hall, Young and other sociologist students of media. Replies tend to be of the 'We're not that gullible' variety. That, however, raises separate questions about the difference between the responses of individual journalists and the collectivity of a news organisation, industry, or entire culture.

In addition, it is perhaps only relatively recently that media critics have become truly aware of the extent to which considerations of house style and aesthetics have come to affect news values not just in print media but in the broadcast sector. Accordingly, as we explore news values in operation across a range of media, this, too, will become one of our principal areas of interest.

With specific regard to Galtung and Ruge's criteria, it a worth taking a detailed look at how they looked at each issue raised – and how their findings have been altered by changes in the media landscape. The world which was occupied by Galtung and Ruge was a quite different place to that which we occupy today. Live television news did not exist per se, nor did real-time contributions from reporters or journalists into radio news programmes. Newspapers relied on material coming in – often by telex, a forerunner of the fax machine – from their own or retained staff, augmented by the major news wire agency services such as Associated Press, Reuters, United Press International or other similar organisations. Press deadlines were determined by the printers, and provided they were met then the pressure lifted immediately. This combination meant that there was invariably time to reflect on events, to mediate them and structure them into a form that was in accordance with the expectation of the readers and with the personal preferences of the senior management of the publishing or broadcasting organisation. In short, there was time for 'the event to unfold itself and acquire meaning.' (Galtung and Ruge, 1965: 53). Today's media climate makes frequency a different matter entirely.

The pinnacle of on-the-fly reportage, live to camera with no time for any process of mediation, was the attack on the World Trade Center on September 11 2001. New York is a base for not just its native media operations – the *New York Times, Daily News, Post, Observer* and countless smaller newspapers – but also to a wide number of broadcast organisations including television stations which are part of ABC, Fox, Warner Brothers, CBS, NBC and PBS, and a wider-still number of radio stations belonging to all of the major national and international players, along with independent broadcast organisations. In addition to these, major international broadcast and print organisations have their own staff based in New York, as do the likes of UPN, Reuters, AP and the other international news-gathering organisations.

In purely practical terms, this meant that the moment news broke that a hijacked aircraft had been piloted into the North Tower of the World Trade Center at 8:46 a.m. local time, almost every news organisation turned its attention – and its cameras – onto the scene. As a consequence, when the second aircraft slammed into the second, South, tower of the Center at 9:03 a.m. the witnesses were watching events as they unfolded, and in many cases running live broadcast events as they happened. Any opportunity for the elapsed time to be used as a gap for the events to 'acquire meaning' was purely coincidental. The reportage, in whatever form it took, was instinctive on the part of the reporters, who knew that this was an event which needed no time to transform into news – and those who watched or listened around the globe as events unfolded knew with equal instinctiveness that there was no need for any mediation; what they were seeing was pure, unfiltered news.

Ironically, mediation came later in the day and was carried out to tone down the impact of some of the images – images which had initially been broadcast live, or photographed and published as quickly as possible. The prime example is that hundreds of people were filmed or photographed as they apparently sought to minimise their own potential suffering by jumping from the burning and badly-damaged buildings. These had the effect of personalising the impact of the attacks, for which Al Qa'eda were quickly (and correctly) held to blame. Subsequent broadcasts of the filmed footage was edited down to depersonalise the events, and images of those who jumped were rarely shown again. That aside, the events were allowed to unfold almost unedited for the first several hours, and the major broadcast media players seemed content to let the story develop live.

Peter Jennings (who, until the onset of his fatal illness in April 2004, was anchor at ABC, where he presented *World News Tonight*) was one such heavyweight brought in by his employer, and who exemplified the initial reaction. Brought onto air almost 12 hours ahead of his usual shift, he led that station's news presentation for a stint that went on, almost uninterrupted, for more than two days, and made comments recalled four years on, in his obituary:

> 'This is what it looked like moments ago' Mr. Jennings said at one point that first morning, as he introduced a piece of videotape recorded moments earlier in Lower Manhattan. 'My God! The southern tower, 10:00 Eastern Time this morning, just collapsing on itself. This is a place where thousands of people worked. We have no idea what caused this'. (*New York Times* 1 August 2005)

Simultaneously, newspapers were attempting to make sense of events – they had the benefit of time before their next press deadlines – and were able to dig more deeply into the background of the attacks. But between these two branches of the media a third phenomenon was beginning to flex its muscles, the web-log. Increasingly known by the easier diminutive of blogs, it is tempting to dismiss these as unstructured rants by amateur would-be journalists. But it is not always thus:

> … with traditional news outlets struggling to make sense of conflicting reports in the minutes and hours that followed the four blasts, many people turned to the internet… Anthony Barnett, editor-in-chief of global politics and culture site *Open Democracy*, which runs its own blog, has also noted the change: 'The blog mechanism has come in since 9/11 and has created quite a natural form' he says. For *Open Democracy* and others, including some traditional media owners such as the *Guardian* and the *New York Times*, the blog provides an increasingly crucial addition to their core online services. (MediaGuardian, 11 July 2005)

However, there is a *caveat lector* attached to that comment; in that same column the risk of the blog developing into a forum for material which 'descended into the raving and the mawkish' was mentioned. The immediacy of a web-log works both for and against the issue of news; things tend to be reported and posted onto the site as they occur, or as they are seen; but this makes no allowance for things not being what they seem. That most bloggers are amateurs, with no formal training or experience in the world of media (and the mediation processes which are integral to that craft), and are what was described in that same Guardian feature as 'the public assuming control of the newsgathering process', can be responsible for some truly vivid images. It can also be responsible for some intrusion into the privacy of others – an issue which the conventional transformation process from event to news, referred to in Galtung and Ruge's initial text, tends to filter out as was the case with people jumping from the burning twin towers of the World Trade Center.

What emerges from these illustrations is that the accepted interpretation of Galtung and Ruge's findings on frequency can no longer be applied with such stringency; the world of communications has moved on from the time when that paper was written. This is an apposite point to take a closer view at each of those criteria.

One aspect of Galtung and Ruge's findings is perhaps the least contentious of all of their posited theories; news only becomes news when it rises above (or falls below – this is a world where semantics can be everything) the base-line of other, 'normal' activities, in other words stands out from everyday, normal, life. As this section is being written, a young man was found guilty of the manslaughter of his girlfriend when she was run over by his jet-ski water sports craft during a Mediterranean vacation, and a woman was charged with abandoning her young children, after she went on holiday, leaving them behind to fend for themselves. These were both exceptional events – at any given minute there will be many thousands of people holidaying *en famille*, and there will doubtless be hundreds of people around the world riding water scooter-type machines safely, without endangering anybody else. Whenever an aeroplane crashes it is news; the many other safe flights, take-offs and landings in progress at that same instance are unexceptional. And so it goes throughout life. Common throughout the majority of news items is that they are essentially negative; the connotation is that bad news is good news.

In 1988 ITN's Martyn Lewis started a campaign to try and reverse this trend, and in his Vauxhall Lecture, said: 'The greatest journalistic challenge is to create the balance between weighing the positive and negative. It is lazy journalism to concentrate just on the negative'. He pursued this theme for some years, attracting comments both for and against his argument. For instance, columnist Minette Marrin noted:

> The newsreader Martyn Lewis must have struck a chord last week in millions of gloomy hearts with his claims that television concentrates too much on bad news. We know that good news is dull and, as they say in the business, not sexy – 'washing-machine ownership increased by 27 per cent in decade', say, would not cut much mustard – but all this dwelling on misery is very wearisome, and largely responsible for compassion fatigue. Television producers even put on items that, however sad, are not strictly national news at all – shots of ambulances at a small accidental domestic fire, for example.
>
> (*Sunday Telegraph*, 2 May 1993)

But Jonathan Freedland, another British columnist, put the opposite view neatly when he said:

> We're interested in conflict. People complain about it. People might remember the Martyn Lewis syndrome, when the TV newscaster complained that all we ever get is bad news and 'Why can't we have more happy stories about cats being rescued from trees etcetera.' He was slapped down and was told, 'That's not journalism'.
>
> (Hetherington Memorial Lecture, University of Stirling, 22 October 2003)

Of peripheral interest is that Lewis's comments were still being referred to 15 years after he first made them. But most significant is the hard fact is that bad news sells newspapers, and draws viewers and listeners to broadcast news programmes. But there are exceptions. Every weekday, the news agency service founded in 1851 by Paul Julius Reuter (to transmit stock exchange prices between London and Paris and which has since grown into one of the world's best-known press agencies) runs a service headlined 'Reuters – Oddly Enough' which gathers together strange, quirky, news items which do not fit into the main news template. Typical of these is that for 8 August 2005, which included the following headlines:

> Shanghai in frizz at hairdressers' electric larceny
> Bounty-hunters snarl Delhi traffic catching cows
> Confusion on Tour of Benelux as peloton loses its way
> Swimmer crosses Lake Superior, conquers Great Lakes
> 'How are the noodles?' Japan's PM asks astronaut
> German guide aims to bridge gulf between the sexes

None of these constitute bad news as we know it; instead they simply illustrate that life can be strange, in much the same way that British broadcaster ITN used to conclude its nightly news programme with a quirky news item. This would perhaps be a skateboarding pig, or a parrot that has learned to squawk the national anthem. The use of this device was intended to lighten the moment, and some might conclude that it was a cynical ploy to subvert perceptions, to give the impression that the people at ITN are nicer than those at arch-rivals the BBC because 'they give us something to smile about and the BBC doesn't'. But as was mentioned earlier, the core value that 'the threshold expands beyond the normal, and the unexpected becomes news' holds as true today as it did when Galtung and Ruge first set down their theories. If only their other values were as simple to follow and to concur with.

The simpler an item, the less scope there is for ambiguity, suggest Galtung and Ruge, adding: 'the less ambiguity, the more the event will be noticed' (1965: 54). But such a theory relies heavily on the ability of a journalist or reporter to take the complex and find its essence, then present that essential fact in a clear and unambiguous manner. A wonderful theory – but one which can be applied only when it is possible to distil such an essence. Given that most news broadcasts and publications are dominated by conflicts or politics – and that neither of those is mutually exclusive: quite the opposite, in fact – and that by their very nature such subjects are shrouded in euphemism, confusion, double-speak, or plain untruths – then the issue of clarity becomes almost an impossibility. Martin Bell, a former war correspondent who later became a full-time independent politician, gave one good example when he précised the difficulties of dealing with Afghanistan resistance to attacks by the Russian army: 'Where's Afghanistan? Who are the Taliban? What's it all about? The British people were lost in a Khyber Pass sandstorm...'. He went on to point out that in the 19th century a politician such as W.E. Gladstone (British Prime Minister) would have been able to spend time addressing what Bell described as an 'informed electorate' and contrasted that with today's politician, who is required to compete with proliferating broadcast media, and essentially get the message across quickly (2003: 170–1).

A subtext to Bell's comments might be that the restraints of broadcast news – where an item rarely gets more than four minutes of airtime, often half that, and as will be seen later a sizeable proportion of that is given over to imagery – makes it virtually impossible to be as clear and concise as possible without leaving out a fair amount of the detail that underlies the event. Journalists writing for 'serious' newspapers – those which allocate sufficient space to a report, feature or article, as distinct from those which rely on short, terse text to accompany sensationalist images – are more fortunate than their colleagues in the broadcast industry, but in many cases the core concept holds true – something must give in the battle between detail and information, and it is usually the detail which loses out.

Part of the problem is that, across Europe and North America – and the rest of the world will doubtless catch up soon – the battleground of politics has shifted from the debating chamber to the world's media: 'politics has moved away from the chamber of the House of Commons, out into the radio and television studios and the columns of newspapers' was how Jeremy Paxman (2002: 125) described the British process. It is likely that similar comments could be gained from pundits in other countries, or from observers of widerranging organisations such as NATO and the European Commission. This shift in place has led to a shift in policy delivery mechanisms, to align with the media which are now being used to win the hearts and minds of politicians' subjects or opponents.

One way in which politicians have found to deal with complex issues is to distil them into what might be described as 'sound-bite politics'. At his party's 2004 national conference, British Prime Minster Tony Blair appeared to display a mild distaste for this device, but was quick to lay the blame for its widespread adoption elsewhere: 'Obviously there are circumstances in which you can't tell the whole truth but the problem for modern politicians is that is the way politics is conducted — if you can't sum it up and get it across in your fifteen seconds you might as well not bother.' (*The Times*, 27 September 2004).

In today's instant media world, there is little scope for nuanced argument, and the sound-bite – which can be repeated *ad nauseum* until the next one comes along – is an established part of the armoury of a wily politician, one who knows that the right slogan-style comment can work for the campaign. There is a further reason for such comments becoming an established weapon in the battle for the hearts and minds of the electorate; the more succinct the comment, the less scope there is for its deconstruction, for the reading into it of any sub textual meanings – real or imagined. Not that such a facility stops the dedicated and the conspiracy theorists. The best example of all is possibly George H. W. Bush (American President 1989–1993) who memorably said in a speech on 19 August 1988, when campaigning 'Read my lips: No New Taxes.' Despite being two phrases, just six words, America's broadcasters and newspapers spent a considerable amount of energy unpacking what Bush said, and trying to find hidden meanings in the phrase. And of course as soon as Bush reneged on that apparent promise, the media leapt upon the contradiction.

Essentially, politicians expect this to happen; news coverage expands to fill the available space, and if that means conjectural analysis of the most straightforward quote, then so be it. But sometimes it can work the other way, too. Tony Benn, who famously quit the British House of Commons 'to spend more time with politics', once wrote that journalists in the popular press are guilty of 'remorselessly trivialising and personalising all the great and complex issues of our day to a level where they almost defy comprehension'. (1981: 115). The corrective, so far as Benn is concerned, seems to be to produce many, often lengthy, books which allow his political views free rein.

So it would seem that Galtung and Ruge, in claiming that clarity is vital, might have mis-read what they were seeing; the situation is far more complex than that, as detailed examination of specific treatments of news items will subsequently show.

Galtung and Ruge put a great deal of effort into establishing the worth of the cultural relevance and social consonance or dissonance of an event. On the face of it, there should be little to argue against these findings. But as ever, time and the changes wrought over the 40 years from the existing topography when Galtung and Ruge carried out their study of news values to the media landscape of today skews that prognosis. Firstly it assumes that there is a homogeneity, a consensus, a general agreement. There is rarely that in a household, let alone in an entire nation. That media are created to meet specific societal sub-groups gives credibility to the theory of clustering, either physically (immigrating groups of a specific ethnocentric background will often move into the same area as existing residents from that background, the so-called ghettoisation process) or by language spoken, by religious affinity or some other form of shared cultural value. Again, this will be investigated in more detail elsewhere within this book.

This means that the likelihood of all items in a news programme or in a newspaper appealing to all members of society in an equally meaningful way is highly unlikely; only when the event is a natural phenomenon of equal interest to all members of a physical society (as happened with the tsunami which struck the Indian Ocean's rim in December 2004) is such a confluence of interest likely.

Cultural expectations vary from country to country, even where there is a commonality of language; while in the USA it is relatively common to see victims of murder on nightly news programmes, they are rarely shown on British television. Similarly in Spanish-speaking South America the threshold of acceptable imagery seems to be set much lower than it is in Spain; the rolling news programmes which ran material based on the Madrid train bombings of March 2004 were sensitive to the expectations of the audience in this respect, while vivid images of damage and death caused by hurricanes is commonplace.

The essential point made by Galtung and Ruge seems to be one of comparison; we as viewers and consumers find either something with which we agree – consonance – and which aligns with our everyday lives – cultural relevance – or it is so far beyond what we would consider acceptable behaviour that its very dissonance creates a news value out of the event. The challenge to editors is to take the findings of journalists, reporters and correspondents, and turn them into something which aligns with what must amount to a greatest common denominator. That such a policy inevitably leads to the ostracism of those outside the cluster determined (or imagined?) by editors is what leads to what appears to be an insatiable thirst in some countries for televised debates based on contemporary news topics; this is not only the expected nations of Britain, Spain, Germany and the USA. The major Arabic news channel Al Jazeera routinely holds live debates, as do other stations as diverse as India's Surya TV, and HITN, the major Hispanic station. This use of live debate (plus its humour-based, ego-pricking corollary the news satire quiz or debate show such as BBC Television's *Have I Got News For You* and its radio cousin *The News Quiz*) is one way in which television and radio schedulers are able to square the circle of trying to impose common values on a diverse audience.

Newspaper publishers have an easier time of this; feedback via the letters page and in unpublished material (opinion polling is one of the several valid and effective tools used) can provide a surprisingly accurate impression of the values of a readership. Unlike broadcast news, which is free at the point of delivery, a newspaper usually requires a reader to purchase an edition. Simple logic dictates that the reader who finds him- or herself in opposition to the views of the paper will simply cease to buy that publication and move to another which is more closely aligned to expectations.

There is one element of Galtung and Ruge's work which is particularly difficult to concur with 'the event-scanner will pay particular attention to the familiar, to the culturally similar, and the culturally distant will be passed by more easily and not be noticed' (1965: 54). But this infers that only events which strike a specific chord with the viewer, reader or listener will create any kind of connection, and thus be valid news. But the opposite is often true – the unusual, that which is completely outside the standard terms of reference, is often of great interest. How else would a theorist be able to explain events such as the release from incarceration of Nelson Mandela and his subsequent rise in a largely bloodless revolution to be president of his country – complete with the overthrow of the hated apartheid regime? Or the reunification of East and West when the Berlin Wall was breached in 1989? The all-too-regular reports of famine and pestilence from all-too-many African nations? The death of Pope John Paul II? The crashing in flames of Concorde? All of these events and many, many others, are outside the standard, domestic terms of reference, but all attract huge viewing figures.

There is, however, another *caveat lector* to observe, one which can modify such a sweeping statement; the existence of a form of cultural xenophobia. Jon Snow, a stalwart of ITN and Channel 4 News in Britain, explained one typical example of this when he described the way that American television news 'mimicked the priorities of the voters [this was prior to the election which was to give Ronald Reagan a second term as President] and it was therefore rare to see a foreign news development anywhere near the top of the headlines.' Interestingly, that observation was triggered by an exceptional event, the arrival on the political scene of Mikhail Gorbachev – an event which gained headlines in the USA even though Gorbachev had not entered the United States of America on official business. The reason for American media interest was simply that Gorbachev was 'A Russian who laughed, and charmed and beguiled all those who encountered him' and who was thus a radical departure from the perceived traditional cold war enemy (Snow, 2004: 231). What is unknown is whether the voters to whom Snow referred had decided for themselves, or, as Max Hastings (2002) observed in a different context already mentioned in this book, the decision was taken by editors acting by proxy – real or imagined.

Galtung and Ruge suggest that if a receiver (their term draws on their initial metaphor of the radio system for the viewer, reader or listener) expects or

The story of the story

There are those who might bridle at the use of the term story to describe a news item, considering it a pejorative term that somehow trivialises its content. This is surely erroneous; while there are always risks attached to the use of the term – for example its association with tall stories and fairy stories – the reality is that a story simply takes a cluster of often disparate pieces, and mediates them, structures them into a cohesive narrative form. This in turn makes it more understandable for an audience which might not have the time or inclination to delve deeply into the nuanced detail of an event or sequence of events, but which may prefer to abdicate that responsibility to a professional.

BBC World Affairs Editor John Simpson, a true veteran of his game, goes into detail about what is happening during this process of mediation, and how it took him time to adjust to it:

It always used to irritate me to hear journalists referring to real incidents in the lives of real people as stories, with all the connotations that the word brings with it: dramatic incident, neatly rounded narrative, a satisfying ending. Gradually, though, I came to realise that the most important function that people like me could perform desires – sometimes both – an event to happen, a weird form of self-fulfilling prophesy will occur and it becomes a news item. This hypothesis is qualified, and placed within a framework of social sciences and human behaviour – these two were coming from a perspective of social science, remember – but the devil is in the detail, in this case one of their primary sources provides the detail which influences what amounts to Galtung and Ruge's sweeping statement. They drew on the work of two more social scientists, Berelson and Steiner, who said 'People tend to see and hear communications that are favourable to their predispositions; they are more likely to see and hear congenial communications than neutral or hostile ones. And the more interested they are in a subject, the more likely is such selective attention' (Galtung and Ruge, 1965: 62). So that's all right, then. Or is it? In reality, this hypothesis needs to be looked at in conjunction with the next of their posited theories, which provides a sense of perspective.

Galtung and Ruge consider that an event which is unanticipated or which is rare sets it apart from other more mundane occurrences. That process sees it changing from simply something that happens to something which becomes news. Buried deep in the subtext of this pair of theoretical explanations is the notion that everyday events or occurrences are of no real interest – save possibly to those who are carrying them out or those for whom they are being executed – and it is only the exceptions that become **worthy** of being called news; and even there, only if those events are of specific interest to the audience. The inference is that items which do not connect with the audience are unworthy of being considered as news items – but that comes into conflict with the issue of audience coalescence mentioned above, and leads to a further issue – that of planning a publication or a broadcast to appeal to the broadest possible audience. This is where the skill of the editor comes into its own; there is the understanding that 'you cannot please all of the people all

was indeed to tell stories. Not in the sense of making up comfortable lies to keep the viewers happy, but of providing an accurate digestible way to make sense of the confusion and apparent chaos of everyday life. (Simpson, 2002: 95)

So even old hands are recognising that stories need to be told, rather than news items simply being reported. An American academic adds:

What is news depends on what makes a good story. The news media's view of the world is influenced, and at times it might be said even distorted, by what Syracuse University Professor Thomas E. Patterson calls the 'situational bias' of journalism... Journalism's biases lie mostly in five areas: in favor of what is new, what is bad, what is dramatic, what is most readily available, and what can be readily understood... (Grossman, 1995)

While it is tempting to lump news stories into the giant bin marked 'entertainment' rather than that marked 'current affairs', it would thus be a mistake; all that is happening when a news story is constructed is an interpretation of the Lord Reith diktat to inform,

(Continued)

of the time', but what an editor can do instead is try to please the broadest number of those viewers, readers or listeners for the maximum length of time. A major section later in this book details the process of news item ordering and sequencing, so we will not preclude that here; suffice to say it is an acquired skill which owes at least as much to experience and understanding of audience demand and expectation as it does to the work of Galtung and Ruge.

Once an event has become news it gathers its own momentum. This might well have applied in the days of Galtung and Ruge's initial research, but these days? Probably not. The repetition suggested by Galtung and Ruge has evolved into rolling news, which is broadcast, web-cast or published through a wide range of media – few of which existed when the initial research leading to *Structuring and Selecting News* was being carried out. There are still rolling news items, but these follow developments of a story, rather than simply repeating the core facts. The death of Pope John Paul II is one of the best example of recent times – news coverage of that event seemed to be almost endless – but what happened there is typical of what happens in most circumstances. Either some new development is unearthed, or the matter becomes subsumed by other news stories until it disappears and goes from news to history (meaning that it will always be considered as a news item in strict descriptive terms, but will go from being current news to archived news). Galtung and Ruge referred to the fact that a news item continues to exist as a news item because once the channel has been opened (another radio analogy) it cannot be closed again. But what happens in the real world is that events become overtaken by more events. Even the papal demise shifted in emphasis. If the Galtung and Ruge premise was followed, headlines and leader comments would have been 'Pope Latest: Still Dead' or words to that effect. What actually happened

educate and entertain. For those still unhappy with the notion of the news as a story, take heed of the words of Tessa Jowell, Britain's Secretary of State for Culture, Media and Sport, presenting a Government Green Paper (an early part of the legislative process) concerning the future of the BBC:

> ... we make clear the importance of entertainment to the BBC's mission ... The BBC should provide a wide range of content, across every genre, trying to reach the greatest possible range of audiences. Where possible, it should make subjects accessible to new audiences. Its programmes should set standards, especially in news, for other broadcasters to aspire to ... [and] 'informing ourselves and others and increasing our understanding of the world through news, information and analysis of current events and ideas'. (Jowell, 2006: 9–16)

Which seems to suggest that the British government is in accord with media practitioners, recognising that the creation of a narrative form is entirely justified as a means of generating accessible content within news programmes.

with the Vatican story is what happens to all other rolling news items – the emphasis goes from the initial news content to a sophisticated blend of opinion and editorial (usually referred to under the combined term of op-ed), obituary, and retrospective feature. The only hard news items surrounding the late Pope's lying in state tended to be the arrival of dignitaries in readiness for his funeral; everything else was op-ed material; what the Pope's lasting legacy will be, what the Pope meant to people he had met and places he had visited, who his successor might be, and so on. Similar processes are common to all rolling new topics; the initial news item leads, but while the key theme remains a constant the rolling nature of the event means that new angles are constantly being sought.

The best way of studying this process as it evolves is to listen to hourly radio bulletins, and be aware of how the sequencing of news items gradually shifts throughout the day. This also touches on the next of Galtung and Ruge's hypotheses, that of the composition (or as we journalists think of it, programme structure or sequencing) of news packages. This is such a complex issue that an entire chapter has been devoted to it, and we will not look into that matter here. What is worthy of serious investigation is Galtung and Ruge's final element, that of the role of the élite.

Galtung and Ruge suggest that the higher the public profile of a country or person, the more importance it enjoys in terms of newsworthiness. This is not to be confused with Noam Chomsky's theory of élite media – to which we will return momentarily – but is concerned with the way in which places and people who come under that nebulous title élite will be far more probable of gaining news coverage. They go on to point out that the more an event can be seen 'in personal terms, as due to the action of specific individuals' (1965: 56) then the more likely the event will become a news item. They additionally

The new news value system

Relevance

The significance of an item to the viewer, listener or reader.
This is broadly aligned to Galtung and Ruge's somewhat clumsy term Consonance. Relevance will vary considerably, and it is this aspect of the news value system that is instinctively deployed by professional news-gatherers, who will often claim to 'know the audience'. A small overnight fire in a school in Des Moines, Iowa, will be of automatic interest only in its immediate locale; somebody in Dartford, Kent, will have no interest whatsoever in that story. If, however, that Des Moines fire was caused by a terrorist cell during attempts to crate an explosive device that they intended to deploy on a transatlantic flight to London Heathrow airport, then it achieves relevance to a much broader audience. And a local journalist that failed to make that connection, and spread the story via the major press agencies, would not be considered to be doing his or her job properly.

(Continued)

state that if the event (or its consequences) can be viewed in negative terms, then the greater likelihood there is of that event becoming a news item.

Although David Beckham had still to born (and would not be so until a decade later) when Galtung and Ruge produced their theory of news values, the sort of headlines that were generated when that venerated football player was accused of indulging in extra-marital relations with female members of his retinue (including the exchange of what some might consider risqué mobile phone text messages) were spot-on to the target of their hypothesis. Former US President Clinton's alleged involvement with the White House intern Monica Lewinsky was even closer to the bulls-eye of Galtung and Ruge's theory of élites; it combined not only a high-profile individual but also a high-profile nation. Central to this élite value is the premise that 'ordinary' people do not make newsworthy subjects. Had it been a footballer from one of the many non-league amateur soccer clubs who had been caught sending 'hot' text messages to a female associate, or even the president of some (to Western eyes) obscure African or South American state who had been accused of indulging in oral sex with a junior assistant, then there would have been less media interest in those events. Or at least not outside the immediate vicinity of where they occurred. But because they were one of the world's most high-profile sportsmen and the incumbent of the most powerful public office in the world respectively, they were given the appropriate level of international coverage.

As with various other of the hypotheses raised by Galtung and Ruge, their interest was rooted firmly in social science studies, rather than in their intrinsic value as a determinant of news. There is a key Marxist agenda at work here. As the Communist Manifesto put it 'Society as a whole is more and more splitting up into two hostile camps, into two great classes directly facing each other: bourgeoisie and proletariat' (Marx and Engels, 1987: 23). With Galtung

Topicality

Is it new, current, immediately relevant?

If it is not, then it has no place in a newspaper or a news broadcast – unless it is a new twist on an old news item. For instance anniversary pieces relating to earlier events (such as the 2005 coverage of the end of the Second World War, the August anniversary of the death of Diana, Princess of Wales, the anniversary of the September 11 attacks on the World Trade Center) in which case there will be a different agenda at work

Composition

How a news item fits with the other items that surround it.

This is an indicator of how news is increasingly being treated as another element of show business; a good news editor will ensure that there is a natural order of content, a spread of items in a broadcast or a publication, with minimised duplication. There will not, for instance, be three similar stories unless they can be merged into a cohesive single report, and there will almost certainly be a blend of domestic and international stories in and Ruge the élite has taken the place of the bourgeoisie, and the reading, viewing, listening public that of the proletariat.

Marx and Engels also flavour the work of that other proponent of élite theory, Noam Chomsky. In the case of the latter, his theory is rooted in the notion that news is determined by élite newsmakers:

> The élite media set a framework within which others operate. If you are watching the Associated Press [AP], who grind out a constant flow of news, in the mid-afternoon it breaks and there is something that comes along every day that says 'Notice to Editors: Tomorrow's *New York Times* is going to have the following stories on the front page.' The point of that is, if you're an editor of a newspaper in Dayton, Ohio and you don't have the resources to figure out what the news is, or you don't want to think about it anyway, this tells you what the news is. (Chomsky, 1997)

This strikes us as a damning, or at least condescending, interpretation by Chomsky of the policies, philosophies, attitudes, and most of all professionalism, of media editors. Also, it makes no allowance for the existence of independent media agencies, the Reuters and APs of our world, that routinely, regularly and constantly feed not just the major players but many smaller organisations with material from which they can choose. AP will flag what their own editors feel is the most significant new item, but they rarely second-guess the intentions of the editor of the *New York Times* – there is too much competition within the media for any organisation to simply follow, herd-like, the guidance of a news agency editor, and for them willingly to subscribe to a common theme. It is for this reason that high-profile newspapers will change their lead item between editions, and broadcast organisations change their lead between bulletins; part of the commercial rationale of publishing and broadcasting is centred on the need to ensure that the gain a commercial advantage (meaning that somebody will buy this newspaper instead of the

a news bulletin. An increasing trend is to take the lead story and worry the life out of it in newspapers this will involve the use of multiple authors to each provide their own piece of the picture, while in broadcast news (where time allows) there will be several different journalists in different places, and often also a second 'talking head' alongside the anchor in the studio who will provide additional colour, usually taking the form of an expert opinion

Expectation

Does the consumer expect to be told about this?
Would it do the consumer a disservice if the item is not present? Anything which is likely to affect the equilibrium of the public falls under this banner; the knowledge that a sex offender is living in close proximity to a school, a medic that starts killing off his patients, a bomb factory in a suburban housing development, all of these are examples of information that the public will expect to be told of, either on a local level or as a national (or even international) news item, dependent on the severity of the example. A brief *caveat lector*: there is a great danger of 'me too' being applied under this umbrella; because a news item is running on one news service, then all others feel that they too must run it.

(Continued)

others on the news-stand) or will tune to a particular broadcast organisation rather than the alternatives on offer.

Part of the skill of a high-profile editor is judging the mood and expectations of the customer base (the audience or readership) and delivering to them the news that they expect to read, see or hear. Chomsky is looking for an agenda which subverts the instincts of an editor to produce a programme or publication which meets those expectations; the thrust of his argument is that everything can be traced back to financial issues. However, Chomsky's argument is not specifically against the editors of the élite media or those he claims are prepared to follow the agenda-setters; it is instead against the corporations (often, but not always, with a core activity divergent from media activities) which, he suggests in that same talk, are responsible first and foremost to themselves and the generation of profit, and that 'you have to control what people think' in order to achieve this level of economic dominance.

It would be naïve to disregard completely the agendas of both Galtung and Ruge and Noam Chomsky, but it would also be foolish to read too much into them. The reality in terms of élite theory within the news industry is that the higher the profile of the person, place or event, then the more likely it is to attract the interests of an audience. Editors simply recognise this better than many, and the mainstream media continues to do what it has always done, and concentrate on higher-profile stories as the centrepiece of their leading news items. Op-ed columns and specialist programmes or publications cater for those in search of greater detail or a more divergent news agenda, and the variations within broadcast or publishing operations provides sufficient choice for the consumer to decide which particular element of the élite content is of the greatest interest to them.

Unusualness

What sets it apart from other events which are not reported?

Dog bites man is a fairly regular occurrence, but man bites dog is such an unusual event (it breaks with all expectations) that it would qualify as news. Anything which is out of the ordinary, which is unexpected – or is something ordinary done by somebody who would not be expected to do it, such as a famous politician shopping in a local liquor store (as once happened with Norman Lamont, a former British Chancellor of the Exchequer, an event which generated substantial news coverage) – will qualify. Similarly, outrageous conduct by somebody who the public expects to act with probity (such as the beating by a group of four Los Angeles police of Rodney King, a stop-and-search suspect), or the repeated drug-taking antics of pop singer Pete Doherty will also qualify as unusual behaviour, in that it breaks with expectations of normal social behaviour.

Worth

Does it justify its appearance in the news?

A family group sitting around a table discussing world affairs is of interest only to that family – but a group of high-profile politicians sitting around a table discussing world affairs

Conclusion

These various hypotheses of Galtung and Ruge were absolutely fine for their time and in their intended context of social and behavioural studies, specifically the way in which world conflict events were reported. But as Bob Dylan once put it, *Things Have Changed*. The approach to the delivery and packaging of news has altered with the passage of time, and the shape of the media in the 21st century is quite different from how it was 40 years ago. Furthermore, the geographical constraints of the Galtung and Ruge project of 1965, where they concentrated solely on Norway, work against their validity today; the emergence of borderless broadcast and publishing operations has seen to that. This spread onto a far broader canvas – the whole of the developed world, rather than simply Norway, a multiplicity of media rather than just four newspapers – calls for a fresh set of values. These values will vary from medium to medium, and from each individual package to the next. Subsequent chapters will determine the peculiarities of each.

Before doing so, though, the authors feel that now is the time to reveal the ideal headings for a news value system that is applicable to today's media landscape – a place which Galtung and Ruge would probably not have been able anticipate when they compiled their original set of headings and qualifiers:

Relevance
Topicality
Composition
Expectation
Unusualness
Worth
External influences

will impact on the lives of many others. Ergo, the first is not news, the second does qualify as news. This is an aspect of the news value system that encompasses all of Galtung and Ruge's élite theory elements. When they first set out their system they were thinking only in terms of élite nations, but in the intervening years since they first published we have witnessed the burgeoning of celebrity, an all-encompassing term which can be applied to everybody from politicians to pop musicians and soap opera 'stars'. The whole notion of celebrity is a contentious one that is being debated in a variety of academic disciplines but one issue remains; news editors remain convinced that readers and viewers are interested in reading about celebrities – and the more salacious the story, the greater the interest. Leaving aside exceptional behaviour by ordinary members of the public, most news is centred on either élite people or on organisations, a catch-all term that covers everything from businesses to nations.

External influences

Is the content of a news item pure, or has it been corrupted by pressure from outside, such as a proprietor, an advertiser or politician?
This is debated in far greater detail later in the book; for the purposes of this 'quick guide', suffice it to say that there is a long history of the press and broadcast industries coming under pressure from outside the industry.

There is additionally a need to tailor these to suit the medium as well as the message, developing certain elements at the expense of others. Each of these justifies a considerably more detailed explanation and qualification. That process follows in subsequent chapters.

How to Study News Values

What Factors Govern the New System?

2

In the light of these observations in Chapter 1, let us now begin to assess some of the issues which will help us determine what sort of framework, if any, may be suitable to replace Galtung and Ruge's framework.

Selection and positioning of news stories

In any consideration of news values, the selection and subsequent positioning of news stories is clearly going to be one of the most fundamental factors – in whichever medium we are working. So let us remind ourselves of some of the issues which will affect the outcome of these deliberations, in relation to any given news story. For example:

- What other stories are around?
- Are there any similar stories around?
- Have there been similar stories recently, or are there any definitely in prospect?
- The frequency of appearance of the story's protagonist(s).
- The presence of a themed period of news stories – or a campaign.
- The options available for story treatments.
- … And a wide range of other possible variables, which we will consider in detail in later chapters.

News story variables

To assist our initial review of what may be the relevant areas of investigation, let us take a few tentative steps into the world of news values in practice. Let us do so in the first instance by taking a couple of news stories of a type likely to be encountered in many television, radio and print news contexts.

Story One

MP comes out against European Single Currency

So, what factors will affect its possible selection and eventual placing?

- Where is he or she the Member of Parliament (MP)? This is an especially valid issue to local and regional media, but could conceivably have national implications.
- What is the status of the MP? Is he or she a back-bencher, minister, or ex-minister?
- What is the history of controversial pronouncements from this MP on this topic or others?
- Does this pronouncement indicate a change of mind?
- What is the current state of party opinion?
- Are there any surrounding events, such as an impending referendum or a reshuffle of major government posts? Is this indicative of a party or cabinet decision?
- What is the prevailing climate? Europe was major issue for most of 1990s; but has been less so in 2000s; does this indicate a new groundswell of reaction?.
- Is the situation likely to offer any lively visuals or audio? Will the MP (or a political opposite number) be available for interviews? Are there any clips available which will supplement the speech?
- Are there any other factors which will suit a particular medium?

Story Two

Elderly Second World War veteran attacked and robbed by hooded youths

- Is this an isolated incident, or part of a spate of such attacks?
- What potential is there in background discussion of 'yob violence', and are there any prominent individuals available to provide informed opinions?
- How does this story relate to any relevant Second World War anniversary?
- What is the availability of photos, film, audio?
- Are there any other factors which will add weight to the article?

Can we systematise or quantify news values?

Is there any merit in attempting to apply some sort of quantitative or 'statistical' approach to the issue of news values? For example, for domestic national media, is it almost possible to apply a 'value-added' approach to some of the criteria which Galtung and Ruge attached different labels? How much more intrinsically newsworthy to the domestic media is a plane crash in the UK than in Colombia? Is a US plane crash more or less newsworthy than a similar tragedy in France? Clearly, much will depend on fatality and casualty numbers. But what will be the balance between this and notions of the inherent newsworthiness or otherwise of certain nations?

Taking it one stage further, if we agree that a domestic plane crash will take precedence in all but the most exceptional circumstances, can we compile a scale, or hierarchy of nations, regions or continents to assist us in determining newsworthiness? Can we then offset these calculations against casualties to provide something like a measurable sliding scale of news values? For instance, how would the following scenarios be treated in UK newsrooms?

- Plane crash in Oxfordshire. No-one injured or killed.
- Plane crash in Oxfordshire. Five injured, one seriously. No fatalities.
- Plane crash in Oxfordshire. All on board feared dead.

There will, surely, be little difficulty in deciding as between these scenarios. However, which of *these* is the more significant story for a UK national newsroom?

- Plane crash in Oxfordshire. No-one hurt or killed.
- Plane crash in France. One dead, several injured.
- Plane crash in Colombia. 143 dead. No survivors.

At what precise numerical stage does a French or a South American air crash become more newsworthy than a domestic incident? Moreover, just as we may think we are at least approaching some sort of quantifiable approach, what about the other factors that may contribute to the journalistic potency of the story? For example:

- Does the country or region have a history of unexplained plane crashes?
- Is there a potential terrorist dimension?
- Have there been other disasters in the same country or region – even if of a totally different kind?
- Has the news organisation in question recently featured or profiled the country involved?

There will additionally be questions of journalistic logistics to consider:

- What is the quality of pictures or audio to help explain the news story?
- What about the availability of staff or freelances, for *in situ* live two-ways or on-the-spot reports?
- Are there any likely problems regarding physical access to the crash site?
- What about the political background? For instance, if the crash happened in, say, North Korea or Burma, how practicable would it be to report from there? Would there be access to other people's material? If not, what could feasibly be done with the story?

An early (and rather crude) attempt to address this was by 'McLurg's Law' as summarised by Schlesinger (1978: 117):

> ...named after a legendary woman duty editor, [McLurg's Law] lays down scales of news-worthiness for disasters: if crashes occur far away, say in Asia, they are not as news-worthy as if they occur in Europe; and they achieve paramount value if they occur at home, preferably in the Greater London area. It is not only crashes, but also natural disasters of any conceivable kind which are subsumed under the 'law'.

In language too offensive to be quoted directly, Schlesinger quotes the 'law' as judging the following as of 'roughly equal news value':

> One thousand [people from the developing world], fifty [French people], one Briton.

With suspicious statistical precision, the 'law' is quoted as stating:

> One European is worth 28 Chinese, or perhaps 2 [sic] Welsh miners worth one thousand Pakistanis.

Schlesinger (1978: 118) also quotes a TV reporter as recalling the old news editor's maxim: one home story is worth five foreign. Some of these voices from the 1970s (and before) strike a note that is not only jarring to modern suscep-tibilities, but also irrelevant. Not all of what is said, however, despite its unfor-tunate tone, is wholly inapplicable to the early 21st Century news landscape.

With these and many other variables, is it inevitable that we abandon any realistic attempt to quantify or systematise news values? Before we can even begin to assess the continuing relevance or otherwise of Galtung and Ruge, we must turn our attention to areas which were entirely outside their purview, but which, we will argue, are absolutely central to any fresh evaluation of news values.

The role of the news meeting

Most mainstream news organisations will have something like a daily – some-times twice or thrice daily – news meeting. Most working journalists and edi-tors would recognise the vital role that these meetings play not merely on a daily, operational level, but also in giving a news culture to their organisation, giving its own distinctive news value system that sets it apart from its rivals. But how does such a system function? In order to begin to analyse the impor-tance of news and planning meetings it is vital to first look at some of the features that shape it.

Sources of potential news stories

People who aspire to become news journalists, and those who consume news stories, sometimes seem to believe that journalists still spend the majority of their time actively seeking out news stories, working from a blank canvas to compile a Pulitzer Prize-winning report. We have all seen films or dramas in which stereotypical news editors shout to trainee reporters 'Get out on the streets and find me some scoops – and don't come back until you've got them!' Needless to say, neither of the authors of this book – with a combined total of 50 years in journalism and broadcasting – has ever heard a sentence like this delivered other than in jest. So, where *do* news stories come from? And does the nature of their sources tend to contribute to the news values of the organisation? It is worthwhile to look at the most common sources of the raw material with which a news journalist tends to work.

Press releases To an extent that would probably still surprise those outside journalism and public relations, many stories appearing on television and radio news, and in newspapers, originate from press releases – and, increasingly, from video releases. It is vital to investigate whether the extent and nature of reliance on news releases affects news values. Does an excessive dependence on derivative material produce inferior journalism – or simply a different kind of journalism? Does a slavish adherence to the verbatim text – specifically in newspapers – vitiate the purity of news values? Or is it more about the selection of the story itself, irrespective of how originally or otherwise it is written?

'Sources' How much do journalists still rely on tip-offs? And, to the extent that they do, what effect does this have on news values? What, indeed, *is* a tip-off? Again, a diet of fictional newsrooms may lead one to imagine the whispered, anonymous confidence imparted over a crackly telephone line. However, dreams of Woodward and Bernstein's 'Deep Throat'[1] are soon replaced by the more prosaic reality of phone calls from fête organisers and fancy dress competitions. Almost as common are the semi-apologetic offerings by a news editor to his team of a so-called story offered to him by a convivial colleague at the previous night's rugby club dinner, or the like. There are, of course, many other possible sources, which we will explore later – in particular, the increasingly contested space between public relations and so-called spin on one side, and news on the other: and the resultant mix of news values.

Stories and treatments

The other crucial factor at the news meeting – much less frequently examined in academic work on journalism and news – is the increasing importance of news treatments both in broadcast and print news. In later sections we will examine these in detail. Here, we will content ourselves with looking at some of the broader trends – particularly in television and radio news.

In broadcast news meetings, and in informal meetings and exchanges afterwards, considerations of format probably demand at least as much time and attention as discussions of the respective merits of the stories themselves.

Package or two-way? Live two-way followed by package? What will be the videowall[2] story? Have we got two packages back-to-back? Do we need a two-way or a live or as-live clip sequence to break them up? These will be questions much aired throughout any normal news day in radio and television. This will not, of course, be so much the case on days of major breaking news stories.

Newspapers have a broadly similar set of considerations to meet, mainly attributable to the house style of the paper; the lead story is almost invariably driven by the political or social positioning of the paper. That the lead story is a major selling plate is a serious consideration which can overshadow the pure news value of the item, in favour of one which will help gain some kind of advantage over a rival. And what of the illustration that will be used alongside the text? Care will be taken to ensure that there is not a run of similar stories within the main body of the newspaper (different sections have different editors) and that the major op-ed columns are aligned to the overall balance of the paper. The placing of editorial content will also be balanced in the meeting if, for example, a British soldier is killed when in active service in a distant war zone, should this be treated as a domestic or a foreign news story? So, in later sections, we shall look at the crucial implications of all this for evolving news values.

Interactivity

One of the most significant recent changes in news is the rise of interactivity. Again, this is, perhaps, more prominent in broadcast news, but has a distinct relevance in the world of print news too. What may have seemed likely to remain a staple of feature programming is now taking a more prominent role in broadcast news bulletins as well.

It takes more than one form. In television news, stories are pre-selected according to whether they are likely to elicit a strong public response. In that sense, it becomes part of the treatment discussions described above. In radio, such issues have long been present in phone-in programmes – though these are usually distinct from the bulletins themselves. However, in television, interactive broadcasting is now taking a high profile within bulletins themselves. As on radio, there will be requests for telephone, email or text comments; and text votes are on the increase also. We will explore the extent to which the search for 'good' (i.e. potentially high response) interactive stories is affecting news values more generally.

Another, even more recent form of interactive journalism, arguably, is the broadcasters' growing reliance on images sent in from the public. From amateur video footage of September 11, 2001, and the Boxing Day, 2004 tsunami to mobile phone footage of the London bombings of 7 July 2005: accompanied by increasingly direct appeals for material to be sent in. It is much rarer for listeners to provide audio material for radio stations. However, radio newsrooms can use the audio component of material sent to television or online newsrooms.

The rise of interactive broadcasting – and, indeed, the extent to which the interactivity claimed is genuine – is a subject for separate study, and is dealt with in greater detail elsewhere. However, its importance for our examination of news values is clear. Historically, radio news journalists have been able to use material generated by phone-in programmes in their bulletins. The generation and production of that material, nevertheless, has been the responsibility of separate staff: producers and presenters who often work outside the main news-gathering operation. Now, the generation of interactive material is integral to the news bulletin, and is therefore central to the decisions and news judgements made in its compilation.

Timing and pacing of news stories

Another common misconception about journalism is that it is invariably, in all circumstances, a race to be first with a story. We will need to spend time analysing how far the 24-hour news culture has caused journalists – and hence analysts – to reconsider whether this remains the overriding imperative it may once have been.

In broadcast news especially, the timing and pacing of stories has always been a major factor. This will not, of course, apply in relation to major breaking stories. However, in the arena of more mundane reporting, news management comes into play. By news management, we are not, of course, referring to spin and public relations. Rather, to the organisation and deployment of elements of the coverage of a story that will be of maximum benefit to the news organisation, and which will most accurately respond to the audience likely to be available at the time. In practice, this will involve different responses from television and radio journalists.

Example

If a news release about a new health service initiative is sent out, and the story is embargoed until 5pm on Thursday, if it is deemed newsworthy at all, television is likely to give it maximum exposure that evening – not least because the highest audiences for television news are still found in the evening.[3] Radio, by contrast, will probably give it some bulletin coverage that evening, but will save its fullest material for the following morning's breakfast bulletins and news programmes because, again, radio listening is still at its greatest in the morning.

Even when an unplanned story breaks late in the radio day – early evening onwards – unless it is of huge moment, it is likely that journalists and producers working on the evening shifts will be told to 'save it for the morning'. That is not to say it will not be reported. Rather, the relevant protagonists will not be used 'live', but will be lined up for an interview the next morning instead. At best, an evening presenter will be told – as one of the authors can testify from extensive personal experience – to 'keep it brief,' so as to leave scope for a follow-up interview the next morning to contain fresh material.

Tomorrow's news today

We also need to assess the impact on news values of another trend in broadcast journalism. Because television and radio current affairs programmes do not wish to be seen as merely chasing up stories that are already in that morning's papers, they will often 'preview' news that is due to happen later that day:

> The Government is set to unveil new anti-smoking measures...
> Ministers are poised to ban skateboards from pedestrianised shopping areas...
> New figures out today are expected to show...
> In a major policy speech, the West Midlands Chief Constable is likely to call for...

Any idea that news organisations are expected to report only what *has* happened already is long gone. Indeed, by the time an event actually occurs, its significance may well have been pored over on numerous programmes, with clips of various contributors already widely aired on bulletins. This is partly because such events are embargoed (see below); and all major contributors will already have seen the detail, as will the journalists working on the story.

But what are the consequences for news values? The current affairs programmes in question wish to seek a reputation for agenda-setting journalism. They want *tomorrow's* papers to follow up what they are reporting: not to be following up what is already in today's papers. So, although not all reporting is a simple race to be first at all costs, the net effect is to bring forward the chronological centre of gravity of news reporting. It is important, therefore, that the consequences of this are fully appreciated and evaluated in any analysis of trends and developments in news values. We shall look at specific examples, and assess their effect on the rest of the news landscape.

Embargoes

It is worth noting that news embargoes are themselves a fascinating, if often unintended, litmus test of news values in practice. To put it at its crudest, a really strong news story is unlikely to be subject to an embargo, because such an embargo would be unrealistic and unenforceable over any significant period of time. For instance, if 10 Downing Street put out a news release that the Prime Minister intends to announce his resignation on Friday week, and embargoes it until eight o'clock that morning, what are the odds of that embargo holding for a matter of minutes, let alone ten days or so? Embargoes will never work for stories of such power.

So, at what level do they become realistic? It is likely that an embargo on a new set of hospital or school league tables will hold – simply because it is in the interests of the specialist health correspondents not to return to a free-for-all; but rather to operate on an acknowledged level playing-field with their colleagues and counterparts elsewhere. The same conventions broadly apply on occasions such as the publication of honours lists and – with one notable recent exception – the text of the Queen's Christmas broadcast. It is also true that any short-term *reclame* received as a result of a scoop in these areas is likely to be more than counterbalanced by loss of prestige and respect among colleagues and peers. Hence, the embargo system is largely self-policing and self-sustaining. However, there is a sort of unspoken consensus that embargoes will only operate up to a certain level of newsworthiness – hence their usefulness as an aid in determining news values.

For example, with stories of a perceived high news value, a very brief operational embargo may be imposed – or, it may be more accurate to say, requested. The death of a prominent person connected with a news organisation may be released on the news wires a few minutes before its intended time of publication, and the subsequent announcement made on the hour. This happened in the case of the announcement by the BBC of the death of radio presenter John Peel. However, there are no sanctions realistically available in the event of the embargo being breached. Because this degree of micro-management is largely irrelevant to print journalists, it only affects broadcasters. Furthermore, because non-news television stations only break into programming for really exceptional news stories, in practice it will more often be an issue for radio broadcasters.

There are also, of course, occasions where embargoes are imposed on stories of relatively weak news value, where there is, in practice, likely to be little real appetite for scooping or pre-empting rivals. Indeed, in some cases, the appearance of an embargo may be an attempt to increase interest in an otherwise unsensational story. It would, of course, be a matter of professional pride for journalists not to fall for such wiles; though, in practice, it can happen at local and regional level. However, embargoes are also pointers to another important feature in the construction of news values: the balance of power between the makers and the reporters of news.

The balance of power

We observed earlier that it is, perhaps, impossible to attempt to apply any purely statistical or quantitative approach to news values. We also considered, only to reject, the notion of some kind of sliding scale in which one criterion of news-worthiness – say, numbers of casualties, – could be offset against another criterion, for instance physical proximity or political/cultural synchronicity.

Another area where it may, perhaps, be worth assessing the suitability of a sliding scale is in relation to the balance of power between newsmakers and reporters of news. As we shall see, there are some stories where the nature of the newsmakers is problematic. If a plane crashes, who is the newsmaker? The manufacturer? The airline? The body responsible for aviation safety? The pilot? A terrorist? There could be a wide range of possibilities. In other cases, it is much easier to be clear. If the Prime Minister makes a major policy speech, for all practical purposes, there is no dispute as to the identity of the newsmaker.

The question of balance of power becomes relevant to our evaluation of news values, however, when we start to examine individual stories, and how they contribute to the overall climate or culture of news values within an organisation. Let us briefly explain the relevance of the notion of the balance of power in news values. Who wants the publication or broadcast of the story more? The newsmaker or the journalist?

Example 1

To revert to an earlier example, if you are a fête organiser seeking coverage for your event, the overwhelming likelihood is that you will be keener on the publication of the story than the journalists who may have to report it. In normal circumstances, even for the humblest weekly free-sheet or the smallest community radio station, such a story is unlikely to set any journalistic pulses racing. This will all change, of course, if the local MP is shot shortly after opening the fête; or if the local vicar is arrested for picking visitors' pockets. Furthermore, any newspaper or local radio station which packs its news content full of such stories to the exclusion of anything more journalistically potent is unlikely to be renowned for robust news values.

Example 2

By contrast, a story about an MP taking bribes in return for a vote is hardly likely to be reported at the urgent initial behest of the MP concerned. Except, perhaps, as a spoiler story, to spike the guns of another, perhaps more antagonistic or vindictive news organisation already planning to run the story. This is likely to be a story which the reporters and news institutions are keener on airing than its protagonist. As a very broad guideline, a healthy count of exclusives of this nature is likely to be perceived as endowing the news organisation involved with a reputation for very robust news values. This is likely to be true within the broader media class even where some practitioners affect a lofty disdain for sensational, 'kiss-and-tell' journalism.

So, again, is there scope for some sort of sliding scale – however rough – by which the protagonist's reluctance can be offset against the reporter's keenness for the story to see the light of day? Is this any sort of guide to the news value of the story concerned? This, too, is a subject we shall have cause to return to as we conduct our detailed media analysis.

The 24-hour rolling news culture

The rise of 24-hour broadcast news is another major factor which is often pointed to as having radically changed the nature of news values. Let us look at the ways in which this is most commonly believed to occur. In the world of broadcast news, the rise of 24-hour reporting is seen as being responsible for a number of transformations in the way news is gathered, compiled, constructed and consumed. We have already indicated – in relation to news meetings and the timing and pacing of news – how decisions are made and in some cases how decision making is changing.

Quality or quantity?

It is often claimed that 24-hour news means that more news is needed: that more stories have to be found to fill the increased space. We shall examine this proposition in detail, along with the consequent assumption that this inevitably results in a dilution of news values; that more is less. However, we shall also consider whether the real change is that the *same* stories are being stretched more thinly; that the real effect is qualitative rather than quantitative.

This means not merely that stories are repeated more often than before in rolling formats – though that is clearly the case. They are also being subjected to more variations of treatment. A package may be replaced next time round by a two-way or a clip sequence (in radio), or a two-way followed by a package (on television). Interviewee A may be replaced by interviewee B, whose contribution may or may not be equally strong and relevant.

In the case of a potentially major breaking news story, the live two-way will inevitably be much in evidence. In the absence of hard information, the questioning will enter the realm of the speculative. It is at this point that we encounter one of the most frequently-heard observations: that 24-hour news is bringing about a climate of increasingly speculative news values and news judgements. It is often further claimed that this is weakening news values, and leading to a more opinion-led type of journalism than in the past.

Example

One of the most famous live two-ways in recent history was Andrew Gilligan's contribution to BBC Radio 4's Today programme on 29 May 2003, in which claims were made about the government's handling of the dossier on Iraqi weapons capabilities. It is no exaggeration to say that subsequent events brought the debate over the live two-way and the alleged rise of speculative journalism closer to the heart of national debate than anyone could realistically have dreamed possible. All sorts of claims were made about trends in reporting which are right at the centre of our attempts to assess the nature of news values in practice. Inevitably, we shall have occasion to return to this and other specific controversies over the nature of what news is and should be about as we unfold our account of the evolution of news values in the early 21st century.

The rise of 24-hour news and rolling news programmes is also responsible for other, perhaps subtler, changes in the journalistic landscape. In television, arguably more than on radio, the widespread availability of continuous news has brought about changes in the nature of the news programmes offered by the terrestrial channels. The main terrestrial news bulletins are much more self-consciously news *programmes* now. This, of course, harks back to our earlier references to considerations of the *treatment* of stories. But what are the implications for news values if the main daytime and evening news output are thought of more as programmes than as traditional bulletins? What are the ratings pressures? Does the balance inevitably shift further from information to entertainment? Are we taking a step nearer to what Mark E. Smith of The Fall memorably termed *The Infotainment Scan*? The implications of these changes in the broadcast environment are correspondingly significant for the world of print journalism. Many would agree that the entire *raison d'être* of newspapers, already in a state of transition, is having to be re-evaluated even more radically in the wake of these changes in broadcasting and the accompanying developments in news values.

News and comment

It is often said that the rise of the 24-hour news culture has changed the very nature of what people seek from newspapers. We have already observed the widespread assumption that many readers are looking less to find out what has happened than to help them make sense of it – or simply to find out more detail. It may also be that we consciously or unconsciously seek aids to help us decide what our *opinion* of the news is, though the general consensus is that fewer people read editorials than news pages. Research on voter behaviour also tends to show a very fluid relationship between readers' voting habits and the political persuasion of the newspapers they choose.

With all these caveats, it is still likely that the role of the newspaper has changed: and further, that this change has had consequences for the evolution of news values within individual papers and across the sector. Indeed, it is often claimed that tabloid newspapers in particular have renegotiated their relationship with electronic media in radical ways. News from other media – overwhelmingly television and cinema – has an enormously high profile in papers like the *Sun* and the *Daily Star*. The story count and the prominence given to the worlds of soaps and reality television is self-evidently a major change of recent years. Inevitably, this shift is in turn responsible for a major change in news values. There is a suggestion that, while not everybody in the mainstream media is in favour of such a relationship, it is (for the time being at least) locked into the commercial viability of newspapers. As Piers Morgan says:

> We all saw big sales increases through July and August thanks to Big Brother, the most inane television ever made. I remember sitting in my office one night-as bidding for interviews with various occupants of the BB house reached ridiculous proportions, thinking: has it really come to this?
> Is my journalistic career going to depend on whether I can persuade some halfwit from Wales called Helen to take my company's £250,000 and reveal in sizzling detail that she's even more stupid than we first feared? (2005: 383)

This, too, will be an important part of our later researches.

News values in the 21st century

So, as well as our revision of Galtung and Ruge's categories for the message or content of news, we must also strive for a new, separate criterion of news values which takes into account our argument in relation to the growing importance of *form* or *message*. It is no longer enough, in our contention, simply to assess news values in the abstract, as if the demands of the respective medium do not even enter the equation. An increasingly media-literate consumer of news joins forces with an evermore genre-aware set of media practitioners to oblige us to rethink the nature of news values, and the entire context in which we should analyse them.

How, then, shall we approach this task of redefinition? Do we simply label it as a separate category of values of form, or values of the medium? Or does this, too, need to be broken down into multiple component parts? Can we incorporate the issues raised by our discussion of news treatments with the consequences of the rise of interactivity? And does any of this do full justice to the pressures imposed on news values by ratings pressures and advertising?

As we conduct a detailed analysis of news output across a range of media, we shall attempt to do justice to the range of issues posed by all of these factors. Will our relatively straightforward formula of *Values of the medium,* or *Values of form* prove sufficient, or will further subdivisions prove essential to do justice to the range and complexity of the issues analysts now face in keeping pace with changes in the nature and delivery of news? Before we conduct detailed analyses, however, let us examine an interesting exercise in which news values are not just applied for their audience, but judged by that audience.

News values: you decide

At the end of 2005, the BBC commissioned an online poll to discover which stories its online audiences deemed the most significant of the year. It then reported the results as a news story in its own right on the BBC News website. The survey was conducted by Canadian pollsters GlobeScan for the BBC World Service, and asked: 'In the future, when historians think about the year 2005, what event of global significance will be seen as most important?'

Of course, this is not quite the same as asking respondents what they felt was the biggest news story of 2005; but it is near enough to be relevant to our purposes. The poll asked nearly 32,500 people in 27 countries for their choices. Globally, the two biggest events were adjudged to be the Iraq War (or insurgency) and the tsunami of 26 December 2004. These were both the choice of 15% of respondents. Third were the US Hurricanes Katrina and Rita (taken as one story) at 9%. Fourth were the death of Pope John Paul II and the election of Pope Benedict XVI (again, taken as one story) at 6%. Then came the London bombings at 4%; global warming and avian flu both at 3%, and the Pakistan earthquake and the second Bali bombings, each on 2%.

There was further data available, breaking the responses down nation by nation. Interestingly, the London bombings were chosen by 7% of UK respondents, but by 11% in Ghana, 8% in Australia and 7% in Spain. Similarly, the hurricanes were chosen by 15% of US respondents, but by 18% in Afghanistan and Argentina. One of the overall conclusions, however, was how similar overall views were across countries and continents. This, in turn, was taken as a sign of further globalisation. Steven Krull, Director of the Program on International Policy Attitudes, who were involved in the research along with GlobeScan, was quoted as saying: 'The extent to which people in different countries perceive the same events as significant is a sign of how much the world has become globalised (Krull, 2006).

For us, however, there are other issues to address. Are people's choices a result of the increasing prominence of internationally-available rolling news channels? Is there more homogeneity of news output even across international news organisations? And are people's choices at least in part conditioned by the *extent* of the coverage given to each of these stories? Or, rather, is the extent of coverage determined, at least in part, by the news organisations' *perceptions* of what their audiences will expect or find interesting? This goes to the heart of how news values evolve. Are they the practical, instinctive or empirical application of 'news sense' by journalists to unfolding events, or is it a more reciprocal process in which the audiences' predilections are guided by and then in turn catered to by the media themselves? All of these issues will be addressed in subsequent chapters.

Notes

1 Deep Throat' was name given to the person within the White House who provided Bob Woodward and Carl Bernstein, a pair of *Washington Post* reporters, with inside information concerning the role of former Republican US president Richard Nixon in a burglary at the Watergate offices of the rival Democrat Party. Finally identified (by his own admission) in 2005 as former FBI agent W. Mark Feld, Deep Throat was vital in providing information that the Nixon administration had considered buried forever. There was a book subsequently written by Woodward and Bernstein (*All The President's Men*) and there was later a film based on the book, starring Robert Redford and Dustin Hoffman which took that title. This is not, of course, to be confused with the 1970s pornographic movie *Deep Throat*, starring Linda Lovelace – even though Feld's *nom de Guerre* was taken from that film's title.

2 The videowall is the background (ahead of which the news reader sits) which is superimposed on the studio images prior to broadcast. The studio backdrop is often a plain wall (usually a Cromakey, for the technically-minded) and the videowall images are digitally added in the control room.

3 The most recent reliable statistics at the point of writing for news programmes on the main British terrestrial television services suggest that in excess of six million viewers watch the main BBC late evening broadcast (with more than 4 million watching the early evening broadcast) and almost 4 million viewers watch each of the ITN equivalent programmes. There are in addition viewers who watch the news on Channel Four and on Five, and a further constituency who prefer to watch news from one of the satellite broadcasters. See http://www.barb.co.uk/viewingsummary/weekreports.cfm?report=weeklyterrestrial for more details.

National Daily Newspapers

3

Agenda Setters – or Mirrors on Society?

Writing of Britain, George Orwell once pointed out that it is impossible to generalise: '... as though 45 million souls could somehow be treated as a single unit' (1946: 23) and in the same way, it is impossible to make sweeping generalisations about newspaper readers anywhere in the world. It is, however, legitimate to cluster readers – and the logical conclusion is that most newspapers are read by people who wish to reinforce their own prejudices. How else to explain how relentlessly liberal a newspaper is the *Guardian*, or consistently conservative the *Daily Telegraph*? And you can allocate similar political leanings to all of the world's newspapers; every western liberal democracy has newspapers which reflect – or pander to – the diverse political agendas of their readerships. And yes, the use of lower case letters throughout that sentence was wholly intentional; western liberal democracy is a state of being rather that a geographic and political tag: people can be conservative without being members of a right-wing political party, broadly supportive of a left-wing philosophy without being active ideologues, and liberally-minded without being political Liberals.

The spread of newspapers in a democratic country tends to reflect the spread of political views within the populace, and although there are some practitioners within the news industry who would like to feel that they are influential agenda-setters, this is rarely true. Even in (the ever shrinking number of) overtly illiberal and dictatorial states, where the press is controlled and channelled and filtered by its government, it has traditionally had little impact on altering the mindsets of its readers. An example of the effect is to be found in a comment made to David Mould and Elizabeth Schuster who observe that the most obvious difference between Western and Soviet-era journalism is the lack of distinction between opinion and fact: 'The inverted pyramid style and the notion of leaving the audience to reach its own conclusions are still rare; as one reader put it, "I read newspapers so I know what to think about what is happening"' (1999: 190). This infers that the reader is simply 'playing the game' and is not directly influenced by what it printed.

The real skill-set of an editor should have at the top of the list an understanding of audience expectations, along with the sure knowledge that the purpose of the newspaper is to offer up a consistent set of values. These will in turn inform the sequencing of news events, not just in terms of the items' coverage within the pages, but also of the prioritisation process that most closely aligns with reader expectation. Andrew Knight, formerly of the right-leaning *Daily Telegraph*, pointed out that in the case of his own newspaper he felt: '[it] needs to fashion a strategic view of its domestic priorities, its attitudes to local deterrence, and the projection of power' (in Hastings, 2002: 69).

All of which makes the application of the 'old' set of values established by Galtung and Ruge the more difficult to apply. We will therefore begin by applying our revised value system, which take into account the need to tailor these to suit the medium as well as the message, developing certain elements at the expense of others. Each of these justifies a considerably more detailed explanation and qualification. That process begins here and is also applied in subsequent chapters – but meanwhile there is a sidebar which provides a thumbnail overview of each news value.

Taking a single day's output from the formidably large output of the British newspaper industry strikes us as a useful way of exploring this process. But before doing so it is worth a brief overview of the major titles in the British national daily press, and its relative status within the firmament, based on official figures for the most recent period (Table 3.1).

Methodology

The first point is that defining the political leanings of the British newspapers listed calls for what amount to arbitrary judgements, and the bias can shift dependent on issues. Those judgements were based on the political support given during the most recent (May 2005) UK General Election, but also factor in the demographic of audience, and any further clues which might be elicited from reading op-ed columns where these are used; this makes for walking on thorny ground, but mind not – we are wearing stout boots.

We are also mindful that by concentrating on the British press, we risk alienating those readers in other countries. In defence of this policy, we would argue that the British buy and read more national newspapers *per capita* than any other country (although China and India have far greater numbers of newspapers published each day, their respective populations are far higher than that of the UK, and there are barely sufficient newspapers in the USA

Table 3.1   Circulation figures and daily national newspapers (July 2006)

Publication	Circulation July 2006	Political leaning
Daily Express	835,937	Right
Daily Mail	2,310,919	Right
Daily Mirror	1,752,948	Left
Daily Star	889,860	Right
Daily Telegraph	864,377	Right
Guardian	337,907	Centre-Left
Independent	219,535	Centre
Sun	3,343.386	New Labour
The Times	658,243	Right

Source: Audit Bureau of Circulation, 15 August 2005

Note: In addition to the titles listed above there are further daily newspapers; the *Financial Times* (FT) plus the *Scotsman* and the *Daily Record*. These are respectively business-focused, and Scottish-based, and so have been excluded from this survey because their agendas are different to the mainstream. We have excluded the daily free-distribution newspapers in view of the core issue raised earlier in this book that for a study of audience to have validity it requires a commercial transaction to be undertaken by the reader.

that can be accurately described as national) and would also add that a direct correlation between our findings could be made in most other liberal democratic countries.

Given that a number of newspapers apparently subscribe to the notion that a picture is worth a thousand words, that there are huge differences in the pagination of the daily newspapers studied, and that the construction of types of story run in those publications varies greatly, there is a need to develop some form of methodology that will level out the field, and allow some form of qualitative judgement to be reached.

Our process thus begun by selecting a single day – 16 August 2005. This is chosen because it is right in the centre of what is known in British media circles as the 'silly season' when the majority of political story generators (the 'spin doctors' as they used to be known) are on holiday. This means that the news items are likely to be less corrupted than they might be at other times of the year; certainly they are less prone to having been mediated by intermediaries. It was also chosen because Tuesday is a day when there are no extra special sections on either sport or other events which might skew the content analysis.

We continue by defining types of story, coverage being worked out on the basis of column centimetres which include related images. In the interests of simplicity, we have grouped all sports coverage in the sports sections of the various newspapers together under that single heading; we have avoided the temptation to develop the analysis further by breaking that aspect of each newspaper down into cricket, football, rugby and other subject coverage. Where sporting issues have been 'promoted' to the main body of the newspaper we have accounted for them as separate articles. Similarly, we have not accounted for each business story but instead grouped the coverage except where they are given promotion to the main body of the newspaper, and disregarded completely television guide pages and their associated pages, but have again counted in those stories which are in the main body of the newspaper. We have additionally disregarded quizzes and crosswords, gratuitous Page 3 'glamour' pieces, obituaries, readers' letters, consumer advice columns and the like, and we have likewise disregarded the supplementary sections in some newspapers which are feature-based – our concentration has been on news and only news, but does extend to those op-ed columns which relate directly to contemporary news stories. Our initial findings are detailed in Table One, the numerals referring to the number of column centimetres we gauge to have been allocated to each item. We will then proceed to try aligning our findings with the newly-offered criteria and also the criteria established by Galtung and Ruge, in a bid to rationalise and explain the codified system.

The first surprise is that, contrary to what one might expect, not all newspapers gave the same amount of coverage to a similar number of stories; although there is the expected level of commonality with such high-profile items as the child who was buried alive in a tragic beach accident, the withdrawal of Israeli settlers from the Gaza Strip, and the delays encountered by Iraqi politicians in establishing a new political constitution, there was a high number of articles which were essentially unique to each newspaper. We flagged those stories which were given front page coverage by the use of a single asterisk, and we applied double asterisks to those items which were mentioned in the editorial masthead – the true indicator of what truly matters to the editor of the newspaper in terms of setting an agenda. Or just as likely, what those editors think are the most important issues to their readership...

This initial analysis raised some expected issues, of course; firstly the way that the *Daily Star* – a newspaper not noted for its political coverage – led on the weighty issue of increasing women's breast sizes. There was also nothing unexpected in the way that the other populist 'red top' tabloids the *Sun* and the *Daily Mirror* (a newspaper form which, according to former editors such as Kelvin MacKenzie, David Yelland and Piers Morgan, claims to be closest to the pulse of the ordinary Briton) majored on the beach tragedy, or that the *Guardian* gives much space to an education issue and the *Daily Telegraph* (in common with the *Guardian*) puts the cricket story on the front cover. That the *Sun*, *Daily Mirror* and *Star* all major on the cult of celebrity (no matter how obscure that celebrity might be – if they are on television then they are deemed suitable for the description 'celebrity') should raise no eyebrows among those familiar with the red top tabloids. What does surprise slightly is that the two middle-market titles, *Daily Express* and *Daily Mail,* also give a substantial coverage to this news genre. That those latter two newspapers give over a considerable number of column inches to diet and health is more expected. Likewise the *Daily Telegraph*'s predilection for 'Little Britain' stories and the pro-ecology stance of both the *Guardian* and *Independent* all remain true to type.

So how does this relate to a value system? In essence the **expectation** element of the theory structure – the consonance with reader expectations – is right on target, as will be explained when we look at some specific news items. Similarly, there is a consonance to the theory of **composition** in the way that news formats are structured. In this latter respect the strict formatting of the 'serious' newspapers (*Guardian, Independent, Telegraph* and *The Times*) makes for ease of understanding; the protocol followed is to lead with the most important stories (as determined by the editorial staff) followed by domestic news, then international news, business news and sport. In a domestic market this is as the reader expects it to be; the newsworthy, the familiar, the unfamiliar and the more specialised interests in that order. Sandwiched in between are the op-ed columns, reviews, and obituaries – exactly where the reader expects them to be, to the point where a regular reader can move quickly to a section which specifically interests them. This facility has even popped up in works of fiction, such as Vivian Stanshall's radio playlet *Sir Henry at Rawlinson End*, 'She left Sir Henry chuckling over the obituaries in the Times...' (1978) which Sir Henry would use as a measure of ensuring that he was still alive, because he was not mentioned therein (a theme used by many other writers of comedy drama).

Closer analysis of the news genres, and how they are deployed by the editors of newspapers, is of vital importance when it comes to understanding composition. Table 3.3, which details the percentage of coverage given, in percentage terms of total editorial content, to the various main genres of news buffers the Galtung and Ruge notion of composition up against some of their other criteria. Sometimes these colliding elements merge to make sense, other times they repel each other, as might matching poles of a magnet when placed in close proximity. And it leaves some of their criteria out completely.

For instance all of the items covered, and this applies in each section as a whole as well as on an individual item basis, the theory of amplitude holds; all news items are exceptional in some sense or other. But predictability? There is no evidence of this to be found; all of the sections rely to some degree or other on external agencies – which start with a witness to the events or to their immediate aftermath – but we feel that there is no such thing in today's news as a self-fulfilling prophesy.

We wrote earlier of the issue of frequency, in which Galtung and Ruge suggest that time needs to pass between an event occurring and it gaining meaning. Close study of the many items in the various newspapers studied shows that time does indeed pass, but this is not a direct news factor; instead editors make use of the elapsed time to make sense of events, to consolidate facts. And sometimes, to prove events are what they appear to be; as the Jayson Blair[1] event proved it pays to be prudent, and ensure that there is a validity to claimed events. Jon Snow explained why a scoop of his was not run, even though the report had been filed: '"Yours was the only source [explained the Foreign Editor] We knew UPI, AP, and Reuters were all on the flight with you, so we waited for them and when they failed to file we decided you'd got it wrong." Snow went on to say that the item was run once it had been corroborated, but also to describe this sequence of events as "an early tutorial in the ways of journalism"' (2004: 83–84).

A further problem area to us is the notion of Continuum; while there are a number of rolling news stories covered in the newspapers analysed (the Iraqi constitution is a good example, as also is mention of the Afghan conflict and the Israeli withdrawal from the Gaza Strip) these are not simply stories which continue to run under their own momentum; instead the coverage is of further developments. The *Daily Express* coverage of the Gaza story is a typical example. That the Israelis were planning to dismantle their settlements in Gaza was first made known in February 2005, when Israel's Prime Minister Ariel Sharon made a formal statement to that effect. In the *Daily Express* coverage of 16 August the news angle was that protesters had gathered immediately before they were to be issued with eviction orders by their government – 'new' news, rather than the simple continuum of events to which Galtung and Ruge alluded. The *Daily Express* article by Con Coughlin included some contextual background, but was in essence concerned with the actuality, rather than the history – and that actuality was fresh protests, a further development of events driven by the imminence of the deadline to leave Gaza, rather than any sense of momentum of the original event. The same applies with the other rolling news items (regardless of the newspaper being studied), each of which delivers up a fresh set of events connected to, but not simply a continuation of, the original story. So each of those items detailed locates neatly within the **topicality** aspect of the codified system; while the framework is already established, the content is sufficient fresh to qualify as 'new' news.

Not that all of Galtung and Ruge's theories are so far away from reality. Their notion of élite applicability holds good; the indefinable, but undeniable, truth is that 'ordinary' people like to read about 'extraordinary' people. We prefer to describe this as **unusualness**. Value systems are totally subjective – some of us, for instance, will never be able to understand the fascination with contestants on *Big Brother* while others will find it equally inexplicable that we are not interested – but the fact remains that there is what appears to be an insatiable interest in the cult of celebrity. But that, of course, is only part of the élite to which Galtung and Ruge referred and the smaller part at that. When they wrote of élites, they had in mind élite nations rather than people, although doubtless under Galtung and Ruge 'rules' the senior politicians of those nations would qualify as élite in their own right. What has to be borne in mind is that they were writing at a time when the cult of celebrity was in its relative infancy. There were, of course, Hollywood stars (the Star System had been established for something like 40 years when Galtung and Ruge started investigating news values) and the Beatles and Rolling Stones had a real fan following – witness the crowds of screaming teenage fans which met the Beatles when they first landed at New York's Kennedy Airport in February 1964 and the correlative screaming hordes who met them on their return to London Heathrow – but those were exceptions. What certainly didn't exist in the mid-1960s were people who were famous simply for being famous, people who took to extremes Andy Warhol's 1968 assertion that 'In the future everybody will be world famous for fifteen minutes' (in Radcliffe, 2000: 144).

In place of this theory of élite, we prefer to use the term **worth**, which is broader-ranging, and allows for the consonance with the market position (and audience expectations) of new organisations. As an indicator of the new 'élite' the *3am* column in the *Daily Mirror* on 16 August 2005 was a double-page spread featuring items on: Pete Doherty (musician arguably more famous for substance abuse than his music – described as a 'junkie rocker' by the *3am* writers); Kate Moss (model); Tara Reid (who appears in an American 'reality travel' TV show); Charlotte Church (child prodigy classical singer turned pop singer turned chat show host); Paris Hilton (socialite heiress turned TV presenter); Victoria Beckham (former pop singer, wife of football star David Beckham); Fran Cosgrave and Paul Danan (both of whom appeared on television 'reality' show *Celebrity Love Island*); Rob Lowe (film actor); Cristiano Ronaldo (footballer); Isabella Hervey (another socialite heiress); Steve Brookstein (winner of *X-factor*, a talent TV show); Cheryl Tweedy (member of group Girls Aloud) and Ashley Cole (footballer). None of the items in which these people appeared seemed to be particularly complimentary; indicative is that the Paris Hilton item focused on her apparently new predilection for wearing what are described as 'comedy' sunglasses which make her look faintly ridiculous, while the Kate Moss item centred on her having to queue 'like an ordinary mortal' rather than being accorded any special treatment when attempting to buy jewellery in a New York store. Any connection with other news values – the exceptional, the topical, the consonant – are conspicuous by their absence. Instead the impression is gained that these items run as an excuse to justify running the accompanying photographs. It is a case of taking élite theory to its ultimate conclusion; writing about people (and accompanying the text with photographs – or vice versa, the order matters not) who are a little famous become more famous because fame grows on the oxygen of publicity. And the more famous people become then the greater the reason (or the better the excuse) to run yet more articles and items on them. Perhaps this is the third millennium's development of what Galtung and Ruge were thinking about when they wrote of Predictability, of expecting an event to happen being sufficient to actually make it happen.

It is perhaps worth a moment to speculate on the source of these various 'celebrity' (a more accurate term than élite,[2] as élite infers some greater level of social credibility than might be deserved by the people who feature in *3am*. and other such columns) items. The average reader could be forgiven for believing that these are all accidentally-observed events, which happen to find their way to the editorial offices of the newspapers and then into the next edition. The reality is quite different. Truly candid images – with what might or might not be accurate accompanying description – often come from paparazzi, specialist itinerant photographers who know where to place themselves so that they are presented with the best opportunity to gain photographs. These might be airport terminals or restaurants, nightclubs or bars. The noun paparazzi comes from a 1960 Federico Fellini film, *La Dolce Vita* and is a pejorative term. In an interview shortly after the release of the film, Fellini apparently explained that: 'Paparazzo [singular; paparazzi is its plural] suggests to me a buzzing insect, hovering, darting, stinging...' (Celant, 1994:326).

But not all items have their genesis in a paparazzo's photograph; there is also a substantial industry – which is culturally rooted in the Hollywood Star System – of PRs (although these are usually personal publicists the familiar term used to describe them is shared with the bigger public relations industry) which sets out deliberately to engineer situations as a means of ensuring continued publicity for the various celebrities. Such individuals operate within the general value system framework of **external influence**, and the modus operandi of such PRs seems to be based on the principle that there is no such thing as bad publicity.

One of the best-known of these personal publicists is Max Clifford; he is by no means the only one of his type, but he is certainly the one with the highest personal profile. Indicative of his reputation is this extract from a lengthy profile-cum-interview in the *Washington Post*, which refers to his role in the events surrounding Rebecca Loos's claims that she had a personal involvement with footballer David Beckham:

> Three months later the *News of the World*, Britain's largest and most carnivorous Sunday tabloid, broke the story on its front page. Rebecca Loos was quoted as having no comment. But an unnamed 'close family friend' provided a host of lurid details, including direct quotes of what Beckham and Loos reportedly said to each other in bed, plus intimate text-messages sent to her on Beckham's cell phone.
>
> Once upon a time, a damsel whose reputation was under threat might turn to a knight in shining armor or a private eye. But this being the Media Age, she's more likely to call Max Clifford.
>
> [Clifford] stands at the intersection of news and gossip, playing middleman between the famous, those who wish they were and the voracious tabloid press. Some clients pay him to keep their private lives out of the newspaper, others to see their names in print. Reputations get trashed. Saints and sinners alike are disrobed. And money changes hands. (Frankel, 2004)

A more recent observation in the *Independent* seems to say much the same: 'Max Clifford knows where the bodies are buried. From philandering footballers to sex-pest politicians, via kinky bankers and closet-case Hollywood stars, the high priest of tabloid kiss-and-tell has heard it all' (Silver, 2005). It is not unknown for these two elements of the news generation process, paparazzo and PR, to work together as a means of ensuring that the clientele gets the publicity it craves – and some say that it deserves. The tactic referred to earlier, where Rebecca Loos declined to comment but allowed an unattributed person 'close to' her to fill in the blanks is especially invidious, and undermines the integrity of journalism.

One reason why the PR has been able to assume such a significant role in this propagation of myth is because the stories are delivered, ready to use, and often with no price tag for the newspaper to pay. But there is a reaction against this process by more serious members of the press. Andrew Marr neatly summarises this when he writes: 'Journalism needs the unexpected. It needs the unpredictability and oddness of real life. This means it needs real reporters. There is no better protection against the special pleading and salesmanship of the PR machines than decently paid and experienced journalists, trusted inside their organisations to use their judgement' (2004: 384).

This issue of experienced journalists reliant on their acquired sense of judgement – and being trusted to use it – is at the heart of the values used by editors, writers and reporters to ensure that some of the issues raised by Galtung and Ruge are actively disproved. Also working against what has effectively become the 'tradition' for news value analysis is the presumption that all journalists operate to the same rule book. This is very definitely not the case. Leaving aside blatant short-cuts such as those exemplified by Jayson Blair of the *New York Times*, there is the more normal practice of writing to suit the reader expectations.

The varying treatments given to a common topic by three different newspapers ought to provide an understanding of how this works in practice. The newspapers chosen are The *Times* (which tends towards qualified support of the current government) the *Daily Mirror*, a newspaper normally in favour of the activities the incumbent Labour government (though this was not always the case – read up on the back issues of that newspaper prior to the second Gulf conflict, when it was taking a distinctly anti-war stance and was locked in a battle with the government) and the *Guardian*, from the centre-left. The first topic selected is the declared plan by the Home Office to deport the so-called 'preachers of hate', radical Islamic clerics.

The *Daily Mirror* gave the item a prominent position, at the top of Page 2, under the headline '**TERROR TO RETURN**'. Written in a measured tone, the text was dropped over a panel which comprised an image of the Home Secretary in sharp close up to the right of the Metropolitan Police Commissioner Sir Ian Blair (whose portrait was in soft focus). Despite the overall tone of the item, some of the terms used and quotes extracted were a shade more explicit: '... Britain faces the risk of more terror attacks' '... hit by further atrocities' and '... clerics who preach hatred against the West' were all terms used in the short (220 word) piece authored by the *Daily Mirror*'s Political Editor, Oonagh Blackman. All quotes came from either Home Secretary Charles Clarke or Sir Ian Blair, and there was no attempt to include anything by opponents to, or critics of, the scheme.

The Times coverage, headlined 'More extremists to be expelled' was much more substantial – almost 500 words – and was illustrated with a small image captioned as being an individual being put aboard an aircraft for deportation. Given the nature of the topic – which tends to cross political boundaries – it is unsurprising to learn that the article was uncritical of the policy; it too used the term 'preachers of hate' and went so far as pointing out that Muslim leaders had been consulted prior to the plans being made public. There was an avoidance of any kind of inflammatory language used by its writers Richard Ford and Daniel McGrory.

The *Guardian* had the most substantial coverage of the three, and again was totally uncritical in its tone. Headlined 'Clarke threatens to expel more "preachers of hate"' and running to more than 600 words (though without any accompanying image) the article again drew essentially on the quotes from Charles Clarke and Sir Ian Blair, but was the only one to add a third dimension – its writers Alan Travis and Richard Norton-Taylor augmented the core text shared with other newspapers by adding that '... the terms of the agreement were criticised by human rights groups yesterday...' but did not detail which groups, or take any direct quotes from spokespersons.

Those three variations on the same theme suggest that the editorial staff are broadly in agreement with the government's policy – which is hardly surprising, given the underlying horror of potential further attacks to those made on London's transport network during the summer of 2005. Any newspaper which was to be openly critical of the policy to neutralise at least one element of the threat would be committing a form of commercial suicide. But on other topics they are on safer, more familiar, more reliable ground. All three examples are **relevant** to the publications and thus by definition also connect with issues of **composition**, are **topical**, and are, of course, **worthy**. It is worth considering whether there has been any **external influence** brought to bear in the development of these stories; this is likely to take the form of complicit support from the media relations officers of the government ministers mentioned.

In the case of the schoolteacher found guilty of having sex with a 14-year-old male pupil (though not one in her charge – she had never taught him) the *Daily Mirror*'s stance seemed to be sympathetic towards the woman and her husband, inferring that the event was not especially horrifying. Even so, the coverage ran to five-sixths of a tabloid page, and was headed by a reversed-out headline: 'JAILED ... MARRIED TEACHER WHO HAD SEX WITH BOY OF 14' overlaying a 400cm^2 photograph of the woman.

The *Times* restricted its coverage to a quarter page, headed 'Teacher jailed for sex with boy, 14' and ran a small (20cm^2) portrait photograph of the teacher. The editorial tone is slightly harsher than that in the *Daily Mirror* – mention is made of the fact that the teacher is to be on the Sex Offenders' Register for ten years (a fact which the *Daily Mirror* also mentioned) but unlike the *Daily Mirror* failed to add that there is not a specific provision attached to the order which will prevent her working with children in the future. The inference is that there is something a little seedy about the affair ('the boy, who cannot be identified, said that sex took place up to four times a week until last year, when the relationship become public' was one part of the report) whereas the *Mirror*'s approach seems more sanguine.

As for the *Guardian*, while its coverage in terms of column centimetres was virtually identical to that of *The Times* – right down to the image used to accompany the text and the headline '**Teacher jailed for sex with boy**' – it was the only paper of the three to gain a quote from the teacher's father, who explained that 'In my eyes she's innocent. She's just an ordinary person who's been caught up in such circumstances that's escalated.' That the *Guardian* carries a special weekly supplement dedicated to educationalists seems to align with the 'soft ride' that has been given to the teacher.

As might be expected, the *Daily Mail* took a far more remonstrative tone; the headline '**Schoolmistress who seduced boy, 14, is jailed**' gives a good idea of the tone; this was the only one of the four papers to use the term 'seduced'. In every case of reportage of that incident, the tone and language used was consistent with the reader **expectation** of the various papers concerned.

For a real indicator of the agenda of a newspaper, as mentioned earlier, it is necessary to study the masthead editorials; these prove beyond all reasonable doubt where the editorial staff members stand. The *Daily Star*, for example, has brief but excitedly-written pieces on *Big Brother* (the TV programme, not the George Orwell novel), the continued safety of air travel despite two holiday jets crashing within a matter of weeks, and the increasing size of women's breasts. The *Daily Express* focuses on the threat to British health and safety of extended drinking hours, the lack of an abject apology for his country's wartime behaviour from Japanese Prime Minister Junichiro Koizumi, and a tribute to Britain's valiant cricketers. The *Independent* offers up a serious

Genre analysis

Worthy of note is the split of editorial content that was recognised in the selection of British newspapers analysed in this chapter – and how the mass-market red-top titles (*Sun, Mirror, Star*) are biased heavily towards celebrity, domestic and sports coverage, while the mid-market titles (*Daily Express, Daily Mail*) are less interested in celebrity than they are in health and beauty and in business matters. Perhaps most interesting of all is while the up-market titles (*Telegraph, The Times, Guardian, Independent*) have a bias towards business, international events and op-ed, they all have a very high proportion of sports news in their content.

analysis of the problems facing Iraq as it tries to establish a political constitution. This shows that newspapers are written to meet the expectation of their readers, and that their journalists and editors are responding in as responsible manner to events, presenting them in a way which suits those who go out every day and buy their product.

Not that all journalists are paragons of virtue; there will always be those who work harder than most in search of a valid truth, but there will also be journalists who are happy to 'borrow' from other newspapers' coverage (in academic circles this would be plagiarism, a heinous offence; in journalistic circles it can seem to amount to standard practice) as a means of either gaining a fresh angle on a rolling news story, or of spoiling the party of a newspaper which has gained that rarest of beasts, a scoop. These factors all conspire to work against the perceived wisdom of much of Galtung and Ruge's work; this is not because Galtung and Ruge were wrong, simply that today we can look in places that were unavailable to them when they were breaking the ground of their research four decades ago.

But that is not quite all. One aspect of journalistic practice that is subject to considerable criticism is the process of 'cheque book' journalism – paying somebody for an exclusive. In reality this is simply an extension of a practice that starts with buying a source a drink or giving a small amount of cash to a tipster; it is simply that the sums involved can appear astronomical in comparison. They also corrupt the established news values. In much the same way as a political 'spin doctor' or a Max Clifford-style character has already dabbled in the facts, obscuring forever (or at least for long enough to get away with the story) those elements which they do not want to get into the public domain, so too those who sell their exclusive stories to the press in return for a substantial amount of money mediate their information. In realistic terms they

Topic	Red top	Upmarket	Mid-market
Business	6588	1360	280
Celebrity	627	980	4386
Domestic news	5840	3817	4345
Education	403	91	146
Health & beauty	24	2350	730
International news	2669	716	885
International Politics	2419	508	392
Op-ed	470	170	171
Sport	8911	4315	6456
Total	**27951**	**14307**	**17791**

Note: All measurements are for column centimetres of coverage, and relate to August 2005 editions

are selling only their version of events, and autobiography is a dangerously skewed craft which is more prone than most to selective processes of memory. As Laurie Lee once noted: 'No-one else who was there can agree with you because he has his own version of what he saw. He also holds to a personal truth of himself, based on an indefatigable self-regard.' (1975: 52). The established values of good journalism – fact, accuracy, corroboration – are all left behind when the chequebook appears in journalism.

At the end of this exercise – and we would encourage readers to look at the press in a similar way, in search of patterns of behaviour – it becomes obvious that the value systems applied are corruptible by various factors. It will become apparent that the same principles apply to other areas of the media, as subsequent chapters will illustrate.

Notes

1 The *New York Times* writer Jayson Blair was forced to resign as the result of allegations of misconduct, followed by an internal inquiry which proved that he had been fabricating and plagiarising material for certain articles. In the wake of his resignation there were further resignations, including the Editor of the newspaper. For a comprehensive overview of the event surrounding this saga, see the PBS special report at: http://www.pbs.org/newshour/media/media_ethics/casestudy_blair.php

2 According to the current edition of the Oxford English Dictionary élite is: 'A group of people regarded as the best in a particular society or organisation' while celebrity is described as: '1 Famous person; 2 The state of being famous.' (Compact OED, 2nd Edition 2000)

National Television News

The Problem Child of the News Family

Television news has a problem that has arisen gradually over the past decade. From being a simple, straightforward conduit of information, it has been forced – as part of the overall shifting shape of television – to assume a higher level of entertainment content. This does not necessarily mean that the information level packed into any given item or overall show is reduced – but logic dictates that something has to give, and the reality is that the educative element (of the 'holy triumvirate' first laid out in the 1920s by John Reith that *all* broadcasting should educate, inform and entertain) is likely to be sacrificed. In practical terms, this has forced a more liberal approach to the core news value of composition than might otherwise have occurred.

The watershed was 1 June 1980, the day that CNN first went on air. As Ken Auletta put it: 'CNN would make news, not over-paid anchors, the star. It would be on 24-hours a day, viewers would no longer have to wait until 6:30 or 7.00 p.m. to learn what occurred in the nation or the world ...' (2004: 40).

Initially a domestic North American service, by 1985 CNN was global, and for the next several years virtually had the field to itself; where most news organisations were closing down overseas bureaux as a consequence to the end of the cold war, CNN executives realised that expansion would be the key to success, and actively expanded: 'It invested in "flyaway" portable satellite dishes, costing about $250,000 each, that could be carried in a suitcase and used anywhere in the world to "uplink" to a satellite.' (Auletta, 2004: 46)

Today, inspired by CNN's eventual (it was not in profit until it had been in existence for almost a decade) success, there are other global or at last trans-Continental news services (for example, BBC World, Al-Jazeera, NewsCorp's Fox/Sky/Star News cluster) and all domestic or national news services have been forced to raise their game. Or have they really raised their game or simply adopted a 'smoke and mirrors' approach which simply window-dresses what they do? With the proliferation of news services comes commercial pressure, and the response to that is a need to redefine the content of news programmes. Robert McChesney is critical of this trend:

> International news has declined from 45 percent of the [US Domestic] network TV news total in the early 1970s to 13.5 percent in 1991 ... What replaced the expensive international news? The annual number of crime stories on network TV programs tripled from 1990–1992 to 1993–96. In one revealing example, CNN addressed a decline in ratings in the summer of 1997 by broadcasting a much-publicized interview with O.J. Simpson. (1999: 54)

With audience ratings (the number of viewers watching a broadcast) being tied to the success of any given broadcaster or programme, and more competition, there is an increasing trend to repackage the news as a form of entertainment show; how else to explain whizzy graphics, reporters who are both telegenic and witty (thus falling into the cult of personality – the journalist as celebrity)? And there is also the speculative two-way, an exchange between the studio and a journalist on the ground – suggesting that something of significance is occurring, even though there is nothing happening on the ground at that moment.

Analysis: British national television news

It is important in television, as in radio news, to distinguish between the different genres, styles and contexts available. General, all-encompassing discussions of 'television news' are now in danger of missing as many elements as they clarify. As in radio, for instance, there is a huge difference between the style and purpose of a short news headlines bulletin on terrestrial television in, say, mid-afternoon and the main evening news at 10.00 p.m. or 10.30 p.m. Again, there are vital contrasts between the type of news delivered on terrestrial television and that found on continuous news channels. And that is only to speak of national news. Regional TV news is the subject of a separate chapter, so is continuous or rolling news. We shall also examine the phenomenon of even more localised news of the type piloted by the BBC in its Local News initiative.

However, in this chapter, we will focus on the news provided on terrestrial television. We shall examine the news values on display in randomly selected news bulletins. We will also look at the balance between *selection* and *treatment* of stories – one of the factors often neglected in academic discussions of broadcast journalism. In the first instance, we shall compare and contrast two terrestrial news bulletins broadcast simultaneously on the same day – Channel Four News and Five News at 7.00 p.m. We will also look in detail at BBC One's Ten o'clock News and ITV's News at 10.30. These, too, will be from the same day (but not the same day as the previous two). As with the radio bulletins analysed elsewhere, the selection was random, with the proviso that there was no one overwhelmingly dominant news story on the days chosen. It is a journalistic cliché that August is a quiet news month. However, anyone who was a practising journalist in 1990 (Iraqi invasion of Kuwait), 1991 (attempted coup against Gorbachev), or 1997 (death of Diana, Princess of Wales) will soon discount this notion. August, 2006 proved to be an active (though not wholly exceptional) news cycle – with the Israeli–Hezbollah conflict in Lebanon, and the disclosure of alleged air terrorism conspiracies in the UK.

While interesting conclusions about news values can still be deduced on days where one story looms exceptionally large, these tend to revolve around selection of angles on the story and interviewees chosen to illustrate it, rather than on the selection of the story itself. For our purposes, it is more useful to analyse issues of *story* selection in practice.

Naturally, it is not possible to state authoritatively exactly why such editorial judgements are made. Indeed, such is the collusive nature of editorial processes, even the journalists involved may not always be able to pronounce with *absolute* certainty about why and how such decisions are reached. However, we do aim to explore the possible interplay between editorial and aesthetic considerations. Many broadcast journalists accept that such criteria are probably even more influential in television news than they are in radio.

Let us first look at two of the most important terrestrial television news programmes in detail. The BBC Ten o'clock News, and ITV's News at 10.30, both taken from 17 August 2006. In both cases, the concentration has been solely on the national bulletins. In the BBC format, the regional news follows the national section (with a final return for the national headlines). With ITV, the regional news is currently sandwiched within the national news, the bulk of the national news coming first; but usually with a final story and a look at the next day's papers coming after.

Here is the running-order for the **BBC Ten o'clock News, 17 August 2006**:

Headlines

- Police investigating alleged air terrorism conspiracy find a suitcase in woodland near High Wycombe.
- Breaking news of a security alert at an airport in West Virginia, USA.
- Lebanese troops move into southern Lebanon.
- Jail for a mother who supplied her nine-year-old son with heroin.
- Baby boomers turn 60.

(Regional headlines then follow, which do not concern us here).

First story

- Discovery of a suitcase containing bomb-making equipment in woodland near High Wycombe (one of the areas where arrests were made).
  Package: containing clips from a public meeting in Walthamstow (another of the areas where arrests were made). Clip one: Mayor of Walthamstow. Clip two: man described as meeting organiser.

This was then linked to:

Second story

- Terror alert underway in USA (West Virginia). Containers of liquid reported as having tested positive for explosives.
  Live two-way (not illustrated with clips of other speakers).

Third story

- Lebanese troops move into southern Lebanon (but other countries reported as not keen on supplying peacekeeping troops).
  Package: mainly troop footage, but with a brief clip of an unnamed man describing the Lebanese army and Hezbollah as one.

Fourth story

- Mother jailed for supplying her nine-year-old son with heroin and crack cocaine.
  Package: containing police video footage of their raid of her property; plus clips of Det. Sgt. Wendy Fuller of Sussex Police, the boy's grandfather (named), and Matt Dunkley of East Sussex Social Services.

Fifth story

- A level results released. Rise in number of passes and A grades.
  Live studio two-way.

This then linked to:

Sixth story

- CBI warns of too few physics students.
  Package: containing mock-up of a news bulletin in 2026 bemoaning skill shortages; a brief clip of students celebrating their results; a clip of Richard Lambert,

CBI Director General; a clip of Dr. Jackie Hunter from Glaxo Smith Kline; and a clip of Alan Wood, Chief Executive of Siemens UK. The package also contained a brief videowall-type presentation of data.

Presenter trails ahead to YouTube package.

Seventh story

- Jailing of David Morris for murders of two children, their mother and their grand-mother in 1999, after a retrial.
  Package: containing clip of members of the victims' family's reaction; a piece-to- camera with the reporter holding a necklace chain, described as the crucial piece of evidence; a clip of police footage of the accused denying his guilt; and a longer clip of the sister of the mother (Mandy Power) killed.

News in brief

- Arrest of a man in connection with the murder of six-year-old JonBenet Ramsey in 1996. Brief clip of John Mark Karr, the man arrested.
- Deputy Prime Minister John Prescott accused of calling President George W. Bush's policy on the Middle East roadmap to peace 'crap'.

Eighth story

- Baby boomers reach 60. (Pegged on ex-President Clinton's 60th birthday).
  Reporter 'as live' with videowall screen data presentation, then linking into *package*: containing actuality of group discussions with unnamed participants interspersed with clip of Lisa Story, PR consultant, and Ailsa Ogilvy of *Heyday* magazine. At the conclusion, the presenter trails a follow-up piece on the same topic tomorrow.

Ninth story

- Free music videos available on YouTube.
  Package: containing clips of self-published videos, and two clips of Jo Twist from the Institute of Public Policy Research. The package is made to look like a com-puter screen presentation.

Finally, the presenter trails the continuing 10 o'clock News Hour on BBC News 24, before handing to regional news presenters.

The presenter returns with a reminder of the main headlines and a trail for the Ten o'clock News pod cast after the regional bulletin.

Here is the running-order for the **ITV News at 10.30 on 17 August 2006**:

Headlines

- Record A level results, but do they pass 'the credibility test'?
- An exclusive report on the company which 'does your coursework' for £400.
- A man 'confesses' to the killing of JonBenet Ramsey.
- A mother supplies her nine-year-old son with heroin.
- Boom time for City bonuses – 'but are they worth it?'

First story

- A levels. Presenter's cue refers to the repetitiveness of the debate about whether abilities are higher or standards lower.
  Package: containing actuality of access to a 'study factory'; clip of Barclay Littlewood, Chairman of the company; clip of an anonymous student, in shade and with a dubbed actor's voice; clip of Nigel Price, an examiner marking a 'test' essay; clip of Schools Minister Jim Knight; clip of David Frost, British Chambers of Commerce.

Second story

- Man arrested for murder of JonBenet Ramsey.
  Package: containing clip of accused man John Mark Karr; archive clip of JonBenet's parents; clip of District Attorney of Boulder, Colorado; clip of Michael Tracey, University of Colorado.

Third story

- West Virginia air scare. Presenter voices over pictures, and links into clip of Airport Director.

Fourth story

- Deputy PM John Prescott calls President Bush's Middle East roadmap policy 'crap', and the President a 'cowboy'.
  Package: live scene-set from Downing Street, linked into a package containing: clip of Tony Snow, White House spokesman; clip of Harry Cohen, the MP who leaked the comments; clip of Andrew Dismore, 'loyalist' MP. Out of package for brief live two-way.

Presenter trails two stories (mother supplies heroin, Andrew Murray in action).

Fifth story

- City bonuses.
  Package: containing clip of trader in wine bar; clip of Taylor and Peattie, creators of the 'Alex' cartoon strip; videowall-type graphics with data; clip of David Buik, analyst with Cantor Index.

  Markets: FTSE, Dow, Pound against the Euro.

Sixth story

- Mother supplies son with heroin and crack.
- Package containing: police raid video clip; clip of Det. Sgt. Wendy Fuller, Sussex Police.

News in brief

- Mel Gibson escapes a prison sentence for drink driving.
- Pete Doherty faces seven more drugs charges.

Seventh story

- Lebanese troops move into southern Lebanon.
  Package: containing clip of Alain Pellegrini, UNIFIL force commander; brief clip of Jon Braun, Israeli soldier.

Sport in brief: cricket Test latest

Presenter trails tomorrow's papers and Andrew Murray.

Links to regional news.

On return, recaps headlines, reads headlines from *The Times, Daily Telegraph, Independent,* and *Daily Mail.* Then final Sport in brief: Andy Murray wins possibly with help from rule change on disputed line calls (having defeated Roger Federer earlier in the week).

Analysis

So what do these bulletins reveal about the news values involved? First, here are the stories that ran on BBC One and not on ITV:

- Too few physics students (although this was linked to A level coverage which both carried).
- David Morris jailed for multiple murders.

- Baby boomers reach 60.
- YouTube make free music videos available.

And these are the stories run on ITV but not BBC One:

- City bonuses.
- Shares and currencies.
- Mel Gibson escapes jail.
- Pete Doherty faces more charges.
- Cricket latest.
- Andy Murray wins, with help from rule change.

If one thinks in media stereotypes, it might be expected that the BBC would be more likely than ITV to include share and currency news. It is worth noting, however, that BBC News 24 runs items which are not featured on the terrestrial Ten o'clock News, whereas the ITV News Channel has closed down. The BBC Ten o'clock News trails items that are due to be run in the second half of the Ten o'clock News Hour on BBC News 24. These often include sports stories not mentioned on the terrestrial Ten o'clock News. Indeed, during this phase of its existence, the terrestrial Ten o'clock News was not attempting to fulfil the traditional role of the all-encompassing, 'all-you-need-to-know' bulletin, with separate sports and financial/business sections. The ITV News, on the other hand, was (and still is) consciously trying to fulfil that role. Hence the inclusion of the cricket and tennis developments, not reported on terrestrial BBC.

By contrast, there would be less surprise, perhaps, at ITV's inclusion of the Mel Gibson and Pete Doherty stories, and their exclusion from the BBC bulletin. These are relatively minor examples of the kind of stories often cited in allegations of an excessive preoccupation with human interest news, or the culture of celebrity.

However, it is the YouTube and Baby boomer packages which, perhaps, pose the most interesting questions about news values. Neither of these stories is pegged to a development in that day's news agenda. The nearest approximation to a peg for the Baby Boomers piece was Bill Clinton's impending 60th birthday (though it was still a few days off!). YouTube charted a recent development (the availability of free music videos), but, again, was not specifically related to a major announcement that day. Both features also have the feel of self-consciously creative packaging. The use of computer screen-type graphics on the YouTube piece, and the mixture of Videowall and pre-packaged elements in the Baby boomer item, reinforce the suggestion that they are more like magazine programme items than traditional bulletin material.

The Baby Boomer item is part of a series of themed packages: another trend in mainstream terrestrial news bulletins. There is also a tendency for bulletins to commission their own research, or harness expert testimony, and then construct a report, or series of reports, around this. If sufficiently interesting, or if a strong viewer response is provoked, this may also result in the sincerest form of journalistic flattery – a similar or almost identical piece run on the opposition channel.

Earlier in 2006, ITV ran a lead story on 'Cocaine Britain', involving the use of a scientist conducting swab tests on various public surfaces (such as the cisterns of public lavatories) to detect traces of the Class A drug. There was no particular news peg that day. Indeed, items such as this may be recorded days (or even a few weeks) before transmission, for use as the television equivalent of a newspaper 'splash' on an otherwise relatively quiet or routine news day. However, in this instance, at least one regional news programme on the BBC followed suit with its own investigation, and broadcast report, a few days later. Some of the pioneering sociological studies of news (notably Gans, 1979) have written of the 'herd' or 'pack' mentality within journalism. We have also spoken of how news items are sometimes generated within 'brainstorming' sessions in news planning meetings. If, as appears to have been the case with 'Cocaine Britain', the story is strong and in journalistic parlance, 'has legs', then this instinct may well come into play.

What can we deduce from the coverage of the A level results? One of the authors worked in radio newsrooms from the mid-1980s to the mid-2000s, either as a staff or freelance journalist and news presenter. Adequately covering A level and GCSE results was always regarded as a major challenge: not because of any inherent difficulties in the subject matter, but simply in order to make it less repetitive and predictable. This problem became even more acute when the debate around the interpretation of the results itself became predictable. In the 1980s, a steady climb in numbers of passes and A grades began. Initially, debates were staged on news magazine and phone-in programmes, and within news packages, about what soon came to be known as 'grade inflation'. Fairly soon, there was a danger of routinely ringing up the educationalist who would condemn critics of the system for devaluing the hard work of the students, and the pundit who would issue ringing denunciations of 'dumbing down'; arguments soon became as predictable and routine as the grades themselves. Equally predictable were the pictures of students opening their results letters and reacting accordingly (the same scenes were also recorded for radio, and more recently, online use).

In the programmes surveyed, there seemed to be an awareness that visually literate viewers may already have relegated such scenes to the ranks of the television news cliché, and expected something more than scenes of jubilation and a weary rehearsal of familiar arguments. Accordingly, both channels sought new, fresh angles. Both also tend to reinforce traditional perceptions of the bulletins and channels in question. The 'exam factory' was presented with the apparatus of an expose. The physics item explored an issue 'behind' the headline story. Both approaches chime with the self-imposed mission and vision of the channel concerned. These two bulletins *could* have been watched in sequence.

The next two news programmes to be examined were broadcast simultaneously: so only a conscious decision to video one and watch it later could have enabled anyone to watch both of them. (Only a journalist monitoring the opposition, someone who featured in the bulletin, or a media academic is likely to resort to such unusual viewing habits!). The bulletins chosen are from the same week, but not the same day, as the two already analysed. They are Channel 4 News and Five News from *15 August 2006*.

Here is the running-order for **Channel 4 News** *on 15 August 2006*:

Headlines

- The brother of one of the airline terror suspects speaks publicly for the first time.
- British Airways (BA) blames British Airports Authority (BAA) for tourists' lost baggage; the BAA hits back.
- Report from within Israel's war rooms gives a 'bird's eye view' of the Lebanese conflict.
- Details of Lord Levy's appointments diary revealed.
- First footage of Fidel Castro since his operation (showing him celebrating his 80th birthday).

Also:

- Lebanese refugees return home after the ceasefire.
- CCTV footage of one of the men arrested in the airline terror plot is released, as another man is arrested.
  (The second round of headlines read by the secondary presenter).

First story

- Terror plots. Billed as 'exclusive'.
  Packaged report with clips of obscured figure of brother of one of terror suspects. Also contains clip of local mosque spokesman.
  This followed by separate but linked story: CCTV footage of another suspect, taken just before arrests (as news in brief item).

Second story

- Row between BA and BAA over handling terror alerts.
  Package: containing vox pop of passengers; clip of Michael O'Leary, Chief Executive of Ryanair; clip of Ian Aisles, Chairman of Federation of Tour Operators; quotes from newspaper interview with William Walsh of BA read by voiceover; BAA described as unavailable for interview.
  This then followed by live interview with Paul Charles, Virgin Atlantic.

Third story

- Middle East Conflict (Israel–Hezbollah).
  (Second of two reports from either side of conflict).
  Extended *package* by Israeli journalist containing: actuality from Israeli war room, excerpts from conversations, and clip of interview with army colonel.
  This then followed by live (or 'as live') interview with Silvan Shalom, former Israeli Foreign Minister.

Second presenter reads 'the rest of the news' (as news in brief):

- Darren Campbell's refusal to do a lap of honour (including Campbell clip).
- Police consider requesting new powers to punish without recourse to courts.
- Prison officers vote for strike action over pay.
- Pictures of Princes William and Harry are three years old; not new, as claimed by a newspaper (statement by *Sun* newspaper then read out).
- First World War soldier shot for cowardice to be pardoned.

Main presenter trails Lord Levy item before commercial break, and Lebanon report on return. Recaps top three headlines in reverse order.

Fourth story

- Middle East conflict.
  Presenter introduces clips of Presidents Assad of Syria and Ahmadinejad of Iran criticising US and UK foreign policy. This is followed by *package*: containing reporter's encounter with a group of Israeli soldiers (no interview); a clip of Hassan Siklawi, UN spokesman; and clip of a resident of one of the villages attacked by Israeli troops.

Second presenter introduces more news in briefs:

- Clip of David Cameron attacking Government security policy.
- Laptops recalled by manufacturer because of fire risk.
- Smaller businesses who use ebay 'go on strike' in protest at the fees charged.
- Inflation still above Government targets.
- Markets and currencies.
- Weather.

Fifth story

- Lord Levy's appointment diaries.
  Package: containing clip of Shahid Malik, MP; clip of William Hague, Shadow Foreign Secretary; clip of Mike Gapes, Chairman of Foreign Affairs Select Committee. (Issue: is Lord Levy too strong a pro-Israeli influence, and running counter to Foreign Office policy?)

  Trail of Castro pictures (commercial break and programme trail).

Sixth story

- First moving pictures of Castro since operation.
  Package: containing clips of President Chavez talking to Castro; clips of Havana residents.

Headlines recap.

Here is the running-order for **Five News on 15 August 2006:**

Headlines

- Airline passengers' bags go missing, as airlines complain over the handling of the terror alert.
- Police call for more on-the-spot fines for yobs.
- John Terry's first (training) outing as England captain.
- Learn how to be psychic.

First story

- Missing passenger bags.
  Package: including clip of Michael O'Leary, boss of Ryanair; clip of Muslim claiming Muslim passengers are unfairly picked on for security checks.
  Appeal for viewers' experiences of first story.

Second story

- New police powers to deal with yobs?
  Package: including Chief Constable Bob Quick (ACPO, the Association of Chief Police Officers); clip of Declan O'Dempsey (described as 'human rights barrister').

News in brief

- Breast cancer patients at risk from Herceptin.
- Dell recalls batteries because of safety scares.
- Pardon for Private Henry Farr, shot in 1916.
- First pictures of Castro since operation.

Third story

- Latest on Middle East conflict.
  Package: including clip of President Assad of Syria; actuality of reconstruction of buildings damaged in conflict.

Fourth story

- Steve McClaren's first England squad, prior to first friendly fixture. Clip of McClaren; clip of John Terry; clip of Danny Fullbrook of *Daily Star*.

News in brief

- Steve Staunton threatened at gunpoint (with clip of Staunton).
- Andy Murray beats Tim Henman.

Fifth story

- Courses on how to be a psychic.
  Package: including clip of course pupil; course of course tutor; clip of tarot teacher; clip of (sceptical) psychologist. (Visual effects of fortune-telling, dry ice, etc.).

News in brief

- Burglar's attempted getaway stalls in river.

Headline recap, and trail of next day's programme featuring memories of Queen Mother's former equerry.

Analysis

Both bulletins lead on the continuing effects of the discovery of an alleged airline terror plot. However, the two bulletins lead on different elements of it. There is always journalistic kudos to be gained by being able justifiably to use the word 'exclusive'. It would also be broadly accepted within the journalistic community that it is used slightly more selectively by the broadcast media than in the print world. However, it is also possible that Five News would have chosen to lead on the aspect it did (missing luggage) even if it had secured an exclusive similar to Channel 4's. The luggage angle undoubtedly has more 'human interest' appeal than the suspect's brother interview: not only because it can be illustrated with a lively vox pop, but also because it is the kind of development which will overlap most obviously with viewers' own lives and (possibly very recent) experiences.

It is important not to overstate the populist, 'human interest' factor when discussing Five News. This station is distinct from the other three in not having an in-house, 'own-brand' newsroom, and it had fairly recently changed from an ITN to a SkyTV-sourced news operation. This led to speculation about a move further downmarket, though this was not necessarily borne out by results.

This may have been because Five, as a channel, had recently repositioned itself somewhat further 'upmarket'. More art and history documentaries replaced the earlier emphasis on soft porn-related material (football, one of the other notorious 'f's, remained). Indeed, one of the ironies of this period is that Channel 4 continued to air documentaries on porn (often viewed as a popular cultural phenomenon) after Five had largely moved away from that terrain. At the same time, Channel 4 News was often cited as one of the remaining bastions of 'upmarket' news (along with BBC 2's Newsnight).

Five News, nevertheless, highlights the element that will make people relate directly to what is portrayed. Indeed, if the intention is to make viewers say 'That's just what happened to me', then the inference is made explicit by the subsequent direct appeal for viewers to say precisely that to the news team, by contacting them with stories of their own similar misfortunes. The ITV Lunchtime News 'Pulse' feature embraced interactivity in the manner of a radio phone-in. Here, the use that will be made of the information is not made explicit; but the attempt to involve the viewer is equally direct. We refer, in the discussions of radio and of television rolling news, to what some regard as the illusion of interactivity. The same reservations are, perhaps, relevant here.

Let us also consider stories that run on one bulletin but not the other. These are the stories run on Five, but not on Channel 4:

Breast cancer/Herceptin risk. (News in brief).
Steve McClaren's squad (full treatment).
Steve Staunton threatened (clip).
Murray beats Henman. (News in brief).
Careers as a Psychic. (Package).
Burglar's stalled getaway. (News in brief).

These are the stories run on Channel 4, but not on Five:

Brother of suspect speaks (exclusive package).
CCTV footage of another suspect before arrest (news in brief).
Darren Campbell's refusal to do a lap of honour (clip).
Prison officers threaten to strike (news in brief).
Pictures of William and Harry were three years old. (News in briefs).
David Cameron attacks security policy (news in briefs).
Small businesses protest at eBay fees (news in brief).
Inflation above target (news in brief).
Markets and currencies.
Lord Levy's appointment diary (package).

Five News occupies a 30–minute broadcast slot, while Channel 4 News runs for 50 minutes. Statistically, therefore, there are always likely to be more stories run on Channel 4 News. Given this, it is, perhaps, interesting to note how many stories are run on Five and not on Channel 4. This is especially true of sport stories. There is no mention on Channel 4 of the England squad or of Murray's victory. Nor does the threat to Steve Staunton make Channel 4. This, of course, is not a 'routine' sport story in the sense that the other two are. Indeed, even these other two have extra news potential. It is the *first* sighting of McClaren's squad. It is Britain's *new* tennis hope beating the *old* standard-bearer. Nonetheless, they are planning-diary items in a way that the threat of violence against the Irish Republic's manager clearly was not. Is Steve Staunton not familiar enough to non-football fans to make Channel 4, whereas Five viewers can be expected to know of him without extensive introduction?

Channel 4 ran Darren Campbell's explanation of his refusal to join the European Championships lap of honour, whereas Five did not. Five had run aspects of the story earlier, so it may have been seen as insufficiently new or fresh as an angle for continuation. Channel 4, while less prone to run routine sporting developments, is, perhaps, alert to the presence of an issue (drugs in sport) transcending the particular event, which makes it relevant to its own agenda.

The Career as a Psychic package has the air of a relatively timeless 'filler' for Five. There is no real attempt to 'peg' it to a particular development in that day's news. On radio, it would slot readily into a current affairs programme rather than a news bulletin. (Radio One's Newsbeat, or the feature section of a DNN bulletin). Without being consciously presented as such, it has the production values of a planning-diary item pre-scheduled for what used to be called the 'And finally ...' slot. (Although, in this bulletin, it was followed by the 'official' 'and finally ...' – the story of the burglar whose getaway was stalled when he waded into a river. This, however, was delivered as a News in Brief item, not a full-blown package.)

Channel 4's Israeli war room package was longer than normal. It also had music running under the fly-on-the-wall speech elements – giving it a slightly unusual feel, running counter to the 'house style'. It was, of course, the work of an Israeli journalist, not an in-house production, which would have explained its unusualness to the alert viewer. Similarly, the visual conventions employed in the Channel 4 lead package (obscured appearance, disguised voice) are now routine in television journalism. Indeed, they are almost an expected feature in any item billed as 'exclusive'.

By contrast, the production values of the Psychic Careers package are the kind of thing you might expect to be taught on a 'Creative Packaging for Television' course: dry ice, and a readiness on the part of the interviewees to play along with the light-hearted style of the piece.

There were no two-ways, live or recorded, in the Five bulletin; and no set-piece interviews (only clips within packages). Channel 4 News, on the other hand, had two interviews to follow up packages, though no live or as-live reporter two-ways. It is one of the contentions of this book that terrestrial television news has had to redefine its role in response to the internet and rolling 24-hour news. One of the ways it has done this is to make terrestrial news slots more aware of their status and composition as programmes, rather than bulletins. This often takes the form of earlier decisions about logistics, running orders, and the allocation of reporters to particular stories; and a more settled, organised feel to the programme. It could be argued that increased awareness of terrestrial news as programme rather than bulletin has resulted in a widening of the stylistic divide between terrestrial and rolling news. Twenty-four hour news is often criticised for over-reliance on speculative reporter two-ways, often in the absence of hard facts. However, like other observations about so-called trends in television (and radio) news, this tends to occur mainly on days of large breaking stories, rather than on more routine news days of the sort we are examining.

Two further phenomena which are often remarked upon in relation to television news are the increased use of the videowall and the increase in 'citizen journalism'. As we have seen, the videowall is a fixture in the BBC Ten o'clock News, and ITV's News at 10.30. However, it is not much in evidence in these two bulletins. The 'burglar escape' story may be an example of citizen journalism, but little is made of this aspect of it in the programme, and there are no other obvious examples. As we discuss elsewhere, citizen journalism is another journalistic trend which is more in evidence on mainstream terrestrial news early in the cycle of major breaking stories, rather than on a daily basis.

Sunday Newspapers

5

Where News and Reflection Start to Merge ...

Sunday newspapers occupy a special place in western democratic countries. Sunday is traditionally a leisure day for much of the working population, meaning that people have more time to read and enjoy newspapers. And newspaper publishers respond to this by producing substantial papers. As an indicator of the shape of the industry, in July 2006 the correlative figures for similar newspapers, under the same ownership, sold in Britain (which remains the biggest single market for newspapers per capita) were:

Daily newspaper		Sunday newspaper	
Daily Mirror	1,660,151	Sunday Mirror	1,502,414
Daily Mail	2,389,236	Mail on Sunday	2,221,338
Daily Express	833,145	Sunday Express	796,956
Daily Telegraph	897,416	Sunday Telegraph	656,055
The Guardian	370,612	The Observer	457,806
The Independent	250,761	Independent on Sunday	216,175
The Sun	3,207,430	News of the World	3,482,856
The Times	667,496	Sunday Times	1,308,604
Total	**10,276,247**		**10,642,204**

Source: Audit Bureau of Circulation August 2006

What is interesting to note is that, despite requiring the majority of people to make a special journey to purchase a newspaper (during the week most buyers collect their newspapers *en route* to their place of work) the overall figures hold up well, to the point where slightly more newspapers are sold on a Sunday than the week-daily average. Some unsubstantiated research suggests that a different type of individual purchases a newspaper on a Sunday (this is based on the fact that there is an additional million or more copies of daily newspapers given away free at major transport termini) but regardless of the nuance, one fact remains – there is a substantial market for Sunday papers.

In view of the different time constraints which apply to readers of Sunday newspapers, the content tends towards 'softer' coverage; hard news is covered, but in real terms much of the content of the main newspaper – which is invariably supported by additional feature-based material in supplements which are printed on either newsprint or as glossy magazines (for example the *Sunday Times* and the *Sunday Telegraph* use both formats together) – is more reflective. Much of this material can be gathered during the week; it is rare for newspapers to have the same editorial staff working on weekly and Sunday editions, which means that there is more time available to editorial teams working on Sunday editions. As one former editor observed when handing out advice to a new editor: '... get most of the paper done by close of play Friday night because "nothing ever happens on a Saturday"' (Morgan, 2005: 27–8).

This not strictly true, of course, but what *is* true is that diary-based or scheduled events are timed by their instigators to be made public during the period Monday afternoon to Friday morning each week. The majority of such events – many of which are government or public relations agency-led – tend to be concentrated Tuesday to Thursday, and scheduled for early morning release so that they are likely to achieve the maximum coverage across all news media. But the fact that not a lot of hard news tends to occur on a Saturday does not correlate to a relaxed newsroom environment on a Saturday night, when the main body of the paper's news section is about to be finalised. On the contrary, activity can be frenzied – and it is by no means unknown for the outer page sections (which are the easiest to change without upsetting the main content of the paper) to be revised as soon as rival publications' first editions hit the news stand. Driven by intense rivalry which can sometimes cloud judgements, and mindful of the fact that, especially in the high circulation 'red top' and middle-market titles, the headline that can persuade a buyer to choose one title over another can make the difference between viability and failure, it is by no means unusual for 'me-too-ism' to set in halfway through the print run. This might take the form of plagiarised copy – there is surprisingly little recourse to legal action in such situations, as all understand that this is a fiercely competitive marketplace, and this week's victim is next week's offender, or *vice versa*.[1]

Former tabloid editor Piers Morgan explained that the rationale behind the decision one Saturday night to change to a different front cover halfway through the run was simply to spoil a rival's scoop. This change from the *News of the World*'s intended cover story came about before the *Sunday Mirror*'s first edition had been published, but was a calculated move based on information received. 'The reason we knew this, as I now found out, was that we have one of the *Sunday Mirror*'s journalists on our payroll, bunging him £250 a week for a rundown on their stories, and more if he gives us a big one. It's a disgrace, of course, and totally unethical. But very handy'. (Morgan, 2005: 35).

This practice puts an interesting spin on the issue of composition, with the inference that news comes second to the more pressing demand of gaining some kind of advantage over a competitor, or nullifying whatever advantage the competition might feel it has. Which also explains, at least in part, the reason why it is commonplace for directly competing titles to run similar lead stories. Sunday 27 August 2006 proves the exception to the rule; every single Sunday newspaper published in England on that day carried a different lead story:

Mail on Sunday   **'Spy In Your Wheelie Bin'** item concerning plans to embed microchips into domestic 'wheelie' bins, as a means of ascertaining amount of rubbish generated by households.

Independent on Sunday   **'Revolution for Women at Work'** item concerned with proposed government plans to revise policies for working mothers.

News of the World   **'For Sam's Sake'** item related to 3-year old boy whose father was shot dead following a street fracas.

Observer   **'Cameron: We got it Wrong on Apartheid'** item centred on UK opposition leader's *volte face* on a key party policy concerned with attitudes to South African political structures.

The People   **'My Drugs & Booze Shame'** item created around 'confession' of minor pop music singer and television presenter Kerry Katona.

Sunday Express   **'Sinister Hook and a Very Odd School'** item based on intelligence services disclosure that a jailed Islamic cleric had tried to infiltrate an Islamic school at some undisclosed time between 1993 and 2004.

Sunday Mirror   **'Heather's New Nude Shoot'** item exposing revelation that the estranged wife of pop musician Sir Paul McCartney has recently returned to her former career as a model, using the key (unattributed) quote 'remember, she has posed naked before.'"

Sunday Times   **'10m Want to Quit "Over-taxed" UK'** item based on results of ICM poll which suggested that one in five British adults are considering leaving the country as a result of 'failure of successive governments to deliver tax cuts'.

Sunday Telegraph   **'Blunders by NHS Kill Thousands of Patients a Year'** item analysing report by government 'watchdog' agency concerning lapses of care in state hospitals.

What strikes the authors is how all of these items play to type; as we shall see below they all follow the core agenda of the various newspapers in their placing within the publications, and the tone and language of their content.

Beginning with the *Mail on Sunday* lead story, the right-leaning , pro-British (and by definition anti-EU) newspaper gets straight in, by referring to microchips being 'secretly planted into thousands of household wheelie bins' and in the second paragraph to the German origins of the technology. And true to form, the term 'Big Brother' appears on Page One, shortly after the official reason for the chips being deployed, to '"improve efficiency" and settle disputes between owners of wheelie bins over ownership' is discredited by unnamed experts, who counter that the technology will 'enable councils to impose fines on householders who exceed limits on the amount of non-recyclable waste they put out.' An apposite quote from a right-wing politician is used to add weight to the argument posited by the newspaper: 'This is nothing more than a spy in the bin, and I don't think even the old Soviet Union made such an intrusion into peoples' lives' – in that quote, for good measure come such *Mail on Sunday* bogy terms as spy and the cold war enemy, the Russians. This plays straight into the system's value of **external influences**, as these are historically established within its management conventions. In terms of location within the news value system the item is **topical**, meets reader **expectation** (both directly and indirectly, by its appearance and the lexicon deployed during the writing of the piece) and also its **unusualness** (the existence of microchip sensors is not normal practice) and **relevance** (it has a consonance with the 'little Englander' mentality of the stereotypical *Mail* reader who is instinctively opposed to government interference in everyday life) and it is of course **worthy**, in that it has an undoubted value to the readership. Finally, it fits neatly within the overall framework of the *Mail on Sunday*, so meets the expectations of **composition**. Worth bearing in mind are two quotes about news attributed to the Daily *Mail* founder Alfred Harmsworth (later Lord Northcliffe): 'for the power, the supremacy and the greatness of the British Empire' and 'News is what somebody somewhere wants to suppress; all the rest is advertising' (also attributed, *inter alia*, to William Randolph Hearst). This set the agenda for the paper back in 1896, and it has remained essentially true to such a cynical view ever since, despite its various editors.

It is interesting to note that Harmsworth also founded the *Daily Mirror* (in 1903) to follow the same basic set of values, but this newspaper (from which the *Sunday Mirror* started in 1963 to replace the 1915–established *Sunday Pictorial*) has undergone several changes of ownership in its history, and now occupies territory at the opposite end of the political spectrum to the *Daily Mail*. The lead story covered by the *Sunday Mirror* on the day under examination is totally devoid of any political dimension; it is a straightforward 'celebrity' piece – there is a strap-line at the foot of the page exhorting readers to submit stories about stars, suggesting that this a key element of the paper's composition. The language used is simple and direct, and is generally biased towards Heather McCartney, and thus generally opposed to her estranged husband, including a reference to a petty incident on his part, when a solicitor's letter was fired off 'after her cleaner took three half-empty bottles of cleaning fluid from the cupboard' of a home belonging to the 'worth about £1billion' pop singer. That the behaviour of Heather McCartney is inconsistent with what she has done with her life since marrying Sir Paul is sufficient to qualify it as **unusual**. The **relevance, worth and expectation** of the lead item is concordant with the intended readership of the newspaper, and the **composition** issue is also wholly in accord with the newspaper's place in the world, though the **topicality** of the piece is questionable as the event described occurred three weeks prior to publication; doubtless the editor would claim that this is immaterial as the story has only just become known. It is difficult to think that such a story would run in the *Independent on Sunday, Sunday Times, Observer* or the *Sunday Telegraph*. It would, however, have been considered a worthy news item by the *People* or the *News of the World*.

But what of the *Daily Express*? This is a newspaper which has periodically changed its market position and, as has been hinted at throughout this chapter, market position is key to the application of news value systems. The *Sunday Express* dates back to 1918, but the paper on which it was modelled, the *Daily Express*, predates that by 18 years. The *Daily Express* exists, according to Hunter Davies, for the same reason today as it has throughout its history – to rival the *Daily Mail*. And that same ethos permeates the offices of the Sunday editions of the newspaper. The *Express* was founded by Arthur Pearson, the son of an impoverished Church of England curate who met Alfred Harmsworth in 1896 when both worked on a then-popular magazine, *Tit-Bits*. Neither man was friendly with the other, and after starting a magazine in 1890 (mirroring the activity of Harmsworth) Pearson ticked along as an independent publisher for almost a decade. Then in 1900 Harmsworth announced that the *Mail* was selling a million copies a day. 'Pearson was determined to grab some of those readers' states Davies, by starting his own newspaper; 'On 24 April [1900] the first issue of the *Daily Express* appeared' (1998: 28).

As might be expected of such intense rivals, the political agenda of the *Daily Express* is shared with the *Daily Mail* – both come at life from a right-wing perspective (seizing every opportunity to knock the incumbent Labour government), this despite the *Express* having undergone several changes in ownership (and political alignment) during its history. So far as the lead item is concerned this again hits all the targets, being **relevant** to, and within the **expectations** of, the readership (which is considered by the *Express* to be resolutely pro-British, and thus anti anything that is likely to threaten the country's stability and general well-being) and is also unusual, in that the infiltration of a faith school by such a radical and dangerous man as Abu Hamza is not what might be expected. In terms of **worth**, this is justified (at least in part) by the language used in the piece; Hamza is described as 'Hate preacher', 'claw-handed, one-eyed' and to be the leader of a 'twisted cause' – all in the first paragraph of the piece. Using such quotes from the report on which the item is based as the school 'does not provide a satisfactory education ... the curriculum is not broad and balanced' is likely to substantiate the worthiness of the piece with specific regard to its readership. While all of these are likely to be truths, the pejorative nature of the language used is intended to inflame the passions of readers. The majority of the story then concerns itself with the school itself, and its poor showing in a government inspection – again with a view to pointing out the **unusual** nature of the school, which as an Islamist institution contradicts the value system of the average *Sunday Express* reader, who is likely to be of at least nominally Christian background, but not necessarily passionately so. The composition of the piece is again paper-specific. The piece is not **topical**, beyond this being the first time that the information has come into the public sphere. In terms of **external influences**, these exist (in common with the *Mail on Sunday*) in the form of the 'Little Englander' prejudices of the paper's tradition, being opposed to anything which threatens the country's *status quo*.

This notion of external influences permeates other Sunday newspapers, too; the *Sunday Times*, for example. In this case the external influences might be considered more malign, as this newspaper belongs to NewsCorp, which is in turn under the direct control of its major shareholder Rupert Murdoch. For most of its life (since being founded in 1864) the *Sunday Times* has been instinctively right-leaning, but in 1997 Murdoch decided (for what various observers have claimed were measures to protect his own interests) to switch allegiance from the Conservative government of John Major to the opposition, led by Tony Blair: 'Rupert has behaved like a swine and a pig. He doesn't like backing losers and he thinks Major will lose: "Tonight the great announcement has come out that the *Sun* is backing Blair' (Wyatt, 1997). The *Sunday Times* itself, however, did not specifically endorse Labour, remaining nominal and lukewarm backers of the Tories (*The Times* advised readers to vote for the most Eurosceptic candidate in their constituency). From about the first half of 2006 there were rumblings that Murdoch (who 'has changed real political outcomes by covert and strictly irresponsible manipulation' which aligns with 'his notion of corporate good practice' [Page, 2003: 5]) was about to shift support back to the Conservative Party, whose new leader David Cameron is perceived as a possible future Prime Minister. 'The new Tory leader, David Cameron, recently met Rupert Murdoch and the two men were said to have got on well, leading to speculation that the *Sun* could switch its allegiance back to the Tories' (Macmillan, 2006) is one take on forthcoming events, while a slightly different perspective is offered by a member of the Fabian Society, a left-leaning intellectual organisation: 'the Murdoch newspapers, The *Sun*, *The Times* and the *Sunday Times* are likely to revert to Conservative allegiance once Tony Blair steps down as Prime Minister' (Gamble, 2005).

Given this type of political manoeuvring it becomes apparent that we are dealing with the last great surviving media mogul who is both prepared and able to switch allegiance of media under his control to suit his own agenda; a *prima facie* case of **external influence**. It is likely that any switch back to a right-leaning agenda will be easier for *Sunday Times* readers to accept; the tone of language used in the newspaper has tended to be passive when the government has been mentioned, rather than actively in favour of its activities. In the lead item, for instance, the tone is not openly hostile, but nor is it fawning:

'Labour, under Tony Blair and the chancellor Gordon Brown, has shied away from income tax rises, fearing they would frighten middle-class voters' is distinctly neutral in tone, but it would take only a minor shift in grammar to alter the tone. Even at the beginning of the piece the tone is neutral, referring to 'the failure of political parties to deliver tax cuts' rather than taking sides. Again, a minor shift could ally with one or other party, suggesting that at present the paper is following a 'wait and see' policy that could easily shift, without the readership necessarily becoming immediately aware. In the other main NewsCorp English-market Sunday paper, the *News of the World*, the tone is less ambiguous: the lead story is critical of the police (who are under the direct control of the government) and uses such terms as 'blasted' and 'attacked' the Metropolitan Police, in place of the more neutral 'criticised'. In the leader column of the same edition of the paper the critique of government is far more direct than might be expected of a newspaper which is ostensibly supportive of government: 'So it is time the Prime Minister rid our land of immigrant crime gangs, teen thugs and slipshod police work.'

The *News of the World* is a paper which falls somewhere in the middle, with regard to its balance of hard news and gossip; the lead story is **unusual** (not many people die at the hands of thugs on the streets of London each week), not especially **topical** (the attack on which it is based occurred at the beginning of the week prior to publication of the newspaper's story) but the paper managed to gain an exclusive interview with the mother of the dead man's son, which excuses this revisiting of what in some circles would be considered an old story. In terms of justifying the **worth** of the lead article, the item is concordant with a lengthy history of the paper's attachment to causes (it has in the recent past led strongly on anti-paedophile campaigns) and given the stance of the paper, it its with issues **of competition, relevance,** and reader **expectation**, all because of its established place in the pantheon of newspapers published in Britain. In terms of balance of the rest of the content, only some 5 out of 30 news pages are concerned with hard news; the remainder is taken up with 'celebrity' led pieces. The *Sunday Times*, in contrast, takes its news seriously, and in common with the *Sunday Telegraph* keeps its 'celebrity' content to the Diary column, and divides the remainder of the paper between domestic (10 pages) and international (6 pages) news, with the remainder of the main section being given over to op-ed and comment, including readers' correspondence. A value system analysis of the main story shows that it again ticks all the boxes. It is **relevant** and **worthy** in view of its interest to readers (many of whom might reasonably be expected to be concerned with issues of personal taxation) and its placing within the *Sunday Times* would also be **expected**, as this is an issue that fits neatly with the surrounding content. Furthermore, that a high proportion of those polled are seriously considering leaving the country in view of taxation issues is definitely **unusual**.

Moving to the two centralist Sunday publications in the English marketplace, both the *Independent on Sunday* and the *Observer* work hard to be neutral, and to remain aloof from any accusations of hegemony on the part of owners; the *Observer* and *Independent on Sunday* both pride themselves on a sense of independence: 'This is a newspaper with a mind of its own and a voice that's clear. We are free from proprietorial influence. We are not swayed by political affiliation. We, like our readers, have an independent perspective on life, which, we believe, comes through the conviction of our opinions and the excellence of our writing' says the *Independent*'s Editor in Chief (Kelner, 2006) while the *Observer* ultimately belongs to the same group as the *Guardian*, and is inculcated with the same value system as that laid down by that paper's founder C. P. Scott, who famously said: 'Neither in what it gives, nor in what it does not give, nor in the mode of presentation, must the unclouded face of truth suffer wrong. Comment is free, but facts are sacred' (1921).

This neutrality reflects in the editorial content of both newspapers; neither owner influences nor political pressure is allowed to influence the messages within its coverage of event.

Critics of the *Independent on Sunday*'s lead item could argue successfully that this piece lacks balance; its entire content is drawn from the government's issued statement on the matter, and is notable for a lack of counter-argument from opposition political parties – but this is as likely an error of editorial judgement (possibly complicated by the unavailability of any suitable spokespersons, in view of this being a national holiday weekend) than a case of political bias. In terms of **relevance** to the readership, the paper's stance as a publication for people of independent mind to whom women's issues are likely to play a significant role ought to justify the item, making it **worthy** and **expected**. It is **unusual** in that the proposed new rules break with the status quo. So far as a **composition** is concerned the item fits with other, surrounding items; immediately above the story continuation on Page 2 is concerned with education shortfalls for children in care, and facing that page is a fashion item geared to appeal to women readers. So far as the rest of the coverage in the *Independent on Sunday* is concerned, this is a curious mish-mash that seems to contradict the high-ground position to which its Editor in Chief alludes; there is far less hard news than might be expected, and it is carries celebrity gossip (a full page story about the alleged infidelity of a major rock musician, and almost a page covering a movie actor's loss of contract, to provide but two examples) along with lifestyle-driven editorial. Similarly, the international news section is of only limited scope in terms of hard news, with lots of soft news filling; how else to describe a half page on the potential for succession to the throne in Tonga, and a half page on plans for a redevelopment of Moscow's city centre? The remainder of the paper's news pages are taken up with op-ed columns, readers' letters, etc.

The *Observer* leads on a piece that is entirely consistent with the paper's centrist views; the crux of the story is a change of direction to a more neutral form of conservatism, and acts as a lead in to the editorial coup on the paper's part of having the leader of the party write a column for this edition. Covering a newly announced stance on the controversial topic of apartheid (a departure from the past position taken by Margaret Thatcher, a previous party leader) is equally consistent with the paper's standpoint, meaning that the item scores on **relevance**, **topicality**, and **expectation**. It additionally is **worthy** because it indicates a political sea-change, and that is additionally an **unusual** development on the British political landscape. The remainder of the paper is split much in accordance with those other broadsheet newspapers the *Sunday Times* and *Sunday Telegraph*, with 10 pages of domestic news (plus 2 of reflective pieces on the weeks' main news stories), 6 of international news and the remainder being made up of op-ed and other columns, including readers' letters.

As for the *People*, this is a newspaper with no apparent political conviction – and an assessment of its content suggests that hard news appears to be of relatively little interest to its editor, which in turn infers that is what its (840,860 – ABC August 2006) buyers expect. Instead it seems to exist mainly on a diet of frothy 'celebrity' stories – though here the notion of celebrity is stretched to its limits, as it seems to concentrate on minor talents, and those who achieved some modicum of fame by appearing on 'reality' television shows – something that is in itself a questionable notion, as it can be successfully argued that once ordinary people are placed in exceptional situations then they no longer behave as ordinary people, and so the notion of 'reality' becomes corrupted. 'Millions tune in to see people being humiliated, with cash for the person who can stick it out to the end. The very fact that so many people actually enjoy watching others getting hurt physically or humiliated psychologically is disturbing' was how Diana Whaley (2001) explained the system, while Noah Page of the *World Socialist International* took an even more cynical view, describing 'reality' television as a mechanism for creating a career which is: 'not for the sake of doing work that benefits real people, but for the sake of *itself*, and for the 'entertainment' value of achieving it, by any means necessary, at the expense of others' (2005).

Part of the Mirror group (which owns the *Daily Mirror* and *Sunday Mirror* newspapers, as well as Scotland's *Daily Record* and *Sunday Mail*) the *People's* hard news content on the day being studied comprised a 400 word item concerned with hospital care spending reductions, short (75 word) items concerned with a statement by the Iraqi Prime Minister; Iran's nuclear programme; the death of a Taliban chief, and additional support for a peacekeeping force in Lebanon, all on Page 2 of the paper. Further into the paper there were short items concerning the potential cost of recycling rubbish (essentially the same story that the *Mail on Sunday* has as its Page one splash) plus smaller items on the risk of extra-marital affairs; a gift by a member of the British royal family to a charity; a vicious attack on a family pet cat, and a 12-year-old girl's death in a car crash. Further hard news items concerned a serious attack on a four-year-old boy; a hit-and-run death in rural Dorset; a shop manager being charged with drug dealing; the burglary of a top jockey's home and the 'disappearance' of up to three million visitors to the UK from the Eastern bloc. The remainder of the paper's editorial pages were made up of 'celebrity' stories, features, op-ed columns, and a broad-ranging sports section.

Compare this with the *Sunday Telegraph*, a serious newspaper which has consistently pursued a predominantly hard news agenda, leaving the trivial items to its *Mandrake* diary section. The lead story is consistent with the paper's conservative ideology (though former editor Max Hastings claims that under his stewardship 'the *Telegraph*'s rabid brand of conservatism would no longer prevail' [2002:25]) and thus meets all of the idealised values: it is relevant to the readership, and is expected by readers that such news items will be treated seriously by the *Sunday Telegraph* staff. It is **topical** as the report on which it is based was released during the previous week and had been interrogated by *Sunday Telegraph* reporters right up to on-press time, and its **compositional** role is beyond question, as it is critical of the incumbent leftwards-leaning government. That deaths in hospital due to errors or judgement or practice are exceptional qualifies the story as having the requisite unusualness, and it is of course **worthy** in view of its level of interest to readers, who could well take a valid interest in any item that either resonates with their own experiences, or highlights their good fortune in not having such experiences.

As for the remainder of the newspaper's main section, 12 pages are dedicated to 'new' domestic news, 7 to a retrospective review and update of news which has emerged during the week, 8 to international news, and the remainder to op-ed pages, including readers' letters. In common with other substantial newspapers such as the *Sunday Times* and the *Observer*, sections such as sports news, entertainment reviews, travel and business are hived off into separate stand-alone supplements.

Conclusion

If there is a single conclusion to be drawn from this exercise, it is that the boundaries of what constitutes and defines news are more blurred on a Sunday than they are on any weekday; Saturday editions of certain newspapers (The *Guardian, Daily Telegraph,* and *Daily Mail,* for instance) fall somewhere between the two, though hard news content tends to be higher than on a Sunday because they have all Friday's events to work with. It is additionally worth pointing out that in common with our analysis of daily newspapers, the timing was deliberately chosen to make use of a period when Britain's parliament is in recess. From late September (when the party conferences take place) through to the official opening of the new Parliamentary session in October, the amount of political coverage would considerably distort the content of papers – and the same happens again each spring. For the same reason, those newspapers which opt to place their sports coverage in the main body of the newspaper have had such content excepted from this analysis, in the interests of a level playing field.

Those *caveat lectors* aside, similar exercises throughout the year will elicit broadly similar results; the split between hard and soft news, and between real news and coverage of the activities of 'celebrities' will be largely the same, and will be driven by the market position (and thus the editorial stance) of the newspapers studied. There will also be a more reflective approach on a Sunday within not just the op-ed columns, but within the news coverage itself; this is something of an inevitability, as editorial staff are forced to fill pages with what really amounts to news the topicality of which has passed its 'best by' date. Until there is a major shift in policy – such as a mass falling from favour of 'reality' television programmes, for instance, or a completely new ownership status for a newspaper that repositions the paper in its market-place – this is unlikely to change.

Note

1 Interestingly, on the front page of the Business section of the *Observer* of 27 August 2006, was an item which claimed: 'News International, which launches a free daily *thelondonpaper* next month, has accused Associated Newspapers' rival title, *London Lite*, which launches this week, of plagiarism. A senior executive at News International told the *Observer*: 'They have copied from our dummy presentation'. Associated Newspapers responded by describing the claims as 'pathetic' and "Rubbish"'. Significantly, there were no threats of litigation.

Rolling News

The Emergence of Rolling News Brings with it Fresh Challenges to the Journalist and Editor

We have noted elsewhere the increasing enthusiasm for anniversaries, and the consequences for news values. In our detailed content analysis of broadcast news, we have avoided samples of output where one story dominates bulletins. However, it seems useful to study a selection of slices of output where one story *does* dominate, and where there is even more evidence of planning and early decisions. We will examine output from Sky News and CNN (with a brief look at BBC News 24) on 11 September 2006: the fifth anniversary of the attacks on the USA.

We will examine how the day's breaking news was integrated with material already planned for the anniversary, and the differences and similarities between the channels' approaches. The output contains particular strands (like Insight on CNN, and a full-length documentary), which distinguish it from the 'pure' blocks of news of the type we see in our examination of Digital News Network (DNN) radio in Chapter 7.

We will then review some of the more general observations and conclusions about rolling news, and see the extent to which they remain justified.

Here is a selection of output from 9.00 p.m. until 10.00 p.m. on the evening of 11 September 2006:

Sky News, 11 September 2006

Headlines

- Special events held to commemorate September 11, 2001.
- New video from Ayman al-Zawahiri warns of fresh attacks.

- No breakthrough in hunt for killers of teenager Jesse James. Trail ahead to first case under changed double jeopardy rules.
- Appeal for viewers to contact Sky News by webcam or 3G phone (this is specifically billed as an interactive news programme).

First story

- Services and events of commemoration for September 11.
- Extended package (preceded by health warning of images of original attacks on World Trade Centre). Includes: clips of recital of names of the victims; observation of silence; clips of memories from survivors and victims' relatives; clip of ex-NYC Mayor Rudolph Giuliani; clip of Vice President Dick Cheney. During the broadcast of this package, viewers were asked to vote on whether they felt more or less safe five years after the 9/11 attacks (no result was revealed during the selection of output surveyed).
- News in brief of new Zawahiri tape.
- Personal commentary and observations by Sky's Washington correspondent (split screen shows related footage).

News in brief stories

- Police seek more time to question London terror suspect.
- Tony Blair's Lebanon press conference disrupted by protests.
- Mahmoud Abbas announces Fatah and Hamas have agreed on a coalition government.
- Jessie James's head teacher pays tribute to the murdered teenager.
- NHS employees vote on strike action.
- Appeal for interactive comment on: 9/11, death of Jessie James, change to double jeopardy rule.

There was a further News in brief, on repatriation of the bodies of UK soldiers killed in Afghanistan. This is then used as the 'peg' for a review of the War on Terror in Afghanistan since 2001, and in Iraq since 2003.

Package on five years of the War on Terror. No clips, but reporter narrative and footage. Followed by live interview with Jamal Khashoggi, analyst, on al-Qa'eda. Interview then interspersed with contributions from viewers. 'Young Muslim' (male) on webcam, and 'Sky News viewer' on phone. Three-way discussion.

Trail ahead and appeal for more feedback. Commercial break. Weather (Italy).

Sport

Reading v. Manchester City updates, and other football NIBs. Cricket and rugby NIBs follow.

Weather (UK).

Headlines

9/11, Blair protest,
Double jeopardy. Email comment from viewer re double jeopardy.

Commercial break

Second story

- Double jeopardy. Murder of Julie Hogg. Includes: clip of Julie's mother Ann Ming (who campaigned for change in law for many years); clip of tape of police interview with Billy Dunlop admitting to killing Julie; clip of Det. Supt. Dave Duffy.
- Followed by: live interview with Julian Young (criminal lawyer). Trail ahead to sport and appeal for feedback.

Markets

Headlines

Straight repeat of previous set as above.
Newspaper front pages (as available).

Sports update

Further copy-only score update on Reading v. Manchester City.
Clips of Jose Mourinho and Rafa Benitez ahead of Champions League games.
News in brief: Brian Kidd joins Sheffield Utd. Lennart Johanssen defends Sven-Goran Eriksson's record.
Short taped interview with Andrew Flintoff on his fitness for forthcoming Ashes tour; followed by clip of Australian Cricketer Shane Warne.
Rugby latest plus Martin Johnson clip. NIBs on athletics, tennis, hockey and golf.

Viewer feedback

Presenter reads out texts and emails. One is a direct criticism of Sky's news judgement (and news values) in devoting so much time to 9/11 commemorations and only seconds to the servicemen's deaths in Afghanistan. Presenter accepts validity of comment and apologises.

This direct viewer comment on news values clearly opens up a debate with which this book is directly concerned, and to which we will return. When interactivity strays beyond the parameters set by the programme makers and challenges the assumptions on which the programme itself is constructed, it raises interesting questions not just about news values, but about censorship and self-censorship. Even in a case such as this, the interactivity is not genuinely symmetrical. The producer or presenter who chose to broadcast the comment could have chosen otherwise without the audience being any the wiser. In the authors' experience, material critical of a programme being broadcast or of the station itself often brings management criticism of the programme team responsible for broadcasting it. Also in the authors' personal experience, feedback can occasionally be used on air by one producer or presenter to buttress one side of an argument conducted in a pre-programme production meeting where the team has been divided over a matter of news values.

Let us also take a look at what was on CNN that same evening. Here is a view of output between 10 pm and midnight.

CNN, 11th September 2006

Headlines

- Remembering 9/11 Clip of Rudolph Giuliani.
- Rocket fire interrupts 9/11 commemorations in Afghanistan.
- New Zawahiri tape.
- Protest at Blair's Beirut visit. Clip of Blair.
- Abbas reaches deal on Palestinian government.
- Hurricane Florence pulls away from Bermuda.

This was followed by a programme-length documentary billed as a Special Presentation: Remembering 9/11.

Headlines

- Straight repeat of previous headlines.

This was followed by the Insight strand. This consisted of clips from 9/11, linked by the presenter, followed by an interview with a survivor lasting several minutes. After this came a feature-called 'Where Are They Now?', focusing on Giuliani, and senior figures from the New York Police and Fire services.

Commercial break

Then came a section on the toxic effects of 9/11. A report first run in January 2002 was rebroadcast. This was followed by a new package on the same topic. This contained: clips of two survivors now experiencing health problems; a clip of a lawyer; a statement from New York Law Department (who were asked for an interview but declined); and a clip of a doctor.

Markets

Visual only.

Headlines

- Straight repeat of previous set.

There then followed a section on the Ground Zero clean-up and rebuilding operations. First came a package first run in May 2002 on the progress of the clean-up. This was followed by a new package on the plans for rebuilding containing several clips of the redesign co-ordinator David Childs; also, a clip of an architect who contested Childs's plans and vision of the future.

After programme trails, the headlines were repeated. This time, it was made clear that the story of the rocket attack was a CNN exclusive. A CNN team was there when it happened and provided pictures (presumably) not filmed by other outlets. This is followed by:

World sport

- Tennis: Federer beats Roddick to win US Open. Package on match, followed by CNN interview with Federer (interspersed with footage). Includes line on Federer and Woods as dominant figures in their sports. Followed by short piece on their comparative records in Grand Slam tournaments.
- Football. Real Madrid and Barcelona's latest games (Champions League and Primera Liga). Chelsea latest – including clip of Jose Mourinho.

World weather and trail

- Argentine football: referee walks off pitch at league game (corruption/pressure allegations).
- Golf: Ryder Cup players tee up in World Match Play. Cristie Kerr wins title.
- Formula One: Schumacher's retirement announcement, and duel with Alonso for drivers' title. Clip of Damon Hill. Briatore complains of favouritism in Formula One.
- Sport business item: Interview with analyst Rick Horrow. Subjects: tennis – profiles and recognition of Sharapova and Federer. Redskins overtake Manchester Utd as world's biggest club.

Commercial/trail break

- Sporting world commemorates 9/11: Clips of Shane Warne and Martin Johnson.
- 'Play of the Day' clips: one from American football, and one from Argentinean football (soccer).
- Trails.
- Reading v. Manchester City update.

'And finally...'

- International Bognor Birdman contest.

To complete the picture, let us take a brief look at what was on **BBC News 24** at about the same time.

Headlines

President Bush will say later tonight that the War on Terror is not over.
Four men arrested in South London on suspicion of terror offences are charged.
New statement from al-Qa'eda 's Zawahiri.
There was also a section on the impact of 9/11 on the business community.
Package on survivors of 9/11. Clip of Twin Towers waiter, now co-founder of Colors Restaurant; clip of member of 9/11 Families Association; clip of former head of New York Stock Exchange. Pre-recorded interview with CEO and Chairman of Cantor Fitzgerald. Heads and Trail ahead.
Package. Coca-Cola in Afghanistan: new factory in Kabul. Clip of President Karzai.
Package. Dell in difficulties. Clip of analyst. Clip of financial journalist.
News in brief: Telecom Italia to hive off mobile businesses.
Hewlett Packard: concerns over leaks of confidential information.
Glaxo SmithKline: measures to tackle tax debt.
Package. Upturn in oil market. Clip of Qatari Oil Minister.
Footage of reopening of New York Stock Exchange, followed by dialogue between London and New York presenters on market trends since 2001.

Analysis

This selection of pieces of output was made to explore how broadcast news treats events for which extensive planning is undertaken. As important is the response to news unrelated to the main story.

Sky

Sky News is dominated by its 9/11 coverage, but does allot headline space to two other main stories and significant coverage to one of them – the double jeopardy reversal case. This, too, however, is a news item which could have been planned for and placed in the diary well in advance. The line chosen on the third story was more a statement that nothing had happened than a report of an important new development ('No breakthrough in the hunt for the killers of Jessie James').

As we have seen, it was the news of the repatriation of the bodies of British soldiers killed in Afghanistan which prompted the on-air discussion of news values. The viewer's complaint was that far too much time was devoted to the events of commemoration of 9/11, while only a few seconds were given to the soldiers' deaths. The repatriation of fallen soldiers would almost certainly have been known about in advance. Breaking news of deaths in combat would have been unexpected, and would have required instant news value judgements. However, the decision on whether or not to devote resources to the repatriation of the soldiers' bodies would presumably have been a more considered one and, perhaps, in view of the on-air criticism and the acceptance of it by the presenter, one the station may have regretted. Of course, the deaths can nevertheless be seen as a direct result of the 9/11 attacks. This could be used to argue that, as an illustration of its continuing effects, it should have received more prominence. Perhaps the decision to give greater priority to the new Zawahiri tape was seen as having filled the slot for 'effects of 9/11 still being felt today'.

CNN

CNN's round-up of main stories centred almost exclusively on the Middle East (though not solely on 9/11 news). Apart from the immediate coverage of the commemorations, prominence was given to the rocket attack which interrupted the ceremonies in Afghanistan. This was introduced as a CNN exclusive. Viewers are informed that their camera team were on-site filming the commemorations, and recorded the rocket attack – thus obtaining a 'CNN exclusive'. Bonnie M. Anderson in *News Flash* (2004: 103–4) talks about the overuse and misuse of the 'exclusive' tag by American news networks. She describes how even the slightest addition to, or variation from, the material run by other networks is used to justify the use of the 'exclusive' tag. However, on this occasion, it does appear, on face value, to be justifiable. The footage was not run on either Sky or BBC News 24 during the times sampled.

The Zawahiri tape is also run on CNN, as is coverage of the protests against Blair's visit to Beirut, and progress towards the formation of a new Palestinian government. Replacing the London terror suspect questioning and the vote on NHS strike action run on Sky is CNN's account of Hurricane Florence pulling away from Bermuda, which is not run elsewhere.

CNN's overall approach involves a programme-length documentary, followed by packages on carefully chosen aspects of the 9/11 attacks and their aftermath – the effects of toxicity, and the clean-up of the Ground Zero site were the topics addressed (retrospectively and in the present) in the output sampled. The juxtaposition of packages from the past with updated reports is an effective way of reporting developments. Naturally, it indicates continuity between the elements of the event deemed most significant at the time and those covered five years on.

The World Sport section, after rounding up the latest developments in tennis, football, golf and Formula One, and following an interview with a sports business analyst, has a section on the World of Sport remembering 9/11. Shane Warne and Martin Johnson give brief accounts of their memories of, and reactions to the day. Anderson (2004: 155) gives an account of how CNN executives planned to cover the FIRST anniversary of 9/11 by inviting celebrities to comment and be interviewed. Among those on the email list, apparently, were Britney Spears, Justin Timberlake, Jim Carrey, Macaulay Culkin, Ted Danson and Michael Jordan. She cites this in support of her overall argument that we are witnessing a move towards 'Hollywoodisation' of news and infotainment. Presumably, she would also apply her argument to the use of Shane Warne and Martin Johnson. Interestingly, the idea was never pursued in 2002. Have we moved further in that direction, or is an exercise deemed questionable for news coverage more acceptable in a sporting context? Either way, within a few moments, we are treated to clips of the International Bognor Birdman contest – presumably the sports desk's prime candidate for the day's 'And finally ...' item.

BBC News 24

The BBC News 24 top headline story trailed ahead to the remarks President George W. Bush was expected to make later that night to mark the fifth anniversary of the 9/11 attacks. The President, we were told, is expected to say that the War on Terror is not over. (The other two headlines also related to aspects of alleged Middle Eastern-originated terrorism.) Without reading too much into one brief headline, it does embody two features of the rolling news culture that are often criticised. One is the tendency to project forwards, anticipate, or speculate on forthcoming events, rather than to report what has already occurred. The other is to state or report the obvious as if it were a startling revelation. It is unlikely many viewers were shocked out of a complacent assurance that the war on terror had been successfully resolved and put to bed.

Rather like the CNN World Sport section, BBC News 24's World Business Report mixes items and packages on the news of the day with material specific to the 9/11 commemorations. The report on Coca-Cola in Afghanistan is, in business news terms, a 'good news' story. It is also, one suspects, the kind of development that critics would point to as ex-emplifying a form of cultural imperialism associated with the USA in the early 21st Century. The news is presented straight, however, without any reference to potential controversy. It is similar to the kind of stories that used to run in the last days of Soviet Communism and shortly afterwards. 'McDonalds arrives in Moscow' was a typical headline of the time.

The other main piece of 9/11 material was the package of interviews and clips with 9/11 survivors. This avoids the trivialisation criticisms levelled at CNN by Anderson, and provides a range of human interest stories angled to a business news strand. The waiter-turned-entrepreneur, the Families Association member, and the former New York Stock Exchange head provide a useful range of perspectives, and is a good example of how planning for major news stories can be usefully and competently accomplished.

24-hour news

The criticisms most frequently levelled at rolling news are that it is repetitive, that it is too speculative, that it relies too much on the two-way between presenter and reporter, and that it puts more emphasis on speed than on accuracy. On the evidence of our brief analysis, and of much more extensive viewing, this is a partial and rather inaccurate picture of the output. It *is*, arguably, a justified commentary on 24-hour news at times of large breaking stories. Here, the output is often characterised by two-ways long on speculation and short on hard facts. In more normal times, however, the criticism is not especially relevant. Our own sample and a more extended viewing of 24-hour news channels actually reveals extensive packaging and shows evidence of the same diary-driven and planning-based news agenda that we find in terrestrial television news.

Managing the story that won't go away

The death of Pope John Paul II should provide a salutary lesson to rolling news organisations

The death of a pope has a considerable impact on global populations. As head of a major institution – a role without parallel in other major religions – the death of the Pontiff of the Catholic church of Rome could be said to deserve the media attention it gains. Being pope is a quasi-political figure, thanks to the estimated billion-plus members of the Catholic faith, almost invariably believers and followers of the doctrine emanating from the Vatican, who are dotted around the world.[1] So it is unsurprising that the world's media gathered in Rome during the final days of Pope John Paul II's life in March 2005.

But it soon became apparent that things were going over the top. All other news stories for a ten day period (from the final hours of John Paul II through to his interment in the crypt of St Peter's Basilica on Friday 8 April 2005) seemed to be pushed aside; only as the funeral had taken place did other news begin to gain any prominence – and then

The other criticism often voiced of continuous or rolling news is that it now relies on 'citizen journalism', and that such viewer-provided journalism is not subject to the same degree of journalistic checking as conventional, professionally-produced material. In an article written at the time of the fourth anniversary of the 9/11 attacks, Andrew O'Hagan (2005) described coverage of the original attack as providing 'perhaps the strongest example of traditional news values being reduced to an instantaneous display of chaos and incomprehension.' Writing a couple of months after the 7 July attacks in London, he also observes: 'Everyone with a video phone is a journalist now, and it was amazing to see, during the London bombings, the extent to which the main news shows relied on amateur footage'.

This criticism also, however, relates mainly to times of large breaking stories. O'Hagan describes the coverage of the London bombings as 'by and large, an abysmal feeding-frenzy – amateur shock-reporters versus journalists interviewing journalists' (O'Hagan, 2005). It is, perhaps, because rolling news programmes only acquire really sizeable audiences at times of big breaking stories that these criticisms have crowded out analysis of what might be called 'regular' continuous news output. Paradoxically, in the context of our discussion, the opposite criticism is, perhaps, more relevant: that routine coverage is still too diary-based, too pre-planned, too formatted and insufficiently flexible. There is certainly little use of viewer footage or 'citizen journalism' in coverage on more average news days. But, again, as audiences are smaller, and fewer waves are made by routine daily broadcasts, critics (both academic and journalistic) tend to focus on the exceptional rather than the routine periods. Some would argue it is easier to be effective as a journalist on big news days than on routine ones. Similarly, perhaps, it is less difficult (and more exciting) to be a trenchant critic of journalism as it reacts to big crises than when the news values on display are less exceptional and more nuanced.

the main focus was on the marriage of HRH Prince Charles, heir to the British throne and former husband of Diana, Princess of Wales, to Camilla Parker-Bowles the following day. As one wag at the time observed, if Charles was being buried and the Pope was going to get married, then that would indeed be news.

The excessive treatment of a single, dominant news story is something which has become all too common in today's news culture (and is one which we study in close detail in Chapter 12, when we look at the coverage of the demise of a former KGB officer) and indicates a twist on the 'me too' nature of news coverage. Whenever a major international event arises, there follows immediately the process of editors jumping onto the bandwagon, as no editor is prepared to allow any rival to gain an advantage. The corollary to this is the difficulty in getting off the bandwagon again; it is a brave editor who drops a story while others are still working its nooks and crannies for material to publish. Only when the Pope's remains had been interred could the story be safely slipped off the radar.

(Continued)

It could be argued that the selection of anniversary output tells us less about news values than a more randomly selected slice of news broadcasting. However, we look elsewhere at several examples of such output. Indeed, we would argue that the news values and styles of delivery on display in routine rolling news are less different from those in terrestrial television news than is often implied. It is sometimes suggested (even by former practitioners) that rolling news consists almost entirely of live two-ways and speculative journalism, as compared with the thoughtful, crafted pieces transmitted on terrestrial news programmes. To repeat, this is true when big stories are breaking, but not really at other times.

There is scope for more international news perspectives on continuous news channels. Also, because of the possibility of alternation and rotation of stories, items that would be unlikely to feature on main terrestrial news bulletins will make it to air on the continuous news channels. The increasing use of programme strands on 24-hour news also affects the news values on display. Stories will be sought, commissioned and covered specifically for particular programmes that might not otherwise make it to air. Likewise, stories that might have been considered to run on a general news strand may not be covered because the resources are needed for a themed story for one of the strands which would not otherwise have been strong enough for the general news cycle.

Interactivity

We discuss interactivity in broadcast news in a variety of contexts elsewhere. In radio, audience feedback started with phone-in programmes (supplemented

In retrospect, it would be interesting to know whether CNN would toady reconsider the merits of the decision to relocate the entire European service to the Vatican City for the duration of the pope's demise and lying in state. All programmes came from there – including news of other events around the world – and it soon became apparent to viewers that the anchors were becoming increasingly uncomfortable with having to constantly return to two-ways with reporters based just outside the studio. There was an almost palpable sense of relief after the funeral, when the team returned to their home studios across Europe and Asia.

According to the *Global Language Monitor*, the death of Pope John Paul II was the biggest story ever in terms of media coverage; with 100,000 stories filed (and 12 million internet citations) it eclipsed the Asian Tsunami, the death of Diana, Princess of Wales, the September 11 terrorist attacks and the 2004 American elections. 'Perhaps the root of this phenomenon lies in the fact that ordinary people came to be acquainted with this by the listeners' letters). In the late 1990s, email comments were taken, and in the early 2000s, most radio stations set up text messaging facilities.

Broadly, television – and television news in particular – has been slower to adopt viewer feedback as an integral part of its output. Radio news and current affairs programming tends to be more flexibly structured than its television counterparts, so comments can be taken at greater length.

On BBC Local Radio, for example, as well as having a specific phone-in programme, stations were encouraged from the late 1990s to incorporate more interactivity and feedback into speech-based breakfast and drive time programmes: a trend which still continues.

There is more scope for feedback and interactive comment on continuous news than on terrestrial news programmes. We have already seen it in action on Sky News. It is also a presence as rolling text accompanying the pictures on other news channels (another aspect of broadcast news satirised in the BBC comedy *Broken News*). However, it is also becoming a presence on terrestrial regional news as well. For example, BBC Midlands Today, in late 2006, occasionally incorporated viewer comments (email and text) into its bulletins as well as running periodic telephone polls.

The disadvantage of much of this viewer feedback is its brevity and, hence, superficiality. The danger, clearly, is of an endless recycling of phrases such as 'This is a disgrace', and 'I think it should be banned immediately' (almost whatever the topic under discussion!). A programme like Sky Interactive is able to transcend this banality and engage in detailed discussion of issues. However, it is interesting to note that, in the hour studied, there were only two on-air contributors (albeit at some length), and a handful of text and email comments put to air. This is probably comparable with a similar radio news programme, but considerably fewer than on, say, a typical radio phone-in programme.

pope unlike any other in memory' explained Paul Payack of the *Monitor*, adding 'he was a truly global pontiff adept at using the traditional media (and the internet) to his advantage. Evidently, on his instructions, the media was even notified of his passing via text messages and email' (Payack 2005).

That infers a combination of news value factors; it was **relevant** and **expected** in that there were many news receivers who would expect to know of it, it was initially **topical** (in that until his death there were periodic changes in his condition) and it was **worthy**, because of his global significance. Popes do not die very often so it was **unusual**. It might also be argued, given the pope's familiarity with the media system, that there was a degree of **external influence**; the power of the Church and its leader cannot be ignored.

Quite whether these combine to justify the media frenzy that swirled around the story is a matter of conjecture, one that is likely to be debated for some time to come.

Note

1 These can only ever be estimated, due to the lack of a global standard for measuring religious involvement. The *Christian Science Monitor* suggests that 'up to 1.9 billion people consider themselves Christian, while all Catholics are Christians, by no means all Christians are Catholics. Another statistic offered is that prepared by Barrett for, among others, the *Encyclopaedia Britannica*; this suggests that there are up to 2.1 billion Christians. Regardless of the pedantry of data gathering, it is agreed that Catholics are the world's dominant religion, by a ratio of around 1.2:1 over the nearest 'rival' religion, Islam'. (*Top 10 Organized Religions in the World* in *The Christian Science Monitor*, 4th August 1998 edition)

Radio Broadcast News

7

Facing a Set of Challenges and Pressures as the Digital Age Embeds Itself in Modern Culture

In this chapter, we propose to examine a number of radio news outlets to discover how news values are applied in practice. We will also explore the tension between the requirements of the traditional radio news bulletin – or programme – and the demands of the various rolling or continuous news formats now available. We will also consider how the spread of 24-hour news has changed the nature of the traditional news output on analogue radio. Having examined a number of specific examples, we will attempt some conclusions as to how news values evolve and are applied in practice.

Case Study 1 – Radio: Digital News Network (DNN)

Before we conduct a detailed analysis of DNN, let us first very briefly review the recent history of the concept of rolling or continuous news on British radio.

Within the BBC, the idea of a news channel on radio received a major impetus during the 1991 Iraq War. The then Deputy Director-General John Birt decided to split Radio 4's Long Wave and FM frequencies; with normal programming on Long Wave, and continuous war programming on FM. This was quickly and predictably dubbed 'Scud FM' by the journalistic community.

The experiment ended with the conflict. The idea, however, remained a long-term aspiration of Birt's. After he succeeded Michael Checkland as Director-General, he was able to make progress with the idea – resulting

(Continued)

in today's BBC Five Live. This is not, however, in any strict sense, a rolling news channel: though it has the capability of becoming a continuous news channel sporadically, when circumstances justify such a format. There are now many other radio stations which also have the capacity – when required – to become temporary purveyors of continuous news: talkSPORT, and many BBC Local Radio stations, for example. Few, however, offer a genuine continuous rolling news service.

One which did is DNN, the Digital News Network. It operated for 18 hours a day (from 06.00 a.m. to midnight) seven days a week and broadcast on the Digital Audio Broadcast (DAB) spectrum using various elements of the available matrices. This gives service coverage to the following English regions: The North West, North East, West Midlands, West Yorkshire and also to South Wales. While DNN has now been taken over by the bigger LBC station (and from September 2006 rebranded accordingly) the structure of its previous news service provides an effective illustration of how the system functions. We shall examine its output, looking at its remit, its structure, and the resultant news values. In order to get a full sense of how these evolve, we shall examine output on what journalists would regard as a 'normal' news day, and at a time of more exceptional breaking news. We will then compare it with what is on offer on more conventional news bulletins on stations which do not offer a continuous news service. (The successor service from LBC, incidentally, did not provide continuous news: making the DNN experiment all the more interesting and unusual as a subject of study.)

In order to do so, let us first explore the chosen format for the delivery of rolling news. Later, we will make appropriate comparisons with what is on offer from rolling television news channels. We will also consider the station's own editorial policy, and statement of journalistic values. (This, incidentally, will also involve us tackling the fascinating issue of how broadcast media sometimes consciously draw analogies between their own output and aspirations and certain newspapers. Their own positioning in the broadcast news market is often described by analogy with particular newspapers' positioning in the print sector.)

DNN operated in units of 15 minutes. Typically, such a unit would be structured as follows:

Forty seconds of headlines.
A two-minute bulletin.
A one minute and twenty second sport round-up.
A more detailed 'package' bulletin of five and a half minutes.
Business round-up.
Traffic and travel bulletin.
Entertainment news.

These are the standard building blocks of each 15-minute segment. This will then be followed by another, different 15 minute section with the same structural ingredients but with significantly different editorial components. Typically, in the absence of a major breaking news story, block one will run up to a quarter past the hour; followed by block two up to the half past. Block one will then be essentially repeated up to a quarter to; and block two will be repeated up to the next hour. Often, the only differences between the repeated blocks one and two will be any change to the updated live travel bulletin.

This contrasts with the half-hour blocks which are the staple features of rolling television news channels such as BBC News 24. This may partly reflect the greater potential immediacy of rolling radio news; and may also reflect shorter listening spans as opposed to viewing periods – though there is little detailed research on this so far. So, what about story selection, and the application of news values in practice? Let us examine a randomly chosen slice of news output. Here is a 15-minute segment of DNN output from 13.00 to 13.15 on Sunday 23 October 2005.

After three news 'teasers' (flagging up forthcoming stories) comes the main programme:

News round-up

- Birmingham riots. Copy and clip.
- Nigerian air crash. Copy and clip.
- Road crash – police responding to 999. Copy.
- Parrot death from strain of 'bird flu': latest. Copy.
- Latest on Cameron-Davis Tory leadership campaign. Copy.
- 'Waterloo' voted all-time best Eurovision song. Copy.

Weather summary

Commercial

Detailed news

- Birmingham rioting. Package.
- Nigerian air crash. Voice piece.
  (A station promo about a new website is interspersed here. Copy only).
- Hurricane Wilma approaches Florida. Voice piece with wildtrack and sound effects.

(Continued)

Travel bulletin

Showbiz news

- Midge Ure gets his OBE: two clips.
- Jennifer Aniston's new boyfriend. Copy.
- Ray Winstone reveals Brad Pitt and Angelina Jolie are to wed. Copy.
- Johnny Depp's new film. Clip.
- Antonio Banderas gets Hollywood Walk-of-Fame star. Clip.

Headlines (top four from news round-up):

Sport

- Chelsea to play Everton (top and bottom in Premiership). Clip.
- Round-up of other Premiership fixtures and previous day's results. Extra focus on Robert Pires's bizarre attempted penalty for Arsenal. Copy.
- Wembley Stadium on course to open for next FA Cup Final. Copy.

Longer sport piece

Lone yachtswoman to sail around the world 'the wrong way'. Interview.

This is a detailed breakdown of one 15-minute section. After this, it is 'back to the top', with a return to the 'teasers' and news round-up as before.

Meanwhile, because DNN was, by definition, a digital channel, there was also digital text available, which scrolled along the display of a DAB receiver. However, during this period of output, this was not providing one-line summaries of news stories, as is possible. It was concentrating on describing the station, providing details on how to contact DNN, identifying itself for new listeners, and also providing time checks every minute.

At the time of the output surveyed, there were plans to expand the textual service available to listeners, as digital radio technology developed. Generally in digital radio there is more scope to use existing news copy from the broadcast bulletin as part of the rolling text update service, by simply highlighting sections of the copy on the computer after it is written, and sending it to the text facility. This builds on what could already be done at the time surveyed. It was already used for updating sports scores on a number of digital radio channels.

As has already been indicated, this rolling 15-minute block of broadcast output was then followed by another block which was substantially similar, but with sufficient differences to avoid excessive repetition. This may involve slightly different story selection. It may also involve using different audio, or different generic devices, on the same stories. One difference on weekdays was that the sports news section was slightly shorter, and was followed by a brief, usually copy-only round-up of business news. This was deemed unnecessary at weekends.

Let us now have a look at the story selection, and some of the issues raised. DNN was a semi-national chain of radio stations, but operating as local or regional stations in several areas of the UK. The DNN output we monitored was the West Midlands service, based in Birmingham. It happened, therefore, that the lead story was local to the station's output. However, analysis of other news outlets indicates that this story was selected as the lead item on a number of other *national* TV and radio stations. It is relatively rare for stories from a local station's broadcast area to be the national lead as well. In an area like the West Midlands, though, it is more frequent than in other news areas – especially, perhaps, in predominantly rural locations. (This may, of course, be significant in its own right as a phenomenon in story selection).

The Birmingham riots were always likely to be accorded high priority nationally as well as locally. They occurred a few weeks after the twentieth anniversary of the Handsworth riots of September 1985. Racial tensions were also much in evidence in the 2005 disturbances. However, in this instance, the tensions were reported as primarily between the Asian-Muslim community on the one hand and the African-Caribbean community on the other. So the news value was perceived as inherent both in the history of ethnically-derived tensions in the Lozells and Handsworth areas, *and* in the apparently distinctive novelty of disturbances not involving the white community. There were additional features contributing to its journalistic salience. The trigger for the outbreak was reportedly an allegation of a group sexual assault by members of one of the communities on an underage female from the other tradition. However, reporting also focused on the role of a media outlet in the evolution of the tensions. It was alleged that a pirate radio station was the source of the rumour concerning the alleged sexual assault. Reporting naturally also centred on the loss of one life in the previous night's violence.

Thus, for a station like DNN – even the day after the clashes – this was likely to be an easy choice as the lead story (as mentioned, it also led on national outlets such as BBC Five Live, talkSPORT, and the evening news on BBC One television). The choice of the second story was, perhaps,

(Continued)

more finely poised. We talked earlier about the role of numbers in news values. Although anyone of any sensitivity – experienced journalists and academics included – must feel uneasy about discussing human tragedies in numerical terms, it is difficult to assess news values in practice without at least some attempt to address the issues in such a way. Thus, the decision between one fatality in a British police chase and many deaths in an African plane crash does raise interesting journalistic dilemmas. The single road fatality would attract less interest if it had not been the result of a police chase. This is because the issue of whether the public are at too great a risk from excessive police zeal in the high-speed pursuit of alleged wrongdoers is a long-running journalistic item. Also relevant in the other direction are the *numbers* reported dead in the air crash. Journalists would also consider whether the early reports that around half the passengers had survived render it *more* newsworthy than if all had perished. At the time we are analysing, there were such reports. Sadly, they turned out to be incorrect; all on board were eventually reported to have died. Another relevant factor may have been that the reports of the air crash were more recent than those of the road crash. Hence, this was chosen for inclusion in the section of longer reports.

The approach of Hurricane Wilma to Florida is probably best seen through the prism of the two recent hurricanes which afflicted the south coast of the USA. Although Wilma was widely – and correctly – anticipated to be less threatening than its predecessors, it was precisely this recent history which enhanced its journalistic potency. Galtung and Ruge would probably have addressed this from the perspective of predictability: though, arguably, it is precisely the combination of predictability and surprise that marks out stories of natural phenomena such as this. The predictability arises from the ability to track a hurricane's movements in advance; but also from the context provided by a hurricane season, and the arguments about their increased likelihood as a result of global warming. This all allows the logistics factor to kick in. The short-term predictability permits the marshalling of resources, which are correspondingly more likely to be deployed, even if the consequences of the hurricane turn out to be less than expected. This will also affect coverage of the Birmingham violence in national media. Local journalists will be present within minutes or a few hours at most. National journalists will take longer to arrive. In order to get the most out of the decision to deploy them, they will continue reporting for longer than is, perhaps, justified by the merits of the story. This will, as it were, prolong its natural news cycle as a national news story. Such a story will, in addition, have a longer cycle on local media because of its even greater salience, and the lack of comparable local stories.

The reports of the parrot's death, and the implications for so-called bird flu, are also likely to be in strong contention – even some time after the initial reports first appeared. The prospect of avian flu is almost guaranteed to force its way onto most news agendas. (An amusing variant was Tomato Flu, in the satirical BBC series *Broken News*: itself a useful commentary on 21st century broadcast news values.) The day from which our DNN sample is taken was not notable for new information on the story. However, it continued to feature – propelled by its own journalistic potential and momentum as much as by hard new developments.

The Tory leadership story was at a slightly different stage. This came days after the parliamentary votes left the two Davids – Cameron and Davis – as the two remaining candidates. There was almost a sense that the story should be put to bed for a while after its high profile for a number of days. Broadcasters – unlike newspapers – still have a need to be seen to accord the various major political parties proportionate time. So there was an almost palpable sense of relief at being able to downgrade this story before the other parties started to complain or claim to be hard done by. What looked at the time like a relatively rare spell of largely favourable publicity for the Conservatives was drawing to a temporary close. Hence its low profile, and brief treatment.

And what of 'Waterloo'? This story resulted, of course, from a survey. The use of surveys in news bulletins, and as shapers of news values, is a topic worthy of lengthy separate consideration. One serious news programme (BBC 2's *Newsnight*) itself carried a report on the proliferation of surveys at roughly the same time as this sample. They are obviously a staple method of attracting coverage of issues which might otherwise go unreported – in many cases justifiably so! Journalists often profess to be individually cynical about their use. Collectively, however, they remain a relatively easy way of generating interest. And even when the results appear unsurprising – as in the case of 'Waterloo' being named as the best Eurovision song winner in history – they are still frequently used.

What of the Showbiz Round-up? The news of Midge Ure receiving his honour was accompanied by what is almost a cliché of broadcast news: the recipient disclosing diplomatically chosen details of his (or her) conversation with the Queen (or other member of the Royal Family). In this case, this was given a little extra news value by the connection made to the recent Live8 concert, of which Ure had been one of the organisers. However, the remaining stories lack even this degree of potency. Galtung and Ruge would surely have struggled to find any notion – even that of élites – to accommodate this sort of material. *Autres temps, autres moeurs!*

(Continued)

Some – such as the new Johnny Depp film – are essentially press release material illustrated by audio clips. Others – the new Aniston boyfriend and a first parental encounter – are also the likely result of a publicist's informal briefing, if not a formal news release. The story of Ray Winstone supposedly being in the bad books of Angelina Jolie for the 'unauthorised' or 'accidental' disclosure of her forthcoming wedding to Brad Pitt is meant to sound more like news 'in the raw': a celebrity feud. We were led to believe that Ms Jolie had said she wouldn't work with Ray Winstone again unless he apologised for the premature disclosure of the 'news'. The news analyst's suspicions are aroused for a number of reasons. The likely marriage had already been the subject of widespread public discussion and comment. And, if such a contretemps had really occurred, would not skilful publicists have been able to see to it that it never saw the light of day? (See Max Clifford and Angela Levin's *Max Clifford: Read All About It*, 2005, on how to kill celebrity stories.) Even more intriguingly, the story was followed by a brief line to the effect that Jolie and Pitt had been attempting to 'improve their image' prior to the formal announcement of the nuptials! It is unclear whether it was felt such a story would help or hinder this undertaking.

These were the main stories covered in the news and showbiz sections. As we have seen, they were repeated many times throughout the day. Elsewhere, we analyse a sample of non-rolling, traditionally-formatted broadcast news. First, it is worth exploring how different news networks react to large breaking stories. We will begin with radio.

There is a perception that networks which purport to offer continuous news respond to major stories in ways which are stylistically, if not substantively, similar. This may be too simplistic a view. Clearly, the nature of the story will determine the response. However, an example may prove useful.

The second Cabinet resignation of David Blunkett occurred on 2 November 2005. This is a major – though not huge – news story domestically. It also illustrates the options available for news-based networks. DNN naturally led on the story of the resignation as soon as it was confirmed. However, it did so in a very traditional format. In the extended news section, it ran a voice piece from a reporter along with a comment from Blunkett biographer Stephen Pollard, acting as political pundit and commentator. As always, material was recorded, not live.

BBC Radio Five Live, by contrast, went into a more traditional radio rolling news format: a series of live reporter two-ways and guest interviews, punctuated by updates from the studio presenter and a reporter colleague acting as a studio guest. This is the format often adopted by various types of news channel when major stories begin to unfold – and this applies on radio and television.

This will sometimes occasion the abandonment of regular features. For example, on Five Live, talkSPORT, and some BBC Local Radio stations, items such as travel news, sport and business can often be displaced or abandoned altogether. The priority is getting hold of interviewees to comment on the unfolding story. Occasionally, even the otherwise sacrosanct hourly bulletin will be postponed or redesigned to accommodate this.

Elsewhere, however, this does not happen. On DNN, the breaking news was absorbed within routine formats and structures. In the case of the Blunkett resignation, no attempt was made to generate the station's own independent audio. The clips used were taken from DNN's national news partners (Sky, IRN, and various news agencies); and were accommodated easily within the format described above. Would some stories be so big as to result in a fracturing of this format? For example, the 7 July bombings, or – as a large local story – the Birmingham riots or the tornado of 2005?

Some stories are regarded as so important that entire programmes change or are scrapped on stations like BBC Five Live: particularly at unusual times in the news cycle. For example, when the 2001 campaign against the Taliban and al-Qa'eda in Afghanistan was launched, this was on Sunday evening, UK time. Regular Sunday evening output was replaced by emergency programmes presented by broadcasters who would not normally have been on air at that time. A station like DNN would not have to make those sorts of adjustments, because the format is already geared to cope with such an eventuality. Also, with news like the wars in Afghanistan in 2001 and Iraq in 2003, although the exact timing may not be known – even off the record – its imminence is likely to be sufficiently predictable for the necessary logistical arrangements to be made well in advance.

It would clearly be useful to explore in detail the kinds of judgement and decision-making which determines the abandonment of routine formats. Precisely how big a story is required to trigger such a change? Who decides? At what level of the decision-making chain? One of the authors has spent many years presenting and producing news-based programmes on BBC Local Radio and on the basis of that experience, it would often be enough at that level for the presenter and/or producer to decide to overrun with an interview at the expense of a travel bulletin, a recorded package, or something similar. To delay an hourly news bulletin to continue with live reaction would be rarer, and would require the assent of the news editor, or whoever was operationally in charge of the newsroom. To reschedule an entire programme, or replace one presenter with another more suited to news broadcasting, would demand agreement at news editor or station manager level.

(Continued)

How do judgements like these operate within more traditional formats? How do news values operate on more conventional or routine news days? Are there significant differences between the types of rolling news we have already looked at and the more traditional bulletin such as the Six o'clock News or the Midnight News on BBC Radio Four? It will again be necessary to analyse a sample of output on what journalists would regard as a reasonably routine or 'normal' news day. (Such terms are not ideal, but most working journalists will recognise the concept, even if they can seem a little loose).

Case Study 2 – Radio: BBC Radio Five Live

Let us next take a brief look at another randomly chosen sample of radio news output. This is the running-order for BBC Radio Five Live's (11.00 a.m. bulletin on Tuesday 8 November 2005:

Main news

- Latest on Government's proposed terror legislation, and 90-day detention limit. Charles Clarke clip.
- Police anti-terror aids in Australia. Copy only.
- Availability of breast cancer drug. Copy only.
- Underage contraception provision. Victoria Gillick clip.
- French rioting: twelfth night of violence. Clip of pundit.
- Children walking – is it safe? Copy only.
- Latest on FTSE 100 index. Copy.

Sport round-up

- Cricket: latest on England tour of Pakistan. Copy.
- Abel Xavier fails B test. Copy.
- Sven-Goran Eriksson may stay on beyond 2006 World Cup, according to Tord Grip. Copy.
- Castleford Rugby League club appoint new Head Coach. Copy.

This is a short bulletin package – no more than five minutes in total. It was on a day where there was no single dominant lead story. Indeed, the lead changed several times throughout the day. More than one of the stories we have enumerated featured as the lead story during the morning's output. Positioning in such circumstances will often depend on availability and quality of audio material as well as pure news value. Interestingly, even within the BBC, three of the stories included in this bulletin were selected as the lead on various radio bulletins throughout the day: the breast cancer drug, the contraception story, and the terror legislation.

The terror story and the French rioting item had both been running for several days. This was the day after the twelfth successive night of disturbances in parts of France; and the controversy surrounding detention without charge proposals had been the highest-profile political news story in Britain since the resignation of David Blunkett the previous week. Thus, their positioning in a bulletin such as this was likely to be changed, depending on the freshness of the latest angle, the quality of supporting audio, and, as always, the nature of the competing stories.

It should be noted that this sort of hourly bulletin does not aspire to give a comprehensive summary of the day's news, in the way that main evening network bulletins on radio and television do. It is rather intended as a snapshot of the latest breaking news that hour. There is, indeed, a certain amount of pressure in this sort of news environment, to 'freshen' the bulletins from hour to hour. Whereas, on DNN, a large degree of repetition is allowed (because of assumed listening habits), here, a simple repetition of the same stories in the same order and with the same audio would almost certainly be deemed unacceptable – or, at the very least, an example of poor and lazy journalism. On DNN, it is accepted that listeners – even in an ideal world – are not going to listen continuously throughout the day. The station's own promotional material on air encourages listeners to tune in 'three, four, five times a day' for the latest news. BBC Five Live, by contrast, aspires to keep people listening continuously for as long as possible. There is, therefore, some pressure to vary the auditory diet as much as possible – with attendant consequences, of course, for news values. A detailed analysis of the various items is apposite:

Terror vote

The choice of the lead story in this particular bulletin is not too surprising. It came on the day before an important vote on the proposed 90-day detention measure, and the audio clip of Home Secretary Charles Clarke was fresh. The news values of the story derived from debates concerning civil liberties, and the perceived threat to traditions of *habeas corpus*

(Continued)

posed by the proposal for detention of up to 90 days without charge. It also resonated as a result of discussion of the length of Prime Minister Blair's continuance in office, and his political strength or weakness. This, incidentally, had also brought about another shift in news values. Reports of parliamentary proceedings – not greatly in evidence during the first two Blair terms – were more frequent and given a higher profile. This was as a result of two main factors: one, that this was known to be Blair's final term as Prime Minister; and two, the considerably smaller parliamentary majority the Labour Government had in its third term. This caused a partial return to the levels of reporting of parliamentary affairs, and speculation about the outcome of parliamentary votes, which were common features of the later period of the Major Government, from 1992 to 1997.

Terror raids

The second story, although copy only, in a sense followed on thematically. The police raids referred to were also linked to the perceived terrorist threat – this time in Australia. Australia had contributed troops to the campaigns in Afghanistan and Iraq. Although its citizens had suffered in the Bali bombing and elsewhere, its own territory had hitherto been exempt from direct attack. The raids were reported as foiling an attempt to carry out such an attack.

It is worth making the point that broadcast news running orders often run counter to what might otherwise have been intended news values for what might be termed 'aesthetic' or structural reasons. In other words, the police raids in Australia may not have been perceived as the second strongest story at the time; but, because of a thematic link with the lead story, a narrative link was made as well. Whether this represents a distortion of news values, or a sensible accommodation of substance to form, will obviously remain a matter of debate. It is also one of the important themes of this book; and a reminder of the need to amend and update Galtung and Ruge's initial work on news values.

Health matters

The next two stories – the breast cancer drug and underage contraception provision – were among those which later led BBC news bulletins during the rest of the day. They are also stories ideally suited for phone-ins, and other forms of interactive response (email, text) which a station like Five Live is usually eager to invite. They are both examples of what might be termed issues-led news: stories where opposing viewpoints, strongly held, can give rise to lively programming. It was noted earlier that some broadcast journalism practitioners may be tempted to keep this factor in mind when making its story selections. Intentionally interactive features, like the so-called *Pulse* on ITV1's lunchtime news up to 2006, are clearly designed with this criterion of story selection in mind. In this case, the issue of contraceptive provision for underage girls was indeed the topic for a phone-in on the programme of which this bulletin was a part. The story of the breast cancer drug's unavailability from a local health trust's provision was also regarded as a suitable candidate for such interactive programming.

At the time of our chosen bulletin, audio was available for the contraception story – in the form of well-known campaigner on the issue, Victoria Gillick. The breast cancer item, however, was copy only – perhaps because it had only recently broken. If so, this may have accounted for its positioning.

The remaining story – based on a survey about the safety implications for children of walking – was also copy-only. In journalistic terms, this was the weakest, or the story with the least 'legs'. Later in the day, it had largely disappeared from bulletins, and was not widely used either as a topical theme for programmes. The other stories were all supported throughout the day with material on Ceefax and on the BBC web pages.

Case Study 3 – Radio: BBC Radio Four Midnight News

It is instructive to compare the two bulletins we have just analysed with the Midnight News on BBC Radio Four. This aspires to be a fairly comprehensive round-up of the entire day's main news stories, rather than just a snapshot of the leading items at a particular hour. We have chosen to examine the bulletin broadcast at midnight on the night of the 10–11 November 2005. Here are its contents:

Introduction and brief headlines (five stories)

- Terror legislation controversy: alleged politicisation of the police. First: Wrap (Dorrell, Hoon, Brown). Second: Political position of Prime Minister. Voice-piece.
- Jordan bombing. Voice-piece with added wildtrack. This then linked to: Iraq bombings (Baghdad and Tikrit). Voice-piece.

(Continued)

- Man acquitted of murder of Julie Hogg could face retrial. Voice-piece.
- Nurses and Pharmacists to be allowed to prescribe. Wrap (BMA spokesperson, Hewitt).
- New Israeli Labour Leader. Wrap (Peretz clip).
- New German coalition closer. Copy.
- Head of IAEA calls for solution on Iran's use of nuclear fuel. Voice-piece.
- Gender Pay Gap – latest figures. Wrap (EOC representative, Jowell).
- Court verdict: chemicals used to make amphetamines. Copy.
- Game park animals sent to Thailand from Kenya. Wrap (Born Free Foundation representative, wildtrack).
- Plans to demolish Heathrow Terminal 2 and rebuild by 2012. Copy.
- Reports of working groups on Islamic extremism. Wrap (Blears). Copy link to terror bill.
- Interest rates unchanged. Copy.
- Next month's World Trade Summit 'likely to be disappointing'. Voice-piece.
- FTSE and currencies updates. Copy.
- Sion Jenkins retrial (Billie-Jo Jenkins murder) – evidence from ex-wife. Voice-piece.
- Death of Professor Ted Wragg. Copy.
- Serious illness of Lord Lichfield. Copy.
- Coastline of England and Wales at risk of erosion – report. Wrap (pundit clips and wildtrack).
- Review of front pages of next day's papers. Copy.
- Russia bids for 2014 Winter Olympics – in Sochi. Voice-piece.

Headlines repeated

The length of the bulletin is 30 minutes. It is a more traditional bulletin format than the DNN rolling news example we have studied. It also aims to be far more comprehensive than the hourly Five Live bulletin. It sees its role as providing a full account of the preceding day's news stories rather than, as it were, ranking them in order of saliency at that particular time. This, therefore, will bring about a subtle shift in news values. Indeed, it raises a number of interesting issues. Is the lead story likely to be the one which has proved the most significant over the whole day? If so, would that take precedence over a late-breaking story which is much fresher – much more *new* – but not likely to have the 'legs' of the older agreed lead story? For a short hourly bulletin, or half-hourly round-up, there would be little doubt that the late-breaking story would predominate. But for a longer daily round-up like this, it is much more finely-balanced.

Terror votes and Middle East bombs

It is not a dilemma which was particularly acute on the day we have chosen at random. The Jordan bombing – the second story – had been in the news for many hours at this time. The nearest approximation to late-breaking news was the material coming in from Iraq. The attacks in Baghdad and Tikrit were more recent. However, they were not deemed to be important enough to challenge the previously-agreed running-order. Indeed, such is the frequency of reports of this kind that, as was once the case with terrorist incidents in Northern Ireland, they are arguably in danger of being under-emphasised. In this instance, they were joined with the Jordan bombing. Had it not been for this, what would its position have been? Still the second or third report? Or lower? Obviously, we cannot answer definitively. However, the suspicion is that it was 'assisted' up the bulletin as a follow-up to the Jordanian bombings.

As to the means of delivering the news, the Jordan bombing was reported in a voice-piece, with added wildtrack of background sound effects. The Iraq attacks, meanwhile, were conveyed in a straight voice-piece (no wildtrack or clips). The top story, meanwhile, also came in two sections. The immediate developments concerning allegations that the police had been politicised came in the form of a fairly long wrap or mini-package – with clips of major political figures (Stephen Dorrell, Geoff Hoon, Gordon Brown). A second, follow-up piece came in the form of a voice-piece, assessing the political consequences for Blair's standing, and likely continuance, as Prime Minister. This story was in its later phases. The vote had already been lost – heavily. So the search was now on for means of 'taking on' the story. Opposition allegations that the police had taken – or been persuaded to take – an excessively political, even partisan, role in the debate over 90-day detention without charge seemed to offer the ideal journalistic vehicle for doing so. The assessment of Blair's political position, however, was framed more in terms of the overall developments of the week rather than the specific controversy over police politicisation. Since the broadcast news agenda often shifts as a result of the print media's verdict on events, such an assessment can frequently appear different 24 hours on from the immediate post-mortems. A critical mass of commentary and punditry can often alter judgements confidently made in the immediate aftermath of events. Although no radical shift occurred here, there was a confirmation of the initial view that Blair's authority had been seriously weakened by the vote. That morning's papers had confronted Blair with some of the most

(Continued)

apocalyptic front pages of his premiership. BBC Radio News, though phrasing its observations much more cautiously, still reflected this sense of a notable shift in the political landscape.

Treatments of news

We do not need to analyse each story in detail. It is, however, worth remarking on one or two features which assist our understanding of news values in their practical application. The number of format options in a bulletin like this is limited. As we see, all stories are either copy-only or are relayed by means of a voice-piece or a wrap (or mini-package). Unlike current affairs radio *programmes* (*Today, World at One, PM, World Tonight*), the *bulletin* – even a lengthy one such as this – seldom makes use of live, or 'as-live' two-ways. They may occur exceptionally when a really big late-breaking story happens. Their rarity is partly a stylistic choice, and partly also a product of the way the bulletin is presented. These major bulletins on Radio Four are read by members of the presentation staff, who are also responsible for continuity between programmes. They are not necessarily journalists. The presenters of the programmes mentioned are from a journalistic background: they would be assumed to be more confident handling two-ways – in some cases asking follow-up, unscripted questions. The journalists responsible for compiling a bulletin like this would rarely be relaxed about a non-journalistic newsreader conducting any but the most tightly-scripted and briefest of live two-ways. Also, it is now increasingly common for material such as this to be lifted, where necessary, from other outlets. So, for instance, if there were to be an important late-breaking story, audio could be lifted from a two-way just conducted, say, on BBC News 24, or BBC Five Live. Often, where matters are slightly less urgent, audio will have been lifted from an earlier programme such as *The World Tonight*.

In our chosen bulletin, the more conventional choices were made. There may well have been some attempt made to avoid stylistic repetition. So, for instance, we would be more likely to hear wrap, voice-piece, wrap, voice-piece – perhaps interspersed with copy stories – than a series of two or more voice-pieces back-to-back. Even successive wraps tend to be avoided if possible – despite their more varied, less repetitive nature (because, of course, the enclosed audio will be different for each story). A run of voice-pieces, despite the different reporters used, is more likely to become a little wearing on the ear. Too many copy-only stories, back-to-back, are also regarded as undesirable.

So does all this have an effect on news values? Elsewhere, we analyse television news, where, arguably, the role of stylistic and aesthetic considerations is greater than in radio. However, even here, it seems likely that these factors play a role. While the *selection* of stories may be conducted broadly on grounds of news strength alone, the *positioning* of stories may well be affected or influenced by such stylistic features. So, for example, in the bulletin we are examining, the decisions as to where to place the items on the retrial, the nurses' and pharmacists' prescription announcement, the new Israeli Labour leader, and the IAEA announcement, as well as some of the later stories, could quite easily have been made as much on the need to vary format options as on their perceived journalistic strength.

It should be borne in mind that this is not levelled as a criticism of the news values applied; simply as a reminder that the grounds for such decisions are often more pragmatic and influenced by the demands of the medium more than we are schooled to believe.

News sources

Let us also briefly explore the likely *sources* for the stories chosen. How varied are they? Some of them will have arisen from press releases or similar announcements, and are likely to have been 'diaried' for some time. The nurses and pharmacists initiative; the gender pay gap item; the working party reports on Islamic extremism; these are all likely to have been in the planning diary for that day for some time. Likewise the coastal erosion report. The day of the interest rate decision is also predictable for weeks if not months ahead. The meetings are monthly, and the dates are set well in advance. It is also likely that the game park animals story will have been diaried for some time, pegged as it is around the visit of the Thai Prime Minister to Kenya.

Other stories will probably have started off as wire items: the German coalition announcement, and the new Israeli Labour leader. The latter may well have been planned for, however. Although the outcome will have been uncertain, the fact that the vote was happening will, presumably, also have been in the news diaries. Court stories – of which there are two – will also be diary items. The Jenkins retrial, in particular, will be a standing item with a daily reminder for its duration. The amphetamines item may have come from wires, as a result of a report

(Continued)

from a freelance journalist; or it may have been anticipated in BBC news stories as the kind of case not requiring daily coverage but worth reporting on the return of the verdict.

The majority of items, then, will have been on that morning's news meeting agenda. Only the Iraqi bombs definitely will not have been there – along, of course, with the sad news of the death of Professor Wragg and the serious illness of Lord Lichfield (whose death was announced the next morning).

There is much discussion in television news about the so-called 'and finally...' item, a convention not unknown in radio news also. It tends to be slightly less signposted in the case of a bulletin such as BBC Radio Four Midnight News, and the respective demands of the medium involved will also play a role. The nearest approach to such an item in this bulletin was the story about the Russian bid for the 2014 Winter Olympics. Its slightly whimsical nature revolved around the choice of Sochi as the proposed venue – because of its southerly setting, and rather unpredictable climate. Although not the kind of news to evoke laughter or strong surprise, it was nonetheless presented in a slightly different tone from the rest of the news. This particular bulletin will often 'flag up' such a relatively light story by running it after the review of the next day's papers. It is not as formulaic and unvarying as it has become on some television news bulletins. It does, however, recognisably fit into that stylistic niche.

Planning for midnight

As we can see, much of the news will have been decided upon well in advance. This is also broadly true of many of the items in the Five Live and DNN bulletins we have examined. Interestingly, one of the arguments often made to distinguish radio news from its television equivalent is that it is able to respond even more quickly to unfolding developments. This also implies that running orders are more flexible. It may surprise some consumers of news, therefore, to discover how much of the news agenda for a midnight bulletin was almost certainly decided upon – in effect, if not in so many words – the previous morning. In a medium where logistical questions have a faster turn-around than in television, again this may surprise many.

Smaller Markets and Niches

Beyond the Obvious – Special Cases for the News Industry

There is a temptation to think only in terms of national and international newspapers and of broadcast organisations (including internet sites) when news coverage is considered. There are, however, other outlets for news which follow the standard cluster of news values.

Local newspapers

Local weekly newspapers offer a peculiar case for the application of news values. They are usually free distribution, rather than paid for; a trend that can be traced back to the period immediately post-Second World War in the USA, and to the 1980s in Britain, when the realisation that sales of paid-for local newspapers were beginning to decline, and that the ultimate profitability of newspapers covering local issues could be maintained by dispensing with the existing business model of distribution – involving sale-or-return accounting procedures, timed distribution and other expensive administrative burdens – and replacing them with a network of people who would distribute, for a small and fixed fee, free issues to their neighbours. The rationale was that the guaranteed readership numbers would more than compensate for lost cover price revenue, by creating potential for higher advertising sales revenue. It took some time to settle down and there were several false starts, but today the free local newspaper is a fact of life. It has not been an altogether painless process, however. Firstly, profitability has been achieved only by stringent cost-cutting; entire layers of editorial and production staff were removed (a situation helped in no small way by the change from traditional typesetting to direct input, with the journalists sending their copy to the press room from their desktop computers) and the ratio of advertising to editorial was altered, in favour of the former (the rationale is that readers are less likely to complain about more than half the publication comprising advertisements if they are not expected to pay for the newspaper). What also tended to happen was the creation of pooled resources, with an editorial team contributing to several titles in a region.

So far as editorial content is concerned, the focus is invariably at a micro level, with regional or national stories only appearing if there is a direct local connection. One example is the *Stockport Times*, which in July 2006 ran on Page 2 an item developed from a survey-based story which had first run in June in most British national newspapers and which was also the subject of considerable broadcast coverage. The core story related to a table of crime rates published by Reform, a London-based 'think tank'. While originally a news item of national significance, the item that ran on 20 July in the *Stockport Times* related exclusively to a revision of Stockport's place in that table; by having used inaccurate population data in the original survey Stockport was said to be the most likely place in Britain to suffer a domestic burglary, but after Reform revised its raw data Stockport was in fact said to be the 26th most likely place. In terms of news value this is a follow-on story (the original item ran back in June 2006) but the revision was **relevant**, **topical** and **worthy** – and there is also a reasonable expectation on the part of readers that the story will run in the local edition, as it had earlier that week been published in the national and regional press.

In all other news items published in that same edition of the *Stockport Times*, the local relevance and worth are common factors; the lead item concerns a fire at a secondary school in the town, and the second lead is a local athlete from the town who is tipped to be a future European Championships contender. The first of those two items is purely local, while the latter is a local focus on a national issue; the same could be said of articles which cover how the heat wave sweeping across Europe has affected Stockport residents, local schools being involved in national Sport Relief charitable events, a warning against swimming in reservoirs that is a localised response to a national safety initiative, and a serving soldier from a Stockport suburb who has been honoured with the George Cross for his bravery under fire in the Iraq conflict. Other content is more purely local (two items concerned with local schools, one concerning plans for town centre shopping developments, and one concerning a local museum, for instance) and this pattern continues throughout not just this edition of the paper, but most others too. In terms of **topicality**, this branch of the publishing industry is something of a special case; while the news item might be up to a week old, the editorial team tends to think on terms of it being new to this readership, so is topical in that respect. Additionally, the news team will rely on the matter of expectation; if a news item has already run in the nationals or the regionals, or has received broadcast coverage prior to the edition of the local newspaper being published, the readership expects a more detailed (often more reflective) piece on the same story to appear in the next edition of the paper.

In terms of the advertising to editorial ratio, this edition had 40 of its 64 pages dedicated to advertising, and of the editorial content a total of 3 pages was dedicated to advertising-inspired coverage, such as home improvement articles in the property pages. Readers' letters, columns by local politicians and television listing took up a further 5 pages of that allocated for editorial. This is a pattern common to all local 'free sheets' (as such newspapers are known within the publishing industry); while the ratio might be a percentage point different here or there, a 60–40% advertising to editorial ratio is normal. Which leaves little space for true journalistic input; the same core team of journalists and reporters would therefore be under-employed were they not also contributing to several other newspapers in the group. Furthermore, feature-based content is often repeated throughout all editions of a paper within a group or regional cluster, and is often sourced externally; garden centres provide gardening features, DIY stores home improvement columns, and so forth. Content of this type rarely concerns itself with news; its existence is purely to act as a trigger for advertising sales. This pattern is not unique to the *Stockport Times*, it is often repeated throughout the world of local newspapers, and is a formula which works because most people see only one of the papers in any given publishing week, so do not feel in any way cheated by the paucity of content. An indicator of the size of the British regional newspaper industry is that it employs a total of 45,000 people, of whom approximately 12,000 are editorial staff which suggests an average of seven editorial staff per paper, based on the latest data from the British Isles, which suggests that there are 1640 regional newspapers in existence. These data do not include 'table-top' publications, such as those serving small towns and larger villages not deemed to be of sufficient stature to appear in the main list (Newspaper Society; Alden, 2006: 37–9). As an interesting aside which serves to indicate the pressure under which editorial teams can find themselves, it is by no means unknown to find duplication of news stories in the same publication. The authors have noted this on countless occasions, and attribute it to the direct input nature of modern newspaper production, where each journalist will assume responsibility for a page, and might not have time to relate the content of that page to others around it.

Another observation concerns those 'table-top' publications. These tend to be as reliable as the average web-log in terms of journalistic scrutiny. One illustration is a village newspaper serving the home area of one of the authors. This is a monthly publication and its *raison d'être* seems to be the generation of advertising revenue – a concept with which there is nothing wrong in essence, as most publications exist for commercial reasons. However, the editor of this particular publication is a renowned Christian fundamentalist who appears to be in denial of anything but good news. Therefore when two major events in the area (one the murder of a policeman from the village, the other the suicide of a much-liked local general practitioner) occurred, it would be a reasonable expectation that some mention would be made of these; both qualified as **worthy, unexpected, topical, unusual** and **relevant** events. Because they were bad news, however, both were completely ignored by the editor, and no mention was made of either event. This is a sin of omission in newspaper terms, and is sufficient to counter any claim the editor (who is also the publisher) might have to calling that publication a newspaper. Its only salvation is that readers do not pay for the paper; it is delivered free at the end of each month to every home in the village, and mostly used to find a joiner or a plumber, or to become privy to the latest wisdom to come from the pen of the patrician local Member of Parliament.

Magazines

The world of magazines can be broken down into three main sectors: consumer general interest; consumer special interest; and business publications. It is essential to have a basic understanding of the economics of this publishing sector to understand how the editorial content will make use of the news value system.

The first two sectors are almost invariably sell-through titles, while the third is almost invariably free, via a controlled circulation list. The economic cases for these three types of magazine are distinct. General interest consumer magazines tend to rely on a low cover price and a high volume of sales (which is necessary to attract general consumer advertising) to achieve financial viability. Specialists magazines can rely on smaller sales figures and higher cover price, for two reasons: one is that the market will withstand paying more for specialist content than it would for more general material, the other is that the advertising sale is based on the premise that the readership is sufficiently specialised to attract custom advertising. The business magazine works on broadly similar lines, though without the revenue stream from sell-through; this loss is countered by an ability to reach a specialist audience which again attracts custom advertising.

Because magazines are published at no greater frequency than weekly – and many are monthly or even quarterly – their editorial content tends to focus on op-ed (opinionated editorial) features and articles which take a longer view of subjects, rather than on 'hard' news items. But that does not mean that they do not have a news content. On the contrary, almost every magazine has a news section carefully tailored to meet the expectation of its readership – and that applies regardless of the sector in which it is published.

Magazines tend to capitalise on the main distinguishers that set them apart from newspapers. The first of these is a facility to go into greater detail than is allowed in newspapers, because of the greater space that is available. The second is a more informed audience, one which can understand the nuance and the specialist lexicon that is often a feature of magazine audiences, and from which newspapers tend to distance themselves on account of their generalist nature, and also because of constraints on space and time. There will additionally be news items that are of such rarefied interest they will not have appeared in the mainstream media. But to their intended audience in a magazine they are still of interest.

An example is the Autumn 2006 issue of *Renault Magazine*, a business-to-consumer publication produced three times a year on behalf of Renault's British car drivers by Brooklands Publishing, and distributed free of charge to 223,371 homes (ABC July-December 2005). On pages 12–14 of the magazine are 12 news items which relate directly to Renault products or directly to readers of the magazine. The lead item is concerned with a face-lifted Renault model, the Modus, and the second lead is concerned with a new range of accessories for Renault cars; the first of these two items also appeared in other publications (*What Car?* and *Auto Express*, for instance) while the second did not. The same pattern was followed for the other items on the pages mentioned; an item showing the British Prime Minister, Tony Blair, with former F1 world champion Damon Hill received wide coverage, for example, while another piece of text concerned with a new car servicing package was unlikely to appear anywhere else as it would be of interest only to drivers of late-model Renault cars. All 12 news items met several of the values which form the core of our system; all were **relevant** to the readership, and all met with reader **expectations** – readers would expect to see these items mentioned in a title dedicated to the cars they drive. While not **topical** in the true sense, they are generally items which have not been seen elsewhere, and so are sufficiently **new** to readers to qualify as such. They are also **worthy** for the same reason – though a reader should understand the implicit contract that in reading the content, they will not find any criticism of the product. In terms of composition of the overall product, the fit with surrounding items is beyond dispute – all editorial has the common theme of a direct connection to either Renault products and services, or the brand's inherent 'French-ness'. Few of the items are especially **unusual** (the Blair–Hill piece is the exception, as these are two people rarely seen together, and the politician is not noted for his close connections with the world of Grand Prix racing: certainly not since the so-called Ecclestone affair of 1997) but all can be validly classed as news items for the reasons given above. The one remaining value is that of **external influences**. This particular is an interesting case, because many of the news items are there not just because they are considered to be of interest to Renault drivers, but also because the publication exists as part of the overall marketing strategy, and is funded directly by the company. It can therefore determine what is or is not to be included in any given issue – this will have been established before the agreement for Brooklands to create the magazine was finalised. In that sense the publication is corrupted by the values of the key financier, but this is not an area that is likely to worry readers, as there will be a tacit appreciation that they are being given Renault's 'party line' so far as content is concerned. That readers are not paying directly for the magazine is a factor which Renault can use to mitigate any potential criticism.

Virtually every customer magazine follows this same format, which is unsurprising as businesses from airlines to wholesalers consider this medium as part of their marketing strategy. Major supermarket chains, for instance, routinely use customer magazines to promote special offers and to encourage increased footfall and increased customer spend in their stores, with all editorial content relating directly to goods on sale in the store.

Many of the same values apply to specialist retail magazines – though with the considerable distinction that they are far less prone to being subjected to external influences. There will often be a degree of pressure brought to bear by advertisers taking exception to a bad review of a product (many specialist retail magazines rely heavily on reviews of new products as part of their *raison d'être*) but any effective publisher or editor will be able to deal with such eventualities to the satisfaction of all concerned.

When it comes to business-to-business (usually referred to in publishing-speak as B2B) magazines the notion of sharpened relevance becomes even more important. Many of the items which will appear in the news columns of such publications will rarely, if ever, appear elsewhere. An illustration is a typical B2B, *Land Mobile*. This is geared to the world of wireless telecommunications, and is a monthly publication distributed to more than 10,000 key personnel working within that industry. This is a rarefied world; its readership is described by its publishers Symposium as:

> ... named decision-makers responsible for wireless communications in every UK Local Authority, Police Force, Fire Service, Ambulance and NHS Trust as well as specifying bodies such as PITO, MoD and Defence Procurement and various government departments.
>
> The Business Comms Users segment comprises named decision-makers involved in procurement of wireless services and products within areas such as Public and Private Transport, The Utilities, Distribution, Logistics, Construction, Ports and Container Terminals and major corporates, to name but a few. (Land Mobile Media Pack, 2006)

In practical terms, the news content is of interest to few people outside that industry. In the August 2006 edition, for example, there were items on price reductions in the Chinese market for digital trunking; a new billing software package developed to smooth the way in which a specific pay-per-mile insurance scheme can be administered; and a new communications package being adopted by travelling staff members employed by a national fashion chain. None of these are likely to be of the remotest interest to anybody outside the industry at which *Land Mobile* is directed, but for certain (by no means all) readers of the magazine they are likely to be considered highly valuable. These items therefore meet the criteria of being **relevant, worthy, expected** (there is nowhere else that such information is likely to be published) and in accordance with the overall composition of the publication. They are also **topical** in that they are new to the reader, even though these (usually press release-based) news items might be a couple of months old in terms of their creation, given the production cycle of B2B magazines. They are additionally **unusual** in that they are unexpected by the readership, a factor which in itself can be interpreted by trade publication journalists as sufficient grounds for describing the item as news.

A slightly different – though broadly similar – approach is taken by serious retail magazines. The example chosen is *The Economist*, a London-based weekly retail magazine with global distribution, and appropriately international perspective on life. Reaching a claimed readership in excess of 4 million, *The Economist* is geared to provide intelligently-written information to a high-value audience:

> *The Economist* is written for a global audience of senior business, political and financial decision-makers that value *The Economist* for the accuracy of its incisive writing, its international outlook and lack of partisanship.
> Hugely influential, *The Economist's* readership has grown to almost 4 million and includes many impressive names from among the world's opinion leaders". (Economist Media Pack, August 2006)

Rather than describe its news section as such, it chooses instead to use the descriptor 'The World This Week', thus allowing its editorial staff to take a slightly longer view on events. Summarised in rarely more than a couple of sentences – and never more than a single paragraph – this section covers recent events which its editor feels are of **relevance** to its readership. Mindful of the chosen demographic, *The Economist* focuses in two areas only; politics and business. All items are carefully written in the past tense – thus breaking with a tradition in most news organisations of writing in the present tense, which provides the dynamic voice favoured by many journalists. As David Randall points out: 'The active voice is not just more efficient, it is also, as the name suggests, more active' (2000:158). By deliberately eschewing this voice and settling for a past tense it becomes obvious to the reader that there is less topicality to these issues than there might be; although nobody is able to either confirm or deny it, we suspect that the reason for this tone attached to the content each week is a subtle sub-text that readers probably know about these various issues, but deserve to be reminded of their significance at the point of reading the current edition of the magazine.

Among the issues being mentioned in the 19 August 2006 edition were such matters as the latest death count from Baghdad, a reminder that there was a ceasefire newly established between Israel and Lebanon, a précis of fatalities due to floods the previous week in North Korea, an item concerning a computer company with a spontaneous combustion problem with certain models of lap-top, and a new chief executive of a major soft drinks brand. All of these items and the many others on the two pages were covered in newspapers and in news broadcasts during the previous week, and so were not at all **topical**. They were, however, **worthy** and would almost certainly be of direct **relevance** to the readership. Furthermore they related to a number of the more exhaustive op-ed articles which make up the majority of the editorial content of the magazine. This is an approach that has much in common with the news items that appear in the supplementary sections of daily and week-end newspapers, where recent news items will be reprised for the benefit of readers who might not have caught the original text, or who (in the editors' opinions) would benefit from being reminded. In both the cases of *The Economist* and the mainstream newspapers, this pattern has become so entrenched that it now complies with the rules of **composition** that govern overall construction and sequencing of news-based publications.

Online news

There is a temptation to think only in terms of web-logs when the internet and news are mentioned in the same breath. This is erroneous; BBC Online, ABC News and countless other services rooted in mainstream news distribution (usually as broadcasters) have developed enormously successful – though not always profitable – on-line news services which run alongside the broadcast news. There is additionally a fast-growing expectation that newspapers will develop their websites to become the first point of reference; news will go straight to the site, meaning it is instantly accessible to readers without them having to wait for the next edition of the paper.

At the forefront of this revolution is the *Guardian*, Britain's centre-left qual-ity newspaper which founded its online edition (actually a cluster of linked sites) in 1999, well in advance of other major news organisations; it is there-fore unsurprising to learn that it is still perceived as the brand leader in its field. But that in itself was not the main story – that came seven years on, when the decision was taken to prioritise the online edition. This was picked up on across the media world, as one piece suggests:

> Several Australian newspapers are gearing up to follow the lead of British counterparts in putting exclusive breaking news online before it appears in print and devoting more newsroom resources to the internet.
>
> This week Fleet Street fired the first shots in a revolution that will fundamentally change the way newspapers operate and could even hasten the end of the newsprint era. On Monday, The *Guardian* announced that its business journalists and foreign corre-spondents would file copy to the newspaper's online edition before it appeared in the paper. The following day *The Times* followed suit, announcing that its foreign correspon-dents would file for its website first. Both papers expect the main home news sections to eventually adopt the same approach. (Este and Sainsbury, 2006)

Such a move might be considered to display editorial naiveté – yet thus far it seems not to have harmed the print edition of the *Guardian*, and instead is credited as responsible for yet-higher site traffic to GuardianOnline. Dietmar Schantin, the key consultant to a rival newspaper, the *Daily Telegraph*, feels that this is the way of the future, and that newspapers which fail to adapt to this new *modus operandi* will be en route to terminal decline:

> Sooner or later the audience will go somewhere else where they can get what they want . . . sooner or later the circulation will go down until a certain point when this Catch 22 starts, less circulation, less advertising, cuts in the staff, less quality, less circulation and then there will be the need to save money again and inevitably they will die.

Schantin also explained that it is not simply sufficient to run the same content in both editions, 'you don't just copy and paste. You need to add value if you go to a different channel.' What is implicit in this statement and explicit in his earlier one is that there is an economic imperative to generate a workable model; failure to do so will result in falling circulation and eventually the failure of the entire publication. (Luft, 2006–2)

One of the world's leading sites is that of BBC News Online. This has come in for considerable flak from rivals, mainly because of its unique funding model; it is publicly funded (but not government funded – the distinction is key in terms of its editorial independence), which means that it has more than adequate capital to continue to develop almost as it feels fit. Mark Thompson, the BBC Director-General [a role broadly equivalent to chief executive] is unapologetic:

> I believe the case for public service intervention in the digital space – to address what would otherwise be a significant under-investment in high quality content, especially British-made high quality content – has also been made elsewhere.
>
> If you believe that the digital environment, whether DTT [Digital Terrestrial Television], satellite, cable or broadband, will naturally lead to a new and major injection of investment into outstanding British journalism, comedy, documentary and drama, spend some time on the internet or on the EPG [Electronic Programme Guide] and look at progress so far. (Thompson, 2006)

Journalistic excellence – especially in the light of criticism brought about by the 2004 Hutton Report – is something else that is high on Thompson's agenda. In an earlier RTS (Royal Television Society) speech he explained that: 'The key challenges facing the BBC as a broadcaster on the web in the next three years are actually quite straightforward – we must maintain the traditional values of what we offer – independence, trust, innovation, and quality, whilst changing how we offer our content and services so that we remain relevant in the on-demand, digital age.' It becomes clear that far from being apologetic about the commercial advantage that BBC News has, Thompson sees it having a pivotal role in the further development of the internet as a valid and real news channel, one which adds to the Corporation's existing broadcast mechanisms without in any way reducing the editorial standards which are expected of this major media player.

Closer analysis of the way that the BBC uses its online resources can be found in the sidebar to Chapter 12, which looks at the way that a single, but rolling, story is treated over a period of weeks. Meanwhile, what of the other major sites? How do these manage the transition from print to online editions? With difficulty, if Oliver Luft's interview with Dietmar Schantin is to be believed:

As a newspaper you shouldn't copy the BBC, or you shouldn't copy Channel 4 radio. You should do your own thing on audio and video. I think some newspapers are making big mistakes. They just try to be the BBC but they are a newspaper.'

Despite having successfully implemented changes in newsrooms across Europe, Dr Schantin says there remains reluctance in large parts of the newspaper industry to adopt change. He claims that his first job is always to show journalists that audience habits have shifted and to try to take away the fear of the unknown of a digital future.

'For some people it is a threat. The past has shown that when you did an online site readers stopped reading the newspaper. So some journalists think it is cannibalism. But we think that if you do it the right way it enhances the paper, it doesn't cannibalise it.' (Luft, 2006–2)

This suggests that many news journalists, while equipped with all the necessary skills to provide them with paid employment in a major newsroom, do not trust the immediacy (and urgency) of rolling deadlines. Perhaps they are too used to the notion of the deadline that falls late each night, rather than one which constantly shifts. From the perspective of news analysts, this hints at the risk of either a reluctance to dig as deeply into a story as they might have under the 'traditional' model, or a continued reluctance to adapt to new working methods. This in turn suggests that until a new wave of multi-tasking journalists comes along this is unlikely to change. One former journalist, Mark Hamilton, is now a journalism lecturer at an institution in Vancouver. He observed recently that:

> The web frees newspapers from a lot of its restraints: space, fixity, time. But to replace those with an always-on deadline that exists simply to be fed by whatever is available doesn't make sense, particularly as newsrooms get squeezed. By all means, take advantage of the web for breaking news and important stories. But if resources (*time and staff*) are limited, use them wisely for important stuff, whether it's for the web site or the print edition. (Hamilton, 2006)

Significantly the *Daily Telegraph* has met the established journalists part way; there are initially four daily deadlines, presumably so that once they have got used to that more deadlines can be added, until they finally adapt to this new world order. Shane Richmond, the newspaper's online editor, suggested this might not mean more work for journalists: 'But it does mean that journalists will have to get used to working across a range of media. The basic skills of reporting will not change but reporters will need to be comfortable writing for web or print and, yes, some of them will appear in pod casts or on video bulletins.' (Luft, 2006–3)

Conclusion

What these various media forms point to is the gradual convergence of the media industry, which brings a need for more rounded, flexible, multi-tasking journalists. The news gatherers and synthesisers of tomorrow (which is closer than many think!) will need to be adept at working across print, audio, audio-visual and interactive forms, rather than being 'one trick' ponies. This does not, however, infer that there should be any slippage in standards as the shift towards a different presentation form is made. On the contrary, the news journalist inhabiting this brave new world will be expected to work more closely than ever within the value system. Provided he or she has the time to do so, of course; overworking an already-stretched news team is likely to become more of an issue as convergence kicks in – and this is an issue which, it seems, is effectively dodged by many advocates of greater level of interactivity who currently operate outside the media infrastructure

Regional and Local Television News

9

Where Commerce and Community Meet – and Sometimes Collide

Regional television news in Britain, in common with equivalent services in many other countries, is ambling towards a crossroads. Resolutely local in its outlook, there exists within it a fundamental editorial approach that takes seriously its remit to provide news that is of specific interest to its constituency; the over-riding elements of the news value system on which it draws are **consonance** to its audience, and the **newness** to that audience of the items covered. In many ways it is a multimedia version of the local newspaper network. Yet at the same time it seems to be in the middle of a shift from its traditional role of providing exclusively local news, to providing a locally-oriented perspective on news items which make the national agenda.

To gain a sense of the current situation, we have studied the output of five local stations during the early part of week commencing 6 November 2006, concentrating on the main news programmes (rather than the abbreviated 'drop ins' that come at the tail of national terrestrial news programmes) which have, inside their nominal half-hour broadcast slots, the scope to provide detailed coverage of the items they choose to include.

Of these channels, three are familiar (within their regions) and established organisations, while the fourth is newer (having launched on the first of a series of restricted service licences in 2000) and is perceived in some quarters as a model for the future of local broadcasting. channel m Television is a Manchester broadcasting service, and belongs to Guardian Media Group (GMG), a structure which is owned by a trust geared to ensuring that editorial judgements made by any member newspaper or broadcaster remains insulated from any risk of proprietorial influence. This is promoted by the station as a prime advantage it offers over other broadcasters.[1]

Supported by CHUM of Canada, and with assistance from the Media and Performance Department of the University of Salford (which uses the facility for on-air training of its undergraduates) channel m's news department appears to harbour ambitions to be taken seriously, as seriously as other broadcasters in the Manchester region. Stylistically, the news show studied (which was broadcast on 6 November at 17.00, and then repeated half-hourly until 19.00) works at following the model of established news in the region by having a news anchor who stands alongside a large monitor showing clips from news items, and begins with a round-up of headlines, then exposition on the various stories covered, a break, more news, then sport and weather round-ups.

Channel m

Headlines

- Fireworks – an increase in the number of emergency service call-outs compared to the previous year.
- The arrest of a suspect for a murder in the areas going back more than 30 years.
- The emergence of a new martial art-style exercise regime.

The various news items are then covered, item-by-item, with further news items included. The running order and treatment of the various items then proceeds:

Fireworks *Package*: A substantial piece which begins by describing the increase in calls to the fire service and other emergency services, and goes on to refer to incidents at unauthorised bonfires (bear in mind that the timing of this broadcast is immediately after the annual Guy Fawkes weekend that Britons use to 'celebrate' the discovery and foiling of a plot to blow up the Houses of Parliament in 1605) and subsequent injuries. The piece was a mixture of location and interview pieces, wrapping back at the news anchor.

Murder in village on outskirts of Greater Manchester *Package*: Short introductory piece with outside broadcast link, centred on discovery of a man's body in the garden of his home overnight. Mainly speculative, there was no direct input from any interviewees from the local community or the local police. This is likely to be because the incident was in the earliest phase of its investigation process, with only the most basic information being made available to news organisations, and nobody from channel m is prepared to speculate on events.

Guns found in home of former TV 'star' a very brief piece based in studio, with only a single still image of the 'star', a former actor in the popular soap opera *Coronation Street*. Again, it is obvious that there is no official material on which to draw, and any speculation could be considered unwise or possibly even subject to breaking the rules of *sub judice*

New arrest in Lesley Molseed case Package. West Yorkshire police (a geographically adjacent force) have made an arrest relating to a murder that happened 31 years earlier, and for which a man had already served 16 years of a life sentence before being freed when a miscarriage of justice appeal was granted. Supporting the studio-based précis was an outside broadcast from the street on which the murder victim, 13-year-old Lesley Molseed, used to live, and several still images of the victim, the wrongly-accused man (who has since died) and his mother (whose premature death was also attributed to the miscarriage of justice) but no other supporting material.

Posthumous award for policeman Package. Claims by a Police Federation representative that a government denial of requests for a murdered policeman is unacceptable. PC Stephen Oake, a police officer killed in 2003 during an anti-terrorism raid on a house in Manchester, should be honoured for bravery according to his Federation, but the government disagrees. Piece is based around an interview with a Federation official, supported by local politician.

News-in-brief items:

- Airport changes in security demands
- Salford University to move to BBC Media City
- Two new super clinics to open in Salford

School meals are unattractive Package. Claims that the much-vaunted healthy eating at schools campaign are proving unsuccessful. Piece anchored in studio, with vox pop interviews to gain public perspective, but no official response to claims made in journalistic piece. Interestingly, the vox pop contributors were identified, an unusual practice; vox pops are almost by definition non-attributed.

Parkour martial arts Package, introduced as entertainment (and presented on location by the station's entertainment reporter). This is a short piece on a new exercise regime, parkour, a form of urban gymnastics-cum-martial art. A single interviewee (a teenage advocate) and much visual imagery.

Advertising break

Résumé of Bonfire and Molseed stories

Vandalism in Coronation Street *Package* Vandalism and anti-social behaviour in Salford, in a street that shares its name with a major Manchester-produced serial drama. Studio link, location-shot interviews with local residents, and statement (but not appearance by representative) from Police.

Charity fund raising activity *Package*: Outside broadcast from local school which has sought to raise funds for cystic fibrosis charity by some of its pupils abseiling down to pitch from top of Manchester United Football Club's grandstand. Interview clips with participating children.

Studio link to appeal for viewers to make email or phone contact with channel m News.

Weather

Sport special extended sports news with tribute to, and appreciation of, Sir Alex Ferguson (who is celebrating 20 years as manager of Manchester United Football Club) followed by round-up of sports news from all teams in the region. Outside broadcast, but no film action from weekend's games.

Final round-up of headline stories and trail for 9.00 p.m. evening news

There are several distinctive aspects to the channel m News to which we will return. In the meantime what of the other broadcasters whose output was studied on that same night?

Granada

Granada is one of the most highly-regarded geographical sections of ITV, the country's main commercial television broadcaster; it has broadcast continually since 1954 and is one of the few ITV regions to hold onto its original name, despite several attempts in recent years for the Granada name to be subsumed. In terms of presentational style it was unique on the night in question in being hosted by two news anchors who took turns to lead items.

Headlines:

- Murder of two children in North Wales
- The Lesley Molseed murder
- Alex Ferguson's two decades at Manchester United Football Club
- Peter Kay's return to his home town

Murder in North Wales Package: A news item that is obviously still breaking, this item is concerned with the discovery that morning of the bodies of two small children in their home. Although confirming that it was being treated as infanticide by the police, there was little else forthcoming, and was a model of restrained reportage.

Lesley Molseed Murder Package: Using the same source material as channel m used for this story – the arrest of a new suspect – the Granada coverage was more exhaustive, and drew on archive footage of police searching for her body in 1975 plus a more detailed evaluation of the miscarriage of justice that had been attached to the original investigation.

Liverpool, Capital of Culture Package: List of the initial events that have been announced that morning to news media of the city's plans for 2008, when it assumes the role of European Capital of Culture. Mainly an outside broadcast from the event launch venue, the piece mixed expert opinion from politicians with vox pop opinions, and inserted archive shots of several key acts. Back in the studio an appeal was made for viewers to phone in or email the studio with ideas of what else might be incorporated in the year-long festival.

Trail

Forthcoming competition
Peter Kay item

Fire-fighters, bonfire weekend callouts   Package: Mix of studio-based assessment of weekend activities, plus outside broadcast interviews with fire chiefs.

Competition   to win a day trip to Lapland, meeting 'Santa Claus'.

Sport review   Lengthy piece on Ferguson's time at Manchester United Football Club with interview clips from friends and rivals, plus vox pops, followed by review of weekend sport, including piece on bad behaviour of crowds at Everton. Substantial use of live action footage of all major goals across local teams playing in top three national football leagues

Peter Kay   Package. First 'home' appearance of nationally-famous comedian and actor. Substantial one-to-one interviews plus clips of colleagues; item driven by reason for Kay's return to Bolton, which is charity appeal for local hospice.

Weather

Final **round-up** of headlines.

A similar format was pursued on that evening's **BBC North West Tonight**, although it manages to host the programme with a single news anchor:

BBC local television

The British TV landscape has traditionally consisted of national and regional television. However, the advent of digital technology, the internet, and other recent developments have all opened up possibilities for a further layer of television broadcasting. The radio market is already becoming more variegated, having moved away from the model of national and county or conurbation stations which dominated for several decades.

One of the most interesting recent developments in UK television is BBC Local TV. It is a service piloted in the Midlands in 2005–6, and originally intended to be rolled out nationally from 2007. Not available on terrestrial television, but broadcast on satellite and on the internet, its immediate challenge was to differentiate itself from BBC regional television. It did so partly by stylistic means, but also in part by its difference in news values from the more established genre of regional television news.

Structurally, it had some similarities with DNN, the digital radio news service we explore elsewhere. The output came in rolling, repeatable short blocks. Stylistically, it was different from most television news – including BBC News 24, for example – in that in most of its early manifestations it had no presenter. Demographically, it covered a smaller area than its regional cousin: roughly comparable with BBC Local Radio 'footprints';

Headlines:

- Lesley Molseed murder developments.
- Liverpool Capital of Culture.
- Strictly Come Dancing.

New developments in Lesley Molseed murder Package: As with the other two Manchester-based news organisations, the story is based on the new arrest. Making full use of its extensive archives, North West Tonight blends archive footage of the original search with clips from a reconstruction carried out at the time, and incorporates a résumé of the miscarriage of justice.

Liverpool Capital of Culture Package: Built around an outside broadcast from the launch location, with interviews with local luminaries as well as local musicians, the piece is augmented by extensive draw on archive footage of some of the acts which will be performing.

News-in-brief items:

Philomena Ward acquittal Brief piece (illustrated by still image) on acquittal of mother of TV talent show winner.

Fire in Barrow-in-Furness – Brief piece on damage to carpet and furniture retail stores in town at northern extreme of station's coverage region.

Injury to baby by firework – Brief package on injury to child plus damage to block of flats by firework-throwing vandals – Studio voice-over moving footage from outside scene.

Air transit problems Package: Outside broadcast piece on changes in rules for air travellers, and how it will affect passengers travelling through Manchester

though, in some cases, even smaller. There was, for instance, a Black Country service as well as ones for Birmingham and for Coventry and Warwickshire. In Local Radio, there is a service for Birmingham *and* the Black Country and one for Coventry and Warwickshire.

Its news values were also shaped by its own view of its target audience and 'house style'. BBC journalist Tim Burke coordinated the Black Country pilot service in 2005–6. He defined that 'house style' as 'more Five Live than Local Radio, more Newsbeat than Newsnight'.1 The idea, he says was, where possible, to 'let viewers tell their own stories.' Referring to coverage of an incident where a pilot had to make an emergency landing due to faulty landing gear, he observes that the treatment of the story on Local TV and on Midlands Today would have been quite different (so, incidentally, might their position in the running order). They were able to use mobile phone footage, and the reporter covering the story for Local TV was effectively packaging the story on-site.

Narratives, says Burke, can be carried forward more commonly by the use of music and/or captions, in a way not always possible or desirable on terrestrial television. Interaction with the audience is easier and more regular. Reporters go out on a story, and routinely return with another two or three potential items. In the case of Local TV,

(Continued)

International Airport. Interviews with security specialist and with executive at airport (subtext to piece is be prepared to allow longer to travel as security rule changes will lead to delays) plus public response via vox pop inserts.

Trail for another programme   Brief outline of forthcoming item, spoils from RMS *Titanic* being sold illegally, to be exposed on *Inside Out* regional programme that evening at 19.30.

Sport review – Lengthy piece on Alex Ferguson, with outside broadcast, archive footage, vox pops, and interviews with contemporaries and rivals. Minimal round-up of weekend sports events with sports news anchor joined by main news anchor as double-header intro/conversation piece.

Weather

Competition for BBC *Children in Need* (major charity fund raising event due within two weeks of broadcast of this programme) plus associated competition for Strictly Come Dancing involving various BBC news presenters from North West region.

Unusually, this programme had **no résumé** – instead it went straight to closing screen after the final item.

Our fourth subject was Central News from the English West Midlands, once again on 6 November 2006. The final news broadcast to be scrutinised was the BBC regional service for the West Midlands: BBC Midlands Today's main news programme for 7 November. The primary focus of critical attention on these last two items was not to make a *direct* comparison of the news values applied on simultaneous broadcasts, but instead to produce a commentary on the *kinds* of stories run, and the formats used. Hence the decision to analyse programmes from successive days.

as with smaller local radio stations, 'the fact that it was local was almost enough for it to get on.'

As for the absence of a presenter, 'people are more concerned about the content than the way it's presented.' This, of course, is an important observation. If true, it raises fascinating questions about the worth of endless relaunches and set redesigns on national and regional television news. Audiences themselves are also less interested in the distinction between professional roles than broadcasters. Viewers and listeners often use the word 'presenter' when talking about a reporter (and sometimes vice versa). On DNN, the distinction between 'newsreading' and 'presenting' is almost impossible to draw.

Interestingly, however, on the subject of lessons to be learned from the pilot for application in the future, Burke highlights the need for more planning. We refer extensively elsewhere to the increasingly large role of planning in news. Even here, where some of the other industry rules are bent or broken, there is seen to be a need for more diary planning in the interests of efficiency. Naturally, its effects on news values are also likely to be broadly the same.

Importance is attached to the greater presence of 'more authored reports' (from listeners). Although the audience's own news values will not necessarily coincide with those of the

Central News 6 November 2006

Headlines:

- Dudley council estate demolition.
- Rubbish removal truck manoeuvre injury.
- Bonfire night injuries.
- Rhyming slang.

Dudley council estate faces demolition   Package: Clips with: Pamela Finch, protester; Linda Sanders of Dudley Council; Jean Claridge and Jack Yates (whose homes may be demolished); and footage of residents confronting Linda Sanders.

Dangerous bin lorry manoeuvre causes serious injury   Package: Clips with: victim (very brief); victim's solicitor; solicitor for Lichfield Council (employer).

Bonfire Night accidents   Round-up of Cheslyn Hay accident. Short package, with eyewitness clip. Bilston accident: News in Brief; ROSPA safe practice reminder clip.

News-in-brief items:

- Sentence for fatal accident.
- Shooting in Broad Street, Birmingham.
- Hunt for missing boy.
- Restoration of Madeley (the town, not the TV presenter).
- Rod Stewart to perform in Coventry.

Opening of Birmingham's Garden of Remembrance – Package. Vox pop of children; clip of Jim McDonald of Royal British Legion; clip of Rev. Bob Wilkes, Dean of St Philip's in Birmingham

professional journalists, this sort of first-person reporting opens the door to a more variegated, less homogenised set of journalistic perspectives. However, it is still mediated by the selection judgements of the professionals themselves. So, while the range and tone of journalistic voices is wider, the story selection processes remain broadly similar. While other BBC staff make distinctions between 'citizen journalism' and 'citizen news-gathering', here we see a partial removal of one form of mediation (that of the journalist, between story and audience), while another (of news editor between story and audience) remains. The news values may well differ on account of the range of voices aired. The judgements on newsworthiness are still made by the same type of professional.

After the 2005–6 Midlands pilot concluded, the BBC soon let it be known that it would be rolled out as a national scheme. However, this announcement was greeted with dismay by some local newspapers, fears were expressed that it would mean the BBC would have a 'Big Brother' (in the original Orwellian, rather than the 'reality TV' programme sense) grip on local news. As BBC Director-General Mark Thompson announced the proposals in late 2006, newspaper editors and media analysts voiced fears of what one called a 'terrifying monopoly' (Steve Egginton, quoted in *The Scotsman*, 7 November 2006).

(Continued)

Trail

Competition to win trip to Lapland.

80s Hitmakers Tour – Live interview one-to-one with singer Toyah Wilcox.

Children's wait for adoption – Package. Interview clips of adopting parents; Helen French, Adoption Service Manager; footage from Adoption Service video.

Sport review – Reports on Aston Villa beating Blackburn, Birmingham beating Plymouth (with Steve Bruce clip), Derby beating West Bromwich, Wolves beating Southend, Sheffield Wednesday beating Leicester, Crewe beating Port Vale, Walsall beating Torquay, Hereford beating Swindon, and Shrewsbury drawing with Wycombe. Report on Sean Perry's performance for England against New Zealand (Perry is a West Midlands-based rugby player).

Weather

New rhyming slang – Package with vox pops input; reporter asks public if they understand rhyming slang phrases with contemporary references.

BBC Midlands Today 7 November 2006:

Headlines:

- HIV checks recall for tests of hospital patients.
- Teenage driver accident rates.
- Anniversary of Wilfred Owen's death.

In order to sugar the pill, Thompson proposed a partnership with local newspapers, with the BBC buying news and content from local papers, 'We want to draw on the news gathering clout of the UK's local and regional newspapers' (Thompson, 2006), 'For newspapers that want to add sound and moving pictures to their websites, a partnership with the BBC could make a lot of sense.'

Inevitably, this would lead to a further homogenisation of news values. Not only would the same stories be covered: the treatments would tend to converge too. The same interviewees, the same story angles; indeed, on newspaper websites, literally the same packages. Media convergence is already a well-established phenomenon. This example, however, because it is driven by fears of a publicly-funded organisation using those funds to undercut commercial competitors, takes us away from the proliferation of new and fresh voices often cited as a consequence of new media technology. Instead, it threatens a further ironing out of differences between media, and a level of standardisation of content. It also may militate against the use of as many of the self-authored reports that were a feature of the pilot.

Something similar happened in the early years of BBC Local Radio. Some of its early advocates and pioneers were convinced that it would give direct, unmediated access to the airwaves to sections of the community whose voices were previously seldom heard.

HIV tests for over 1,000 hospital patients – Package. Clips of: Dr Rashmi Shukla, Director of Public Health (from press conference); Dr Ian Blair, Health Protection Agency; cleaner at Alexandra Hospital in Redditch; vox pop. Followed by live interview with Dr Steve Taylor, HIV specialist. Help line number broadcast.

Teenage drivers prone to driving accidents – Package. Interview clips with a driver's mother; another driver's father; Matthew Henderson from Brake! (governmental road safety campaign organisation).

News in brief:
Job losses at Celestica, Telford.
Company challenges factory pollution fine.

Trail ahead.

Restoration project at Ironbridge Gorge Package: including clip with Adam Rawling, AMEC Construction.

Young Director of the Year winner Package: Clips of winner Nathan Littlejohn, and vox pop of school pupils. Videowall: presenter runs through Nathan's Top Ten Tips for website success.

Anniversary of [First World War poet] Wilfred Owen's death Package: Interview Clips with: Peter Owen, nephew of Wilfred; Major David Hamilton (who also reads from Owen's poem 'Asleep').

Profile of local church figure a year after [Birmingham suburb] Lozells riots Package: Interview Clips with Rev. Jemima Prasadam, and vox pop of youths she works with.

However, BBC Local Radio newsrooms and newsgathering operations function largely in the same way as other sections of the Corporation. While retaining local autonomy of news values, its output is increasingly harmonised with material acquired for, and run on, regional television news programmes.

Similar fears, incidentally, were also expressed by local newspaper editors and journalists with the advent of UK local radio in the late 1960s and early 1970s. Although there remains a degree of story overlap, local radio news values and priorities remain distinct and separate from those of local newspapers. It remains to be seen whether the same will be true of local television.

Note

For the benefit of those unfamiliar with the two BBC programmes referred to in that quote, *Newsbeat* is the weekday BBC Radio 1 news programme that seeks to meet the cultural expectations of a young audience, while *Newsnight* is a daily BBC2 television news programme which expects its (more mature) audience to have a solid engagement with news

(Continued)

Sport   Look ahead to Tottenham Hotspurs v Port Vale. Clip of past upset from 1988. Clips with: Ray Walker, ex-Port Vale player; and John Rudge, former manager. Report on Stoke beating Coventry in fogbound game. Package on Julia Hubbard's selection for British bobsleigh team. Clips of Julia, and vox pop with work colleagues.

Man builds miniature railway station in his back yard – Package, including interview clips with Phil Green, main subject of story

Weather, and emergency travel flash.

Analysis

When non-journalists (and non-media students or academics) are asked for their accounts of what a 'typical' television news programme is like, it is quite possible that they would come up with something closer to a regional news programme than the national and international material we have studied. The bulletins we have selected contain traditionally packaged and delivered items, no live reporter two-ways, no direct on-air interactivity or feedback (other than a competition result), vox pops, and fairly conventional 'and finally ...' items. (There are occasions, of course, when features such as interactivity/ feedback and two-ways *are* present) but on the nights studied the only such examples were the Granada programme and the BBC North West sport section. Both of these broadcasts drew on the fact that there were two presenters in the studio, allowing less a formal two-way, more occasional informal discussions about specific – and non-contentious – items.

The story content of the Midlands programmes is also fairly typical of regional broadcast news. Although these programmes (as with the Manchester

and current affairs. A useful analogy might be that the former takes a red top tabloid approach to news while *Newsnight* follows a more serious path, more aligned to the *Guardian* or *Daily Telegraph*.

The show business influence

'News as a show' is an increasing fact of life in the broadcast industry
Much has been written about changes in news values in recent years. The discussion has tended to focus on key areas including: celebritisation of news, infotainment, dumbing down, and interactivity (or so-called democratisation of news). A lot has been written about *what* is happening. Less about *why* it is happening. And most of the explanations offered tend to focus on factors such as commercialisation and/or commodification of news.

There is general agreement that mainstream broadcast news has realigned its news priorities in recent years. Most commentators also contend that a similar trend is observable in the mainstream print media (there is an interesting attempt at a defence against the claim in volume 7 of the official *History of The Times*, Stewart, 2005: 613–25). But is ones) were selected at random, they do contain much of what has characterised regional television news over many years. They also contain a high number of stories which could plausibly have run on *another* night. The increasing influence of the planning diary is once again strongly in evidence.

In the BBC Midlands Today bulletin, arguably only the lead item (the HIV recall) *had* to run that day. The others were all more or less flexible. The Wilfred Owen anniversary and the Young Director package had some time specificity, though no effort was made to present them as stories relating to 'today', and the remaining stories were also relatively timeless (of course, this does not apply to most of the sports content). Where attempts are made to attach stories to a 'peg', they are only approximate (as with the clergy profile) – *near* the anniversary of the Lozells disturbances. The stories on teenage accidents, Ironbridge restoration, and the Young Director award seem similarly loosely related to the particular day's agenda.

The Central News bulletin was slightly more closely related to that day's news agenda: but this may have been in part because it was the day after Bonfire Night. The council estate facing demolition, the Garden of Remembrance opening, the bin lorry accident, and the Bonfire Night round-up stories were all more-or-less time-specific. The others – long waits for adoption, and Toyah's 80s tour – were less so.

Both programmes had one live interview. BBC Midlands Today's followed the lead story (the follow-up to HIV recall). Central's was at the other end of the spectrum: the piece with Toyah Willcox. This is the sort of item that would be more likely to run on a feature or magazine programme than on a news-based programme on radio, and demonstrates that broadcast news genres remain fluid. Although we have used the terms 'bulletin' and 'programme' almost interchangeably, the balance seems to have swung further towards the latter both journalistically and stylistically. There was a considerable media

it enough simply to ascribe it all to pressure from advertisers and broadcasting management for the biggest possible audience share? Is it because news is seen as one more exchangeable commodity?

What time is the news on?

Less often discussed is the relationship between news and time. To take the BBC as an example, for much of its history, it was regarded as vitally important that news should be available at a very precise time. Both on radio and on television, major news bulletins would start precisely at the time intended. The Six o'clock News would start at exactly that time, and so on. This is still the case in some places, but is no longer universal or automatic. The BBC Ten o'clock News on occasion starts up to two minutes after the hour as programmes sometimes 'crash' the ten o'clock 'junction', and trails will still be played. Purists and traditionalists may well feel this is even less justified than on commercial channels, where there is at least the argument that advertisers' demands have to be met.

(Continued)

debate in late 2006 when BBC2's *Newsnight* aired a major interview with Madonna, following her adoption of a Malawian child. Was she a suitable topic for the lead item on such a programme? Should an entertainment figure be accorded the same treatment as a senior political or diplomatic figure?

Many people still seem to regard the 'And finally ... ' item as a staple of national terrestrial news bulletins. In fact, BBC One's Ten o'clock News has rarely run such an item in recent times. Even the ITV News at 10.30 does so very selectively. It is only likely to be present if there is strong (or, perhaps, exclusive) visual material. It is no longer, however, a 'slot' for which material has to be consciously sought. In regional television, by contrast, it is still more likely to be encountered. Both our chosen programmes contain such an item: the back garden 'railway halt', and the updated rhyming slang features.

One of the authors spent a decade working in a shared television and radio newsroom at Pebble Mill in Birmingham. During the whole of that period (and beyond), BBC Midlands Today had a reporter whose primary role was to find and report on 'and finally ... ' stories. Although the identity of the reporter changed, and it was never, one presumes, specifically articulated in their contracts of employment, this was effectively their role. There was also a similar figure at Central News for most of the same period, and the picture was broadly similar in other broadcast regions. It was, for all practical purposes, a regular slot that had to be filled, rather than being run on merit, depending on the availability of suitable material.

The presence of viewers' competitions is no real surprise. In the absence of journalistic interactivity, it enables the programme to involve its audience in a way familiar to local radio. The question posed, like many on television (Silent Night, Quiet Night, or Peaceful Night: which is the correct title of the Christmas carol?), is designed to maximise viewer response numbers by being almost impossible to get wrong: thus enabling a sizeable reaction to be

We are not talking here about the occasional overrun caused by a live concert or sporting fixture. We are talking about a routine pattern of broadcasting which, on occasions, puts the needs of programme and channel promotion ahead of the news. Gone are the split-second clock countdowns and the precision timing of the past. In *this* sense, we may well be witnessing the commodification of news even within public service broadcasting. On some terrestrial channels, the news is still struggling to retain its place on merit – i.e. by viewing figures, and by similarity to surrounding programming. This, in turn, is likely to affect the news values on display. If terrestrial news is effectively just another unit of programming, designed not to be too obtrusive in the schedules, then the choice and treatment of stories will reflect this. On occasion, this will result in more lifestyle or celebrity stories, at the expense of the more traditional elite-based news. The more interesting question is not whether this is inherently good or bad, but why it has occurred.

There was, of course, a noisier public debate a few years ago about the timing and positioning of the main evening news bulletins on both main terrestrial channels. BBC One moved its bulletin from 9.0p.m. to 10.0p.m. ITV famously attracted parliamentary criticism for depriving News at Ten of its fixed slot completely, and then moving it to 10.30p.m. The tendency to adopt a looser chronological approach even to these fixed highlighted (to advertisers), and raising further revenue in the process. At about the same time, the BBC programme had experimented with journalistic feedback and interactivity on its follow-up (10.25 p.m.) bulletin – though only briefly.

The story selection itself, despite changes in broadcast technology and programme formats, remains fairly typical of regional news over a lengthy period. Health 'scares' and council 'rows' have been filling programmes such as these for decades. So, for that matter, have local award winners, children waiting for adoption or hospital operations, clergy/community figures, 'eccentrics'; bonfire night accident round-ups, crash stories, and remembrance ceremonies. In regional as in national broadcast news, there are periodic debates as to how much crime should be included, and how the balance should be struck between automatic reporting of local/regional crime and the attempt to reflect a more 'positive' view of the area served by the programme.

Local and regional broadcasters (especially, but not solely, presenters) sometimes see themselves as having a different sort of relationship with their audience from that of their national counterparts. Some of the characteristics of 'embeds' in war reporting, or beat reporters (such as prolonged or intense association with the subjects of their reporting), also apply to local and regional journalists. A more personalised identification can affect the tone, even if not often the substance, of regional news values: especially, for instance, when major job losses have occurred or are threatened; or when a local venue is in the running for a major national or international event. It is probably more often a matter of tone or emphasis rather than outright story selection or omission. Occasionally, it can even feel like overt journalistic campaigning – as, for example, when the National Exhibition Centre (NEC) was in the running as the possible site for the Millennium Dome, or when major industrial sites faced closure such as occurred with Leyland Daf in

slots has received much less attention, but is still symptomatic of the same approach, on a micro rather than a macro scale. The subtext is still that news is a programme, like any other, rather than a specially ring-fenced piece of output.

Accountable news editors?

BBC News has recently started a new range of blogs. Whereas reporter blogs tend to be variants of the stories filed for television, radio and online, editorial blogs attempt to engage with some of the issues covered in this book. They are presumably part of an attempt to render BBC output more 'transparent'. In attempting to do so, they sometimes engage directly with news values issues in a way that was previously only done on programmes like 'Feedback' on BBC Radio 4.

Tellingly, the opening lines of an Editor's Blog entitled 'Citizen Newsgathering', by Jon Williams (bbc.co.uk/news/theeditors: 20 October 2006) reads: 'So just how much should we listen to you – our audience? It's a question all of us involved in the media are pondering right now.' The question is then specifically related to the BBC's relatively

(Continued)

Lancashire and the West Midlands during 1993, and Rover in the West Midlands in early 2005.

This is certainly the case with the coverage on BBC North West Tonight and Granada of the Liverpool, European City of Culture 2008 story; this is a story of national, some might even claim international, significance, but one rooted within their broadcast regions. In the cases of both Granada and BBC news coverage the tone and language used inferred a sense of ownership of the story, a 'this is ours, and we [inferring the whole regional population] are all stakeholders in the success of Liverpool's year as Capital of Culture'. Furthermore, both organisations have been in the past subjected to criticism for being too Manchester-centric (hardly surprising given the city's dominance as a media centre second only to London) and so the opportunity to provide substantial positive coverage to Liverpool was seized with apparent enthusiasm. There was additionally the issue of rivalry between the BBC and Granada; neither would be prepared to have the other cover the story as an exclusive. The result was almost interchangeable coverage; both used the same location (the launch venue of the City of Culture programme) as the anchor point for their items, both used the same interviewees – who will have been made available by the public relations team of the event – and both used similar, and in some cases identical, clips of the musicians due to be involved in the year-long event in Liverpool.

The issue of social cohesion – running programmes that have direct relevance to the community they serve – is embedded in the networks of television stations throughout the UK. As the then ITV Managing Director pointed out: 'Our news bulletins and weekday flagship news magazine programme, *Granada Reports*, are at the heart of our regional output. Our News programmes have undergone a number of changes in recent years, aimed at improving their performance and strengthening the editorial agenda of the

recent tracking of stories accessed on the BBC website. 'How big a role should that play in the decisions we make?' After a brief enumeration of recent big stories, and the mail, mobile phone and video responses received, Williams then distinguishes between citizen journalism and citizen newsgathering, saying: 'It's vital our stories engage with the audience – but we need to be careful our running orders don't become a *Top of the Pops* of news (look what happened to that!)'.

He then contrasts a story about a shot of a walrus feeding on clams on the sea floor winning a photography prize (the second most read story on its day) with a story about EU leaders meeting in Finland to discuss fuels and climate change. The second story, he says, was not in the worldwide top ten. 'But it doesn't mean we shouldn't do it. We should – we must.'

But, as often in discussions of news values in practice, the interesting question, going to the heart of the matter, is: why? To ask the question is not to make a value judgement about whether Williams is right or wrong. It is simply to note that discussions so often stop short of the really interesting and challenging questions. The same issue is addressed, from a slightly different perspective, by another BBC Editor, Radio One *Newsbeat*'s Rod McKenzie (bbc.co.uk/news/theeditors: 20 October 2006).

day... the plans we have for the future will continue to benefit viewers and confirm ITV's commitment to an effective, professional and relevant regional News service.' (Woodward, 2005). The BBC's Director-General has similarly commented on the value of local news, but added to that the dimension that its existence is expected to feed into the rolling news service: 'BBC News 24 offers strong regional coverage, drawing upon the expertise of BBC correspondents across the UK and trying to feature at least one regional perspective or a regional example from beyond London in major stories in order to highlight different impacts in different parts of the country' (Thompson, 2006). Without a strong regional presence it would be impossible to meet such a demand.

The differing geographic bases of the three Manchester-based broadcasters has an impact on the overall structure of the programmes; channel m's coverage is confined to the Greater Manchester region; while of the BBC extends their coverage into the northern edge of the territory (albeit with a news-in-brief piece on a fire in Cumbria) while the Granada broadcast included a substantive piece on murders in North Wales. In this respect channel m is the most fortunate in terms of competition for time slots within the programme, as it is able to cover more stories centred on Manchester, whereas the other two broadcasters are subjected to trawling across a far greater geographic zone, leading to a regional, rather than local, service with the inevitable loss of tight focus. It is interesting that while Granada assumes responsibility for North East Wales, this is outside the territory of BBC's North West team (being handled as part of the BBC Cymru portfolio) even though the two services are run within a kilometre of each other in Manchester city centre. That aside the territories of the two stations are broadly the same, bordering with Midland TV in the south, Borders in the North, and Yorkshire in the east. In both cases it is the main cities in the region that gain the maximum coverage, with the extremes of the regions being covered only in a perfunctory manner.

'So where do we stand on the issue of how much to listen to our audiences – how much say we give them about story selection and running orders? How much do we impose and how much do we interact?' Referring to listeners' text messages, McKenzie says:

> It's not just a lip service thing though, it genuinely makes us editorially richer I believe ... It's made our news agenda stronger and faster: We (sic) were alerted to stories like the dangers of 'Snatch' Land Rovers in Iraq and Afghanistan by our listeners with military connections long before our other BBC network colleagues.

Interestingly, he also says: 'It may not be right for all BBC outlets...[but] I am clear where we stand. Without our audience and our daily dialogue with them – we'd be finished.' One would clearly wish to know more about how this dialogue is actually conducted. As with Williams above, McKenzie is really talking about the traditional journalistic tip-off, suitably technologically updated and rebranded. Is the dialogue also extended to story selection from among stories already known about, to news priorities and running orders, and to how stories are covered? He also refers to its usefulness as a gauge of audience

(Continued)

Another of the interesting aspects of the Manchester-based broadcasts was the way in which channel m's limited resources were highlighted, particularly with regard to the Molseed murder case. The channel m package was made up of studio reading, interview clips with the only neighbour who remembered the original events and who still lives in the street where Lesley Molseed once lived and with newer neighbours who have subsequently become aware of the proximity of events in 1975, and still images from a photographic library service. In contrast both the BBC and Granada packages made a great deal of use of what was originally locally-generated archive footage (although some of these same items were used in the night's national news programmes, these were part of much shorter pieces) which shows 'ownership' of items. If there is a subtext, it is that longer-serving broadcast organisations tend to be better resourced.

That the Lesley Molseed item has also featured in the main news programme on national television (which can be explained in news value terms as being based on several exceptional characteristics, notably that a child had been murdered, the man originally found guilty was the subject of a miscarriage of justice, and that both he and his mother were broken by the events and both subsequently died) brings another question: why repeat the same story? One explanation is that the regional news services assume ownership of the story due to its local consonance – especially as they are likely to have produced much of the archive material. Another is that it offers the opportunity to go into greater detail, the local service not suffering the same time constraints brought about by competing stories. A third explanation is that a proportion of the viewer base switches onto the local service drop-in towards the end of the national news, and so is assumed to have missed the nationally-broadcast item. This infers that the item is new to the viewer, and

reaction to stories. So, in essence, the primary role of the audience is still as a provider of tip-offs and feedback. Not that different from the picture in the days before text and email.

Meanwhile, another blog, this one by Kevin Marsh, editor of the BBC College of Journalism (bbc.co.uk/news/theeditors: 14 June 2006), reported: 'Apparently 32% of BBC staff don't think news organisations should be more open with audiences.' Marsh goes on to criticise the 32%. In justifying this, and providing examples of bad practice, however, he draws all his examples from the world of newspapers, concluding:

> The demand for news – facts about the world that professional journalists have gathered, verified, made sense of – continues to grow. The organisations that will do best at servicing that demand among developing audiences will be the ones that show their workings.

Apart from anything else, this is an interesting take on the process of newsgathering and distribution. Many critics, one suspects, would wonder whether a number of questions thus qualifies its inclusion in the regional broadcast as well as being in the national programme.

What is of interest is that each broadcaster had a 'scoop' story that none of the others carried. The reason for this could be any of several reasons, the most common of which is active public relations activity; channel m's piece on Stephen Oake, for instance, is likely to be rooted in a close working relationship between an influential member of the editorial team and the lobbyist on behalf of the Police Federation's local office, and similarly the Peter Kay story on *Granada Reports* is rooted in a good working relationship between the comedian/actor (whose regionality is a vital aspect of his success) and the programme team – but it might also be extended to include PR activity by the charity. Such close relationships are common throughout the news business (reporters who have nurtured police officers to feed exclusive pieces of information, sports writers who work closely with players, managers or agents, and so forth) and are more commonplace than many viewers or readers might realise. They are accordingly responsible for certain organisations carrying more of a certain type of news story than their rivals.

Teletext

At the beginning of 2007, Teletext, the news text service accompanying ITV, reorganised its services and organisation. One of the main changes was to institute a separate 'And finally ...' section. Although, as we have seen, the 'And finally ...' item is not quite the universal presence in television news some believe, this nevertheless represented another step in the routinisation of the final story. As with many other elements of broadcast news, the hunt was now officially on for stories to fit the generic brand and house style.

are begged by that simple phrase 'made sense of'. What degree of mediation and interpretation may lie hidden in those simple words! And how much of the 'workings' can ever really be shown? Reasons for running the story? For its positioning? For its treatment? For the choice of interviewees and visuals to illustrate the story? No news organisation would ever be able routinely to provide such information. But it is only by addressing them that we begin to get a sense of news values at work.

Here is another example. Daniel Dodd (bbc.co.uk/news/the editors: 24 May 2006). 'Some callers ... asked why Tuesday's rise in profits at Marks and Spencer was reported so widely.

The answer is simple: M&S is an iconic High Street brand ... Broadcast or print, we are all agreed that M&S is a story. It's a store that everybody knows, one of those British brands that everyone has heard of and has a view on ...'.

Again, the approach is simple assertion – 'we are all agreed...'. We note elsewhere that some academics regard journalists' own assertions as largely based on instinct and professional hunch. The contrasting approaches are discussed in Hetherington (1985).

(Continued)

Conclusion

Regional and local news programmes are an integral part of the broadcast industry in the UK partly because there is a legislative or regulatory requirement to do so,[2] but also because they help maintain a sense of localness (and thus viewer loyalty) that is an ideological proximity to the value of regional and local newspapers. But there is another reason for its continued existence; the expectation that national news organisations will maintain local bureaux to feed into the national system, but will at the same time justify their existence and will be considered as more trustworthy by a local public, which accords with Herbert Gans's (1979: 142) assertion that in stories that go on to assume national significance, 'local power-holders charge the national media with unwarranted meddling'.

The primary news value to all local television news is that of its **relevance** to a local audience; all other aspects of the system are subsumed by this. Perhaps best of all, it has managed, thus far at least, to remain immune to what journalist Kate Adie describes as a vulnerability to changes brought about by shifts in: 'commerce and intellectual fancy, and ... fashion and technology' (2002: 402). Quite how long it will be able to continue to be the preferred mechanism for the population of a region to receive moving images of events in their area is unknown; what is certain is that, by engaging with viewer feedback mechanisms and by integrating with the relevant website(s) it is attempting to move it forward while remaining true to what it has always been; the broadcasting equivalent to Giuseppe di Lampedusa's 'If we want things to stay as they are, things will have to change'. (1960: 40).

We have already remarked upon the lack of sports news on BBC1's 10 o'clock News. Shortly after the programme we looked at was broadcast, Craig Oliver addressed the issue on the site (bbc.co.uk/news/theeditors: 28 September 2006). 'Do we have a duty to do it – given that many sporting rights are not now available to terrestrial TV? Should that squeeze out other news? The audience feedback we get when we do sport on the Ten is almost universally negative. At a recent major focus group people seemed to be suggesting that they expected sport on local, but not national, news.'

Oliver is too tactful to comment on this rather eccentric piece of focus group research. But he cannot hide his frustration at the failure to show, for example, the Xabi Alonso goal scored for Liverpool from his own half. How extreme must the sports news be before it appears on this programme? Or is it only when sport can be packaged as news or can be portrayed as raising issues beyond sport? (hooliganism, racism, drugs).

Meanwhile, for a discussion of the seemingly eternal question of whether 'Big Brother' is newsworthy, see the blog by Matt Morris, Head of News, BBC Five Live

Notes

1 There might, however, be another agenda behind channel m; according to Philip Reevell (2006) 'The corporate thinking behind the channel is to maintain GMG's dominant media presence in Manchester, where the company owns the *Manchester Evening News*, a range of weekly newspapers and the ManchesterOnline portal. So with ITV, BBC and GMG spending substantial amounts on their local offerings, Ofcom's "Digital Local" report, published in January 2006, was able to conclude that "we anticipate that development of local content services will continue strongly." Note, however, the language here – local content, not local television.'

2 All British television and radio broadcast media are expected to provide a degree of public service content, which extends to the provision of local news supply and broadcast. The Broadcasting Act 1990 and the rules for organisations governed by Ofcom are worthy of further study – the latter organisation is currently engaged in pubic service broadcasting in a digital age, and again puts news among its primary expectations for meeting its public service remit

(bbc.co.uk/news/theeditors: 24 May 2006). 'It's worth doing BB if it raises an interesting issue, or if something actually happens. So yes, it is news ... sort of.' Issues such as ... ? ' ... a feature on Tourette's Syndrome; ... what it's like to come out when you're a Muslim.'

So, do they cover it because it fits in with the perceived Five Live audience more comfortably than, say, the Ten o'clock News on BBC One? If the station asked its audience if they wanted to hear Big Brother news on air, would they approve? ' ... we were pretty sure what the texting constituency, or a majority of them, would say: "No Big Brother, thank you"'.So if we thought the audience (or at least the texting constituency) would vote against, why on earth would we cover it? 'Well ... because it's news. Sort of.'

So, ultimately, we still end up with the same answer from the editors.

'It is news.'

'Why?'

'Because it just is!'

The Rise and Rise of Citizen Journalist

10

How User-generated Content is Shaping the Agenda, or not

It has been suggested that the days of traditional news journalism are numbered – that the citizens will assume ownership of the news. This is an interesting phenomenon – but it does not automatically follow that the established linear model of news gathering, editing and dissemination will wither away eventually to die, redundant and unloved. On the contrary, it is entirely possible that the old order will triumph because of its understanding of, and adherence to, a value system that is rarely followed by individuals who set themselves up as reporters and chroniclers of news. It can be argued that the role of the citizen is, and will remain, an adjunct to the existing news system. At issue is the ownership of news. In the past (and that means any longer than 15 years prior to the publication of this book) for an event to become news, it was necessary to wait until the broadcast of the next edition of television or radio news, or the next newspaper was published. Today, events can be posted for instant access onto the Internet in close to real time, moving from a 'by appointment' process to one of instant access. And many of those instant reports are generated by enthusiastic amateurs, or citizen journalists as they are increasingly known.

The turning point in the emergence of citizen journalism is accepted as being September 11 2001, at a little before 9.00a.m. in the morning, local time. When the first hijacked aircraft slammed into the side of the World Trade Center's North Tower, it was not a professional news crew which provided the initial images, but members of the public using digital cameras and ordinary, domestic video cameras. Those same eyewitnesses were subsequently drawn upon to provide accounts of what they had observed to professional news gatherers, but there was an almost immediate backlash from the public, who resented the editing process that was rapidly introduced – editing that is a standard part of news mediation practice. Since that time, whenever there has been a major event of international significance – the fall of Baghdad, the Madrid train bombings, the Asian tsunami, London's Underground bombings – ordinary citizens have provided early images and accounts. And every time there is a wave of complaints that elements of the story provided by eyewitnesses have been subsumed by news professionals.

Accordingly, the role of the citizen in the journalistic process is an issue of increasing concern to industry professionals. On the surface, many news industry professionals seem to take a liberal, 'anything goes', stance in the face of this threat to their livelihood – but it could be argued that a liberal is somebody whose interests have never been threatened, and as soon as citizen journalists begin to impact on the earning potential of professional journalists then the amateur news gatherers come in for criticism. What doesn't help is that nobody seems to know quite where citizen journalism is located; the plethora of internet sites and other media forms such as web-logs (more commonly referred to as blogs) and pod casts confuses the issue, and few provide a geographical address, preferring it to be out there in the void of cyberspace. One typical comment was from Neil McIntosh who explained that: 'For many media executives, citizen journalism has taken on the characteristics of the Beast of Bodmin Moor. It's out there, the consensus is it has the capacity to be quite vicious if you cross its path but, so far, nobody's seen much of it' (McIntosh, 2006).

The proponents of citizen journalism understandably take a positive view of the role of the individual in the news dissemination process, the most concise of which came from author Dan Gillmor, who wrote in his own blog that: 'I'd argue that some coverage, however amateurish, is better than none at all' (Gillmor, 2006–2).

Television news journalist Jon Snow, speaking at a conference in 2006, was reported as saying that input from viewers was 'gold dust flying our way' and added that:

> The biggest problem was sorting though the volume of information viewers were supplying. Of course, there's loads of rubbish out there, but in terms of its impact on traditional media, it's not a problem. The only issue is how do we manage it and how do we reconfigure the newsroom to do so. Facilitating feedback and transparency had helped democratise journalism. You begin to look back on what you were doing and you think it was so undemocratic, it was so unresponsive, it was so arrogant. (Stabe, 2006)

Snow is not alone; there are others who also see the 'old order' as hegemonic. Typical comments are those centred on the perception that the process of professional newsgathering and dissemination is too closed, too ready to work to its own agenda – something which has been interpreted as a lack of transparency. But just as there are critics, then so there are also defenders:

> Is more transparency always better, or are there dangers lurking within an otherwise healthy movement? In short, is the pressure for explaining spiraling [sic] out of control?

The reality might easily be that critics of the old system are small in number, but are especially vociferous – disproportionately so, it might be argued. One enthusiastic news and opinion self-publisher (which is simply a further variation on the notion of citizen journalism) is Bill Ardolino, who publishes *InDC Journal* from Washington. 'Being an independent journalist is a hobby that sprang from my frustration about biased, incomplete, selective, and/or incompetent information gathering by the mainstream media,' he is on record as saying (Friedman, 2006: 46). But such a damning indictment of the old system might as easily be perceived as nothing more than the ranting of somebody who could not make it onto the staff of an established publication. It might also be argued that the one-man nature of such operations does not provide the resources for a balanced, considered view of events.

Writing after Michel Foucault, one academic observed that there exists an assumption that: 'the conventions of news writing do not simply chronicle the world, but that they constitute certain claims to knowledge about such matters as the audiences for news texts, the position of journalists in that world, and the relationship between audience and journalist' (Matheson, 2004: 445). This infers an important part of the professional news gathering process is to contextualise events, to frame them within the value system – and that begins with its relevance not just to the intended audience, but also to surrounding events.

A simple illustration is the rolling story concerning Iran's development of its nuclear fission processes. This is a story of international significance which began in the 1990s and which will continue to run into the foreseeable future. In essence the nation of Iran (which has been treated with much suspicion for several decades by various powerful Western governments, ever since a religious-inspired and -led revolution overthrew the autocratic 'Peacock Throne' government of the Shah in January 1979) in 1974 began to construct (with much help from the German Government, and that nation's Siemens KWU business) a pair of nuclear power stations near Bushehr, 400km south of Tehran. A decade later during the Iran–Iraq war one of the reactors was damaged several times during an air raid, severely crippling the unfinished installation. A decade of relative inactivity followed, while the Iranian government sought to gain international help form Germany and from Spain; neither country was prepared to carry out the work, apparently because of pressure brought bear by the American government, which was distinctly hostile towards what it perceived as an Islamist fundamentalist regime controlling Iran. Finally in 1995 an agreement was reached whereby Russia would provide the technology to allow the Bushehr facilities to be developed, and start to produce electricity. Given the wary (some might argue suspicious) nature of relations between the USA and Russia this was not likely to be received with anything other than caution.

Tensions between Iran and the west heightened progressively throughout the rest of that decade, in part because of the dawning realisation that, while Iran had acquired a number of intercontinental ballistic missiles ostensibly for defence of the facility against attack from its various perceived enemies, those missiles would be capable of carrying nuclear warheads. And those warheads could be developed as part of the nuclear fission programme that Iran says is being carried out purely for purposes of electricity generation. Various diplomatic moves were thus accelerated, with a variety of government and non-governmental bodies involved; at the point of writing there are threats of sanctions against Iran, and threats of attack both to and from Iran. The situation is complex and layered, and of significance on a global scale; any attempts by a citizen journalist to provide a balanced and useful article on the subject would require resources which could draw on not just local knowledge from inside the Iranian government, society and nuclear industries, but also the American and Israeli governments and society, the United Nations, and NATO. Such resources require a major news organisation with contacts that are rarely within the grasp of any individual. At best, a citizen journalist would be able to provide only a small part of the story, perhaps an exposition of feelings within the country of Iran or the view from within Israel, a country which feels threatened by any of its neighbours gaining a nuclear weapons capability. This is just one example of why the traditional media model is likely to survive, regardless of the protestations of advocates of citizen journalists. Almost every other news issue, to be fully understood, needs to be viewed from a position of greater perspective that that achievable by most 'civilians'.

Furthermore there is the issue of commitment. Most citizen journalists are enthusiastic amateurs in the true sense of the term, in that they rarely get paid for their output. To gain a broad base of background requires commitment in terms of both time and money – resources which few individuals can provide on a long-term basis. As one of the world's higher-profile citizen journalists, Salam Pax (The Baghdad Blogger) pointed out in an interview after his blog had ceased to exist, he would resume his chosen career and become an architect, and another blogger, Xeni Jardin, states that 'for most bloggers, blogging is an unpaid labor of love. Some blogs include advertising or "tip jars" (online cash donation systems), but the dilemma of how to earn a living from blogging is largely unsolved' (Jardin, n.d.).

Much the same point was made more recently by Kim Fletcher (2006) who stated in relation to online editions of newspapers, that: 'It raises the biggest internet question of them all, which is how to make money – enough money to fund proper journalism – out of that on-line readership. That last is the question that taxes all managements.'

All of which suggests that even the most high-profile blogs – which, to recap, are the main outlets for the work of citizen journalists – are transitory in nature, and are subjected to the same time constraints that all hobbyists will be familiar with. Only those with the required combination of sufficient free time and adequate funding will be capable of sustaining their output – content provided by the rest will simply fade away as the pressures of everyday life overtake the producers. And besides, as Edmund Burke once said: 'It is a general popular error to suppose the loudest complainers for the public to be the most anxious for its welfare' (Burke, 1769).

In an ironic twist, it is the closed, insular, non-professional nature of web-based media that can work for the interests of pressure groups. In much the same way as small electoral turn-outs in elections can provide an easy route to power for minority interest groups, the web-log is also endowed with a disproportionate sense of power. Writing recently in an English newspaper, a radio presenter referred to critiques that appear in blogs – and to which he feels too much relevance is attached: 'the majority of views contained within these silly little circles of self-appointed experts would, in bygone times, have been written in green ink and composed entirely of capital letters. Then, of course, nobody would have read them' (O'Brien, 2006). It does not take a great leap in imagination to realise that this phenomenon of amateur, narrow interest web media is an ideal channel for the propagation of minority interests who feel almost duty-bound to bypass the established channels of paid media and democratic process, and push forth their ideas for change in what could be described as a 'Fifth Estate'.[1]

And what of the matter of publishing blog-based content? Where does the responsibility for its validity and truth begin and end? BlogBurst is a service which is at the forefront of media convergence; it syndicates blog content and links it to newspaper or publisher websites. According to Eric Newman – the ultimate head of BlogBurst – when speaking to Editors' Weblog in December 2006, the true value of a blog within the journalism framework resides in its 'ability to bring new content to newspaper websites.' He cites the example of Reuters, a traditional media company with strict editorial guidelines, and the freedom it enjoys to use and link to opinionated content gained from blogs without having to endorse it; this is because in Reuters' view, that content stays part of the BlogBurst syndication. But is this not simply a cop-out on Reuters' part? If Reuters is happy to validate the content then it ought to stand up and say so – and if it is not, should it run it in the first place?

One respondent – unnamed – to that item said that:

> They have found a way to please both the blogger and those in search of hard news. Blogs are often seen as a place for people to simply place their opinions without any real evidence or support of what they are saying. Linking blogs to credible news publication sites

is just what some skeptics need in order for blogs to seem entirely legit. Also, by only inviting certain bloggers it allows for a large number of prank and insincere bloggers to be taken out of the equation. Blogs are coming into journalism whether people like it or not.

Fine words – but this suggests that by attaching the content to Reuters' site a validity is gained, something which may not be justified – and something which is definitely not claimed by Eric Newman.

Push or pull?

One of the main arguments put forward in favour of the citizen journalism model is that it is more closely aligned to pull, rather than push models of news delivery; in place of the old order of news being selected by editorial teams who have by cumulative experience become attuned to the expectation of their readers, the new order allows news receivers to draw in only those items which are of direct relevance to them; in other words, they determine how specific news items fit best by achieving consonance within their own value system. But is this the correct approach? One argument is that posited by Peter Bale of *Times Online*, who stated in a recent article that 'one of the main objectives of the newspaper is to give people journeys that surprise them' and that the process of 'pull model' personalised newspapers leads to what he describes as a 'dull' newspaper (Bale, 2006). A concurrent observation is that a move over to a pull model will bring the risk of 'individuals not extending beyond preconceived world views' (Matheson, 2004: 459).

In reality, the pull model might be viewed as simply a further development of the focus groups that were – and in some areas still are – used by organisations as a means of attuning news programme or newspaper content to its audience expectation. Focus groups were first used in the consumer goods industry to help shape proposed products (and to aid the commercial viability of such products by eliminating some of the risk) with mixed results; the automotive industry still reverberates with the horror that was the Ford Edsel project, where a completely new car was developed during the 1950s with the intention of creating a product entirely in tune with pubic demand. However, even as the project was being developed it become apparent to certain Ford executives that tastes had changed, and that the car's integrity was also being compromised by attempts to put too many elements of public taste into the finished product. The car was a dismal failure, and as Walter Hayes put it so succinctly, the prime example of 'How not to do it' (Hayes, 1990: 71–2; see also Lacey, 1986: 486–2 for a broader explanation of the process adopted by Ford).

Yet despite the misgivings of some members of the industry, there are still those who are moving rapidly towards a greater level of involvement. Trinity Mirror, a media group which owns some 240 regional newspapers, recently appointed its first head of multimedia. Michael Hills obviously expects to develop a cohesive strategy for the use of public-generated content alongside more traditionally-gathered material, as he explained to the *UK Press Gazette*:

There is going to be much more of a focus on being inclusive, rather than publishing to an audience at a time you specify, and giving the audience the news diet that you decided. There's going to be a bigger focus on interacting with that audience, answering to them, and using a lot of the stuff that they produce for you. I think the distinction between professional journalists and citizen journalists may become a little blurred. Rather than seeing the content that citizen journalists provide as being useful exclusively on a website, papers can start looking a lot more to use some of that content in print as well. (Stabe, 2006–2)

Dan Gillmor summed up matters nicely, quoting in the Introduction to his book *We The Media* (2006) his friend Tom Stites's observation that citizen journalism is the province of:

A rather narrow and very privileged slice of the polity – those who are educated enough to take part on the wired conversation, who have the technical skills, and who are affluent enough to have the time and equipment.

Gillmor then continues, making the point that:

to our discredit the journalism business and society at large have not listened to them as well as it should. The rise of the citizen-journalist will help us listen. The ability of anyone to make the news will give new voice to people who've felt voiceless – and whose words we need to hear ... In the end, they may help spark a renaissance of the notion, now threatened, of a truly informed citizenry. (Gillmor, 2006: xxix)

But Gillmor is an avowed advocate of citizen journalism. Journalist Michael Buerk points out what can happen when this same philosophy of public consultation is taken too far in news organisations, when analysing the perceived decline in quality of American news coverage:

The market research established that people wanted news to be 'relevant' and exciting and (this was inferred rather than spelled out) not too intellectually troubling. The networks closed down nearly all their overseas operations. Foreign news disappeared from their news programmes, which soon largely consisted of crime stories and health scares ... Maybe this is one reason why a lot of Americans seem to be ignorant, and unconcerned, about what is happening in the rest of the world. If television is, even partly, responsible for that detachment, then the failure of news programmes has consequences for us all. (Buerk, 2004: 413)

Buerk's colleague Martin Bell states that: 'Television is no more morally neutral than the people who control it ... so the camera is also a force for good or evil' (2004: 35) and it is in that later comment, the way in which truth can be manipulated, that seems to offend the value systems of bloggers and other citizen journalists. These private individuals, free of the editorial processes that can shackle the truth – and bear in mind that in all areas of life there is often a filtering process exercised by media-literate originators of information in politics and business – claim that they are able to put forward something which is somehow more pure, and unadulterated. But there is a danger in buying into such a naïve ideology.

One of the issues that militates against excessive corruption of truth in professional news publishing is the level of competition that exists between rival broadcast or print organisations. A constant theme of the various memoirs of professional journalists is the element of competition (which can border on internecine warfare) between representatives of various news organisations; the desire to gain the upper hand – the scoop, or at least the minor extra snippet of information that provides a tiny advantage – raises the level of news provided to readers, viewers or listeners. It is rare for citizen journalists to be involved in such a competitive environment, and while the citizens might have the advantage of intimate knowledge of a situation or event, and also have the time to compile a reflective account of their chosen topics, they rarely have access to a broader view of events.

In a recent Editorial in the *Columbia Journalism Review*, the comment is made that:

> Competition is good, remember. It nourishes aggressive reporting and distinctive, creative approaches. With a lack of competition in the local news and information business, too many papers, even some of the more ambitious ones, allowed their voices and personalities to wither. Too many editorial pages toned it down and slid into the inoffensive and boring. Too few embarked on crusades. Corporate owners, too, encouraged a play-it-safe culture. Too many newspapers rounded off their ragged edges, but lost the spark. When the advertising and readership began to recede, so did resources, and those weak habits and attitudes began to reveal themselves like the fish on the beach before the tsunami. (March/April, 2006)

But this presumes that the element of competition leads to better news; it could equally be argued that there is abundant proof of what might be termed 'me too' news, items which are covered by all of the media in a country on the implicit understanding that to not cover an item would indicate some form of weakness.

There is, however, always a risk of duplicity hiding behind the façade of subjectivity that is claimed by citizen journalists when they claim a more direct line to the truth. While it is easy to claim that citizen journalists are beyond the corruption that affects professionals, this is not necessarily so; a prime example was centred on a heath fire in South West England in Spring 2006. The fire was given coverage in several media, including Sky News and The *Guardian*, accompanied by an image which described 'wild animals, silhouetted by the bright orange inferno in a photograph taken by a local resident ...'. Unfortunately, the image was subsequently reported to be not of Canford Heath in Dorset, but instead of forest adjacent to Bitterroot River, Montana – and was taken on 6 August 2000. Or was it a fire in Yellowstone National Park from 1988, or one in British Columbia in 2003? Whichever, the fact is that the animals in the foreground of the image were elks – not a species native to rural Dorset. 'The picture editor said it points to a problem with citizen journalism. Picture agencies have draconian rules about altering pictures or passing them off as something they are not [...] there are no such rules for the citizen ...' (Mayes, 2006). This directly contradicts one of the claims of this emergent medium: '"we can fact-check your ass!" is one of the cries of the blogosphere' (Lemann, 2006) which infers that it is the old, not the new, system that is given to corruption.

There are also those in power who are reacting to the unfettered nature of citizen journalism. On example is the Malaysian Prime Minister, Abdullah Ahmad Badawi, who told a press corps gathering that 'If information in blogs, websites and online portals were incorrect, bordered on slander, caused disturbance or compelled the public to lose faith in the nation's economic policies, their authors would be detained for investigation' adding that 'we cannot allow such matters to flow through uncontrolled'. While denying that he was directly seeking to create a control mechanism, Abdullah asked 'where in the world is there such freedom, where one can freely spread incorrect information and slander without having to own up to it?' (McIntyre, 2006).

But Abdullah's campaign is lightweight when compared to the process of imprisoning internet journalists, as highlighted by Kim Pearson in the Annenberg School of Journalism's *Online Journalism Review*:

> A new report from the Committee to Project Journalists finds that increasingly, online journalists are being imprisoned for their work, causing an increase in the number of incarcerated journalists for the second straight year. CPJ said that as of December 1, 49 of 134 imprisoned journalists worldwide work via the internet – the highest number in that category since CPJ began keeping records in 1997. Print journalists remain the largest category of imprisoned journalists; 67 print reporters, editors and photographers are behind bars, CPJ said. China, Eritrea and Cuba top the list of governments responsible for jailing journalists, but the United States is responsible for incarcerating two journalists without charges, as part of the War on Terror ... [Abi Wright of the CPR added] 'I think there's two things going on. First of all, there are more people writing and doing journalism online. Secondly, the perennial offenders, China and Cuba, in particular, are just saying an increasing, or ever-present, I should say, intolerance towards reporting and dissent in any form, and online in particular' (Pearson, 2006)

Citizen journalism or user-generated content in broadcast news

The debate about the role and prominence of citizen journalism fairly soon moved from the private to the public sphere. As individual broadcast journalists and producers were actively encouraged to increase the presence and profile of such material, discussions on its future occupied increasing space in media columns and editors' blogs.

One of the early subjects was precisely whether it should be referred to as 'citizen journalism' or as 'user-generated content'. The point was addressed directly by BBC editor Jon Williams in a blog called 'Citizen newsgathering' (bbc.co.uk/news/editors'blogs, 20 October, 2006). Williams wrote:

> It's been called citizen journalism – I prefer to think of it as citizen newsgathering. It's an important distinction – and one that goes to the heart of the debate. It's vital our stories engage with the audience – but we need to be careful our running orders don't become a 'Top of the Pops' of news (look what happened to that!).

Just over a month later (weekend of 25–26 November 2006), BBC News 24 launched what it described as its first interactive programme, highlighting user generated content. Ironically, one of its opening features of the new programme, called 'Your News', was

It is such issues of accountability – whether malicious or inadvertent – that lead to suggestions that citizen journalists are just as vulnerable to 'biased, incomplete, selective, and/or incompetent information gathering' as Bill Ardolino feels afflict the old media reporters and journalists. It might also concur with the assessment of a difficulty reconciling 'the tension between writing author-itatively *for* a public and writing *to* a public' (Matheson, 2004: 453, italics in original) which suggests that the skill lies as much in the quality of writing up gathered information as it does in its intrinsic content. Which leads logically to assumption that: 'The form [online journalism in the shape of a web log] should be taken, then, as indicative of certain kinds of change, rather than anything like a model for online journalism' (Matheson, 2004: 461).

The answer might lie in a hybrid between the linear and citizen models, of the type that has been developed by OhmyNews in Korea. Oh Yeon Ho founded OhmyNews in February 2000. There are now more than 50 reporters and editors, with 'a legion of 36,000 "citizen reporters"'.

> Our slogan is 'every citizen is a reporter'. We've created a new kind of journalism. We call it 21st century journalism, two-way journalism. So the readers are no longer pas-sive. They are very active and participate to say what they want to say' he told CNN. (Lu Stout, 2006)

OhmyNews is a mediated site, meaning that incoming material from citizens is edited and cross-checked for its validity, balance and accuracy by staff of OhmyNews, and all contributors agree to a code of conduct that includes the following key points:

1   I recognise the editorial authority of OhmyNews' in-house editing staff.
2   I will share all information about each of my articles with the OhmyNews editing staff.

a Top of the Pops style countdown of the top ten stories clicked on by news con-sumers. Also in the programme were pictures and video clips sent in by the audience, and ideas for stories the BBC should be covering. In the accompanying Editors' Blog, BBC News 24 Controller Kevin Bakhurst described the new format as 'work in progress', and as being on 'a short pilot run', but also as 'the first news programme entirely driven by our audience'. While one might legitimately question the use of the word 'entirely', it was still an interesting staging-post in the development of user-influenced news agendas. The central item was a viewer's film about his attempts to honour his late wife's request to donate her tissue to research. At almost the same time, how-ever, there was a significantly different view from the assistant editor of Channel 4 News, Martin Fewell. Speaking at the Westminster Media Forum (14 November 2006), he said: 'My view is that blogs and user-generated content, nine times out of ten, will be complementary to traditional news. I don't believe it can be the provider of high-quality, impartial news that people want'. A slightly more informally-expressed tirade against user-generated content (or UGC, as it was already becoming known) came from Jeremy Paxman on Newsnight (Wednesday 29 November 2006). He criticised the 'Oh My Newsnight' slot, saying: 'In the meantime, it's [the programme] all available on the

(Continued)

3 I will not produce name cards stating that I am a citizen reporter of OhmyNews.
4 When an article I submit has or will be simultaneously submitted in another medium, I will clearly state this fact to the editorial staff.
5 I will accurately reveal the sources of all quotations of text.
6 Citizen reporters who work in the field of public relations or marketing will disclose this fact to their readers.
7 Legal responsibility for acts of plagiarism or unauthorized use of material lies entirely with the citizen reporter.
8 Legal responsibility for defamation in articles lie entirely with the citizen reporter.

OhmyNews publishes in Korean, English and Mandarin, and has laudable aims and ambitions – it sets out to give the broadest possible array of news, but news that has been edited, cross-checked and validated. So does that make it any different from mainstream news organisations, in any other respect but its financial and commercial model? The evidence suggests not. Content mediated by OhmyNews is edited and filtered, to negate any ambiguity and to clarify the inherent message – the ideals to which all journalists and editors should aspire, regardless of the medium deployed to distribute content. The only essential distinction between OhmyNews and other news organisations is that its key contributors are unpaid, while other news organisations rely on professional staff journalists and reporters.

Another way around this issue is a method of newsgathering developed by an American journalist and publisher, which bridges the old and 'new' models and has the additional benefit of increasing circulation of his traditional print publication (*The Chi Town Weekly News*) by a claimed 10 per cent month-on-month since its December 2005 launch:

> While working as a reporter on *The Chicago Tribune* [Geoff] Dougherty noticed that good quality local stories were being overlooked, or not covered at all, as international and statewide news took up space in the paper. [He then realized that]: 'There is a big demand for

website, along with the editor asking you to send us some bits of your old memories and the like, so we can show our version of Animals Do The Funniest Things. Goodnight', (Telegraph.co.uk, 1 December 2006).

Meanwhile, on New Year's Eve, 2006 (repeated on 2 January 2007), for the first time, ITV ran a news review of the old year consisting entirely of UGC clips. Naturally, its priorities were somewhat different from the more conventional compilations of journalistic highlights offered by other news organisations. Some of the same themes, and their implications, were addressed by Peter Horrocks, Head of BBC TV News, at the Reuters Institute for Journalism at Oxford University, 28 November 2006 (bbc.co.uk/news/editors'blogs, 30 November 2006). He argued that UGC was only one (and not the most interesting) of the ways in which 'wider audience interaction, technology and changing audience perspectives and consumption are changing broadcast journalism in far more profound and interesting ways than simply providing … an extra information source'.

In discussing the ability to monitor click response to BBC Online stories, and the information provided by focus groups and viewers' panels, he asks: 'As some of the stories the online audience loves are ones that the TV News audience says it dislikes, what should a programme editor choose to run?'

ultra-local information. It is perverse really what news focuses on' he said. 'People are most interested in what is happening down the street. 'But most of the prestige and resources goes into reporting things that are farthest away from us. It is about correcting that balance'. Dougherty – who has twice been nominated for a Pulitzer Prize – left *The Tribune* to start a more radical approach to local reporting with *The Daily News*. He decided to hand the reporting process to the readership, offering to train people living in Chicago's boroughs to write stories about what is going on in their neighbourhoods.

'in a city the size of Chicago there is no way to have a reporter covering everything that is going on. So to have someone that lives in a neighbourhood, who knows the people, and knows the issues, and is going to that local meeting because they are interested, and then can write something afterwards, now that is the real beauty of this'. Currently, he has 15 reporters throughout the city, none of who are professional journalists. He is the lone full-time member of staff. (Luft, 2006)

By merging the traditional print newspaper medium with a new means of gathering information, Geoff Dougherty seems to have happened up on a workable compromise, one which draws on the advantages of an enthusiastic group of citizens (albeit with a degree of professional training) but which also has the checks and balances of a professional approach, adhering to traditional news value system rules. Which is not to say that the old system is foolproof; far from it, as the chapter on media ownership and other external pressures explains in greater detail. For now, suffice to heed the opinion of Robert McChesney, who states: 'No credible scholarly analysis of journalism posits that journalists have the decisive power to determine what is news, what is not news, and how news should be covered'. Instead, he suggests that media professionals 'tend to internalize the values, both commercial and political, of media owners' (McChesney, 2004: 100). While Robert McChesney was looking at the specifics of the American media system, there is an almost global validity to his comments; such is the nature of today's media that all but the smallest news organisations belong to national, international or global corporations.

However, as with so many of even the more thoughtful journalistic reflections, Horrocks shies at the crucial fence:

> Some would argue that editors should just ignore confusing audience information and use professional judgement to decide what is important or interesting. And of course for the most important stories that's exactly what they do. Few audience surveys or click statistics ever indicate the Northern Ireland peace process or conflict in Sri Lanka are desired by audiences, but we need to cover these stories.

The two most interesting issues raised by that excerpt go unanswered. What exactly is the *nature* of that professional judgement? How is it arrived at? Is it instinctive or empirical? And *why* do 'we' need to cover 'these stories'? What sort of development in Northern Ireland or Sri Lanka? How big does the breakthrough have to be? How new, different, or enlarged do the manifestations of the Sri Lankan conflict have to be in order to command coverage? The truth is, they are still subject to the same considerations of newsworthiness as other stories.

It is for this reason that we (apparently pedantically) questioned the use of the word 'entirely' in relation to the 'Your News' programme referred to earlier. For, of course,

(Continued)

In some countries, even the role of the editor is coming under question. 'The problem that some see with the traditional editor in the interactive world is that it's only one person who is deciding what stories get researched and eventually published. Obviously, the decision of one person is not going to appeal to everyone' explained Andrew Heyward (the former President of CBS News) in a speech to the Poynter Institute on March 2006 (Heyward, 2006). The core argument against editors is that they perpetuate the hegemonic nature of news organisations, even when they are working with citizen journalist sources.

What does differ from country to country, though, is the impact of citizen-generated content. Writing recently of the pull model of news acquisition, Charles Arthur gave an example rooted in British culture: 'John Prescott [British deputy Prime Minister, and avowed 'working-class' man] plays croquet! [a game with middle- or upper-class connections] Do you care? Maybe. Will you pass it on? Hell, yes. Someone is evicted from the BB [*Big Brother*, a constructed reality TV show] house. Do I care? No. Will I pass it on? No: it is not news to me. For others, it is. News is a subjective commodity' (Arthur, 2006). *Big Brother* has developed a massive network of sites which contain web logs and other opinions directly related to the show throughout Britain – and the indications are that a similar phenomenon is repeated in the other countries where localised versions of *Big Brother* are broadcast. Interest from outside those places, though, is limited – as might be expected of a programme with distinctly localised cultural significance. This feeds perfectly into the **relevance** aspect of the news value system, which holds that only something of direct relevance to a news receiver has any value as a news item – everything else is an abstraction. And for every single example such at that above, there will be dozens of other, localised illustrations which centre on content which rarely crosses borders, except to satisfy the needs of expatriates in search, or in need, of a connection with home.

numerous journalistic decisions are still required to be made before UGC can be broadcast. Is it of broadcastable technical quality? If not, can editorial considerations result in the suspension of normal rules? Does it meet legal requirements? Are there too many submissions on the same subject areas? Is a right of reply needed/ available/desirable?

The mediating role of the journalist is still important in dealing with UGC in broadcast news. What can appear, from the outside, as an unmediated transaction between consumer and provider is usually much more complex than that. It is incumbent on broadcast providers to acknowledge that news value judgements and other mediatory factors are still at play. Indeed, to purport to offer a product as transparent when it is really equally opaque, but in a different way, is itself a potentially misleading form of journalistic practice. In the interests of viewers, listeners, and other news consumers, it is important that claims of democracy, transparency and accountability are not overstated.

It is possible that the exercise, for broadcasters, is as much about presenting an appearance of a symmetrical, transactional relationship between themselves and their

One area which is attracting a good deal of interest is that of transference of information from blogs and other sites, to mainstream news. At the point of writing one academic study is being undertaken by a team working under our University of Wolverhampton colleague Professor Mike Thelwall, with publication due in 2007. Among the topics that are expected to feature in this research (and in other similar programmes being pursued at other institutions) is the work of Dave Panos's Pluck, which in April 2006 established a business to syndicate content from blogs to mainstream news organisations:

> BlogBurst, as the service from blog technology company Pluck Corp. is known, includes headlines and articles for use by newspaper publishers in the news or feature sections of their online services, as well as print editions.
>
> Pluck initially has signed up Gannett Co., *Washington Post, San Francisco Chronicle, Austin American-Statesman* and *San Antonio Express*. Eventually, the Austin, Texas-based company will offer BlogBurst editorial materials to niche business and overseas publications. (Associated Press Reporter, 2006)

In his rationale for this development, Panos – an internet veteran who co-founded Pluck in 2003 – explained that: 'Newspapers are looking to BlogBurst to provide expert blog commentary on travel, women's issues, technology, food, entertainment and local stories, areas where publishers may not have dedicated staff' (Associated Press Reporter, 2006).

Such specialisation is likely to be the area where collaboration is at its strongest between the old and new models. What remains certain at this point is that any transfer of information from blogs to mainstream news outlets will be mediated via traditional channels, with editors maintaining the ultimate arbitration role. Which in turn means that regardless of the ideals of the individuals who generate the original content, it will still adhere in its final form to the news value system.

audience. Further, that it is the audience itself which is the intended recipient of that message. In other words, presenting an illusion of unmediated journalism is itself part of the message of redefinition of that very relationship. Responsiveness to audiences and to the community is arguably more of a watchword now than ever before. So, while user generated content has a genuine journalistic role to play, it also reinforces the perception of a closer bond, and of a less paternalistic approach. Individual broadcast journalists now find themselves under real pressure to expand the quantity (and quality?) of user generated content in news and current affairs programmes. Perhaps one of the real imperatives behind the UGC 'revolution' is to reinforce that perception of a transactional, symmetrical relationship. Convincing the viewer and listener that the relationship is different may, perhaps, be more important than actually changing the relationship itself. With UGC, as with other forms of interactivity, communicating a revised view of the relationship becomes almost as important as the output itself.

Note

1 For the benefit of those who are unfamiliar with the terminology, the established mainstream media is often referred to as the Fourth Estate; this locates it beneath the First Estate of Church, the Second of Nobility and Aristocracy, and the Third of Commoners. This is based on Thomas Carlyle's evaluation posited in several of his early essays and leaflets and in his 1841 book *On Heroes And Hero Worship and The Heroic in History* and is in turn based on an evaluation of the ancien régime of the French pre-revolutionary hierarchy. It has also been attributed to Irish philosopher Edmund Burke (1729–1797) who spoke and wrote widely on matters of the British, American and French constitutions

Corruption of Values

11

Truths, Half Truths, Lies, Censorship, Coercion and Spin

In an ideal world, the news would be a true, valid, accurate and reasoned account of what happened. In the real world, it is rarely thus. Leaving aside the simple truth already mentioned that every individual has his or her own processes of witness or recall, there are various external forces at work which can corrupt whatever baseline of purity is applied – and anyway, that baseline is never consistent as it will vary from one publication to the next. These forces are considerable, and can vary from the political (with a small p) agenda of the management, to the nature of the source of the story, to any processes of mediation which have gone on the background before the story has broken through into the journalistic world – usually by public or media relations intermediaries – and to attempts to provide inducements which might alter the perception of a story.

As an indicator of the way that news values can be skewed by proprietorial interference, this is an excerpt from Piers Morgan's autobiography-cum-diary, which relates to sequencing the pages of the *Daily Mirror* in March 2004. He had acquired a first-hand account from a former prisoner of his experiences when detained in Camp X-Ray, Guantanamo Bay, Cuba:

> To justify the hefty £40,000 price tag, I cleared the first seven pages for his account of life inside Guantanamo Bay. A bit over the top maybe, but it was fantastic stuff. Then in mid-afternoon, news came in that Madrid had been bombed – ten explosions on four trains in three stations [this was obviously an error of recall because the news broke early in the morning, before 9:00 am]. At least 59 people were killed, and it was complete carnage down there. But the general view was that it was an ETA attack, and therefore a localised terrorist incident, like the IRA would be in London.
>
> This clouded my judgement and I kept the Camp X-Ray interview where it was and stuck the bombing up by the masthead and on a spread back in the paper.

It was only when it became clearer that Al Qaida [sic] had probably done it that I realised how bad our paper's news values looked in the first edition. [...] As I sit here watching the news at midnight, I know I've really fucked up this time. (Morgan, 2005: 440)

This extract shows two of the distortions that can affect an editor's judgement; one is the corrupting influence that getting 'value for money' after paying for a story can elicit, the other that of local consonance. Regardless of whether or not the attacks were the work of ETA there were still 59[1] people dead; the sub-text might be that by relegating this story to the background, well behind one which was concerned only with a single person, then the *Daily Mirror* valued those victims of the Spanish atrocity at a whisker over £700 each. But there was another agenda at work; the *Daily Mirror* had been a vociferous critic of the 2003 invasion of Iraq – running critiques of varying strength and vituperation since the spring of 2002 – and this had undoubtedly influenced the decision taken to order that edition of the newspaper in the shape it appeared.

The approach displayed and discussed by Morgan shows how several of the key new news values that we have identified can be corrupted; **topicality**, **expectation** and **worth** are all not given the attention they might in different situations. In normal circumstances the Madrid story would have gained its due prominence as it met a wide number of values – it was topical, it was unusual and worthy of in-depth coverage, readers would expect to see it at the front of the newspaper, and it would have an integral role to play in the **composition** of the newspaper.

This situation was by no means the only example that had influenced Morgan during his years as a newspaper editor; earlier in that same book he refers to a situation where his then employer, Rupert Murdoch, advised strongly against running an image of the body of Ronnie Kray, a notorious London gangster, lying in state prior to his funeral service. Morgan was persuaded that this was a poor idea for his then newspaper, the *News of the World*, and relegated to the story to inside pages, instead leading ('splashing', as the vernacular term has it) on the eating disorder of Victoria Countess Spencer, the sister-in-law of Princess Diana. This latter decision was to come back and haunt Morgan, when he was duped into running a fabricated story 'planted' by Earl Spencer, which in turn led to a Press Complaints Commission ruling against Morgan – a ruling apparently supported by Rupert Murdoch, whose remonstration was published by the Commission. Morgan's diary contained the rather telling comment: 'Bloody cheek. None of this would have bloody happened if he hadn't stopped me doing Ronnie Kray's dead body' (2005: 78).

The spectre of interference by proprietors is nothing new, of course. Throughout the history of the structured media there has been a suspicion that those who control the finances of the organisation will be prepared to corrupt the news process to their own ends. Certainly Lord Beaverbrook, once owner of the *Daily Express*, was famed for pursuing what Ian Hargreaves (2003: 109–10) describes as 'maverick political causes' and which led to Stanley

Baldwin's oft-quoted criticism that newspaper proprietors enjoy power without responsibility. Vernacular histories are littered with similar claims concerning the behaviour of various individuals, some of which are valid and some not. But not everybody says it invariably happens:

> Is the English press honest or dishonest? At normal times it is deeply dishonest. All the newspapers that matter live off their advertisements, and the advertisers exercise an indirect censorship over news. Yet I do not suppose there is one paper in England that can be straightforwardly bribed with hard cash. (Orwell, 1946: 29–30)

Countering that opinion was the example provided by journalist Fergal Keane (2005: 130) of his former employer the *Irish Press*: '[Irish politician Eamon de Valera] understood that if he was to have a realistic chance of coming to power he needed his own propaganda outfit. The *Irish Press* slogan was *The Truth in the News* – which was true except when De Valera's interests came into conflict.' That same observer also noted the effect of oppressive, and state-condoned, religious hegemony from the Roman Catholic church: 'The newspaper became more inward looking and conservative, genuflecting to the alliance of church and state, a mouthpiece of the ruling establishment rather than a watchdog' (2005: 130).

Other forms of hegemony also exist. There will doubtless be examples of advertisers attempting to bring pressure to bear on newspapers and independent (for which read commercially-funded) broadcast organisations, but there are few, if any, illustrations of success on record. With the publication of *Fast Food Nation* by Eric Schlosser (2001), the fast food chain McDonalds found itself subjected to intense criticism concerning the healthiness (or otherwise) of its standard fare. The expectation was that the business would fight hard to defend its position, possibly by using the threat of withdrawal of advertising revenues. In the end this did not happen, and instead the company reinvented its menus to counter the bulk of Schlosser's criticism. It is likely that there was a realisation that withdrawal from the advertising marketplace would do yet more harm, and leave the field open to its business rivals.

The rise of the personal publicist

A further indicator of the nature of news distortion – and in particularly news which is centred on celebrities – can be found in a brief excerpt from a recent interview (by John Preston) with Max Clifford, the publicist:

> I wondered if it was possible for him to define the pleasure he gets from exposing someone's indiscretions. Clifford does not hesitate. 'With David Beckham [shagged the PA] it was money. A lot of money. With Jude Law [shagged the nanny] I was able to use that to do all sorts of deals for other clients of mine. I could say to an editor, I'll give you this story if you help me publicise something else I'm involved with. With David Mellor [shagged an actress] it was the pleasure of helping bring down the Conservative Party. With Jeffrey Archer [allegedly shagged a prostitute, then told whopping shaggy-dog story

to cover it up] it was the pleasure of doing something that no one on Fleet Street had managed to do. (*Sunday Telegraph Review*: 3, 25 September 2005 whole comments)

That explains the rationale behind Clifford's *modus operandi*, but there is more to it than his simply delivering up stories to tabloid news editors. For a start, it would be naïve to assume, even for a moment, that Max Clifford is ever providing solid, reliable, unmediated information. *Au contraire*, the information will be skewed towards the agenda that Clifford is pursuing on behalf of his client – and it would be difficult for an editor to gain contradictory information which would give a fair and balanced account, because Clifford effectively acts as gatekeeper. Secondly, there is the *quid pro quo* arrangement referred to in his comments concerning actor Jude Law. This infers a subtle contract between the editor and Clifford to accept information at face value, as failure to do so would result in the additional material being made available. In realistic terms, the news values for the item are being controlled from beginning to end by Clifford, whose reputation has been carefully constructed over a lifetime of working as a conduit that looks after the interests of his client base at the expense of truth and absolute veracity.

In an authorised volume that bridges biography and autobiography, Clifford shows that there is a degree of contempt for the public he dupes with some of his fabricated stories. Referring to the English comedy entertainer Freddie Starr, who achieved notoriety via the totally constructed tale that he had eaten a friend's live rodent (and in the process generated one of the British newspaper industry's most memorable headlines of all time: **Freddie Starr Ate My Hamster** in the *Sun*, 13 March 1986) Clifford explained his rationale thus: 'I thought it was fantastic publicity [for a performer whose career was 'already declining']. I also reckoned that most of Freddie's fans probably couldn't read or write, and the few who could wouldn't care what he ate' (Clifford and Levin, 2005: 108).

Clifford is by no means the only player in town; he is simply the best-known in the British media landscape. And he goes to some lengths to prove that he is not amoral, that there is a degree of honour in what he does and citing as one example: 'In the late '90s a woman came to me wanting to sell her story about a brief affair with a senior Labour politician. The man in question is somebody I both like and admire. I wasn't impressed with her and I told her I didn't want to take her on. When she left I rang him and had a chat. It soon became obvious that he'd briefly been swept off his feet by her, was basically happily married, and that if it came out it would have completely devastated his wife and family' (Clifford and Levin, 2005: 07). He then went to some length to advise the politician how to best avoid the story being corroborated, and effectively killed off the story.

There is a feeling that the power of Clifford is at least on a par with that of other 'spin doctors'. But not all editors are as compliant as those of certain tabloids. For example, when discussing the former media aide to Margaret

Thatcher, Bernard Ingham, in one of his editorials from 1990 in the *Daily Telegraph* Max Hastings said that: 'Like most politicians' press officers, it is Mr Ingham's role to act as a purveyor of half-truths to the nation's journalists, but it is the business of the journalists to seek out the other 50% ...' (Hastings, 2002: 174).

As fearless and uncompromising as Max Hastings' views are, it is likely that only those who are able to withstand the onslaught from such sources – and are able to actually gather and then use contradictory or expository material – will do so. Others who either care less or are forced by unholy alliances into compliance will simply go with what they are given. So who is to blame?

One former national newspaper editor, today free of commercial pressures to pursue his career as a BBC current affairs expert, is under no illusions:

> The truth is, across the industry, we have seen a huge increase in 'Here's One I Made Earlier' journalism, the journalism of people sitting in front of screens in airless offices on the outskirts of towns, under the lash to be productive – that is, to churn out repetitive stories by rote, lifted from rivals or from the Internet or press agencies, and massaged to fit that paper's particular audience [...] Journalism needs the unexpected. It needs the unpredictability and oddness of real life. That means it needs real reporters. There is no better protection against the special pleading and salesmanship of the PR machines than decently paid and experienced journalists, trusted inside their organizations to use their judgement [...] So the most important thing is to hire more reporters – front line people who are inquisitive, energetic and honest. (Marr, 2004: 383–4)

The former political spin doctor Lance Price, who spent nearly three years working for Alastair Campbell and thus for Prime Minister Tony Blair, also gives a number of accounts of how his office were economical with the truth in order to save the reputation of the Prime Minister. Price was writing about events surrounding the breaking of a story that a prominent politician, Ron Davies, had allegedly been involved in cruising on London's Clapham Common in search of sexual encounters with complete strangers. The matter had been brought to the team's attention by the local police. He explained that:

> TB [Prime Minster Tony Blair] and AC [Alastair Campbell, head of communications in the PM's office] quickly conclude that he [Davies] must resign for a 'serious lapse of judgement', although Ron denied it had anything to do with gay sex or drugs. He fiercely resisted but was eventually persuaded he had to go.
> The story we put out was significantly different. That the first we'd heard about the incident was from Ron himself and that he'd concluded he should resign, which TB then agreed to. The media knew there must be more to the story than they'd been told. It took until lunchtime to convince them that actually we agreed with them, but we didn't have any more salient facts than they had. Which was true. (Price, 2005: 124)

Whatever the situation – and bear in mind that this is just one example – the whiff of manipulation comes wafting through Price's words. Another remedy for this corruption has been touted as the web log (or increasingly, blog) and its close cousin the wiki. On one level these phenomena can be claimed to offer clean, clear, unmediated, immediate and passionately subjective coverage of events. This is based on the premise that those who write blogs and wikis are deeply immersed in the situation about which they are writing, and are not subjected to the conventional processes of editorial 'interference'. But does this mean that veracity is always to the forefront? Not necessarily so, according to Jody Raynsford's interviewees for a recent DotJournalism column:

> 'It's like all stuff on the web,' Mike Smartt, editor of BBC News Online, told DotJournalism. 'Dissemination of information is great, but how much of it is trustworthy? They are an interesting phenomenon, but I don't think they will be as talked about in a year's time. Web logs provide a very good service at pointing people at other trusted web sites by filtering the news in a way – you might be interested in this, because you are interested in that. Some of the personal ones are quite good.'
>
> Lloyd Shepherd, chief producer for Guardian Unlimited, feels web logs have a role alongside the usual news output, but are not journalism: 'Blogging is not structured in the way journalism is. People are putting their views out in a relatively unprocessed manner. The two main things that separate blogging from journalism are the personalisation of the voice of the blogger and the lack of the subbing workflow you would expect to see for any print or online publication'. (Raynsford, 2003)

Besides which, who is to say that the blogger is genuinely impartial? That they are immune from any external corrupting forces? This analysis of a 2004 American political blog suggests that there is scope to question the inferred independent nature of the medium:

> The power of blog buzz has been far too effective to escape the notice of political strategists. After the 2004 campaign, a former aide to unsuccessful Democratic presidential hopeful Howard Dean said that Moulitsas (Daily Kos) and business partner Jerome Armstrong (MyDD) had been hired to work on Dean's Internet campaign, 'largely in order to ensure that they said positive things about Dean' on their blogs. 'They never committed to supporting Dean for the payment,' wrote the aide, Zephyr Teachout, on her own blog, 'but it was very clearly, internally, our goal.'
>
> Moulitsas and Armstrong freely acknowledged their work as paid consultants, but fiercely denied that posting on their blogs was part of the deal. Moulitsas also took issue with the suggestion that his work for Dean, or any other candidate, would be unethical. 'I never claimed to be free of bias', he wrote on his blog. 'Ultimately, I trust you all to take what I write with the proper grain of salt, fully appraised of whatever conflicts of interest I may have ... I have to make my living, and if I can do so helping Democrats win elections, I can't imagine anything more exciting and fulfilling'. But Perlmutter questions the ability of a blogger to remain true to his or her own opinions while on the payroll of a campaign. 'Will he be likely to say, "Boy the campaign really screwed up?" Or [will] they start saying things they don't believe because it's the party line?' (Palser, 2005)

Of course there are routinely similar criticisms laid at the feet of professional journalists. In the specialist area in which one of the authors of this book has operated for much of his career, the motor industry, there is a lengthy tradition of editors, journalists and reporters being flown, almost always either in club class or on private aircraft, to exotic locations to test-drive new cars prior to their launch. It is routine that exclusive (for which read expensive) hotels are used as the base for the test programme, for meals to be of cordon bleu standard, and for a gift to be provided at the end of the event. All of this is at the expense of the motor manufacturer, which might budget as much as £15,000 per head for each journalist – an amount which could easily be perceived as sufficient to distort impressions of the car being launched. But this is not the case; reviews, when they appear, are consistently critical, and there is no tendency whatsoever to gloss over any defects. The reason for this inconsistency is that such extravagant launches are the common currency of the industry and have been for many years. As one public relations director put it when asked about negative reactions to a new car: 'we just have to bite the bullet, and put up with it'. There has been a suggestion that the opposite might happen – that if a manufacturer was to break with this tradition and run a low-budget campaign it might work against them, but this too is unlikely. From this author's perspective and extensive knowledge of that industry, the process is simply of fulfilled expectation, and there is no corruption involved; where a car has deserved bouquets it has gained them, and when there have been brickbats due they too have been delivered with the requisite force. As this is written the DAB radio that was the gift from one manufacturer plays in the room, and notes are being made using the Mont Blanc pen that was a gift from another; one of those cars was given a positive review, the other not. And neither judgement was influenced by the provision of the gifts (which were of broadly similar value) or indeed by the shape of the launch event, one of which involved staying in a five star hotel in Florence, the other staying in a five star hotel in St. Remy du Provence. The good car gained a favourable review, the flawed one had its weaknesses laid bare in print.

The same applies in other specialist areas; travel, most notably, but also restaurant, music and theatre reviews. In all of these aspects of the industry and others besides there is a culture of providing for the needs of journalists without those journalists ever having to pay out of their own pocket. Occasionally publications will take an independent stand and insist on paying the expenses of their staff, but such occurrences are rare, and will become rarer still in this climate of financial constraints on editorial budgets. Some new organisations, writing from what others consider to be the moral high ground, are totally opposed to anything free. Typical is this comment from the Associated Press's guide to its value system:

> We do not accept free tickets to sports, entertainment or other events for anything other than coverage purposes. If we obtain tickets for a member or subscriber as a courtesy, they must be paid for, and the member should reimburse the AP.
>
> Employees should politely refuse and return gifts from sources, public relations agencies, corporations and others hoping to encourage or influence AP news coverage or business. They may accept trinkets (like caps or mugs) of nominal value, $25 or less.

One area of journalistic activity that is increasingly perceived as being vulnerable to corruption of values is war zone reportage. In the early days of battle coverage the process was very much every man for himself (it was not until the 1930s that women managed to break into this world) and some people, most notably Winston Churchill, built early reputations for fearlessness that would serve them throughout their days. But Churchill did not always manage this without attracting criticism: '[Kitchener] clearly regarded him as a young whippersnapper who was "publicity seeking" and "medal hunting"' (Jenkins, 2001: 35) and, as was inferred during Churchill's period in South Africa during the Boer War, Churchill was happy to vacillate, to skip between an army officer rank and the independent status of being a war correspondent depending on which would be the more advantageous to him at any particular point. (Jenkins, 2001: 55–8).

During the Second World War the combination of rising adverse criticism from, increased number of and danger to, war correspondents led to the genesis of what we now accept as standard procedure, the embedded journalist. This is essentially the process whereby a journalist or news crew is temporarily attached to a military unit, which assumes responsibility for the safety of reporters and affiliated staff. But there is a trade-off; in return for this enhanced security, all news reports are shaped by the military, and subjected to a form of censorship. The process has been refined still further in the past two decades, partly in response to the increased number of news gatherers that are attracted to war zones. Today's version is the reporting pool. A good description of this is to be found in freelance journalist Michael Kelly's excellent book on the first Gulf War:

> The pool system has been organized by the US Central Command (CENTCOM) after six months of meetings with American media bosses, and it works like this; the journalists in each medium – print, television, radio – chose from amongst their number a coordinator who then chose journalists for assignment to various military units. The journalists were escorted by public affairs escort officers and subject to Department of Defense rules and orders. They filed reports which were sent back to Dhahran, were censored by the Joint Information Bureau, and then became common material available to all members of the pool. [Kelly then continues by explaining some of the restrictions applied to journalists.] News media personnel who are not members of the CENTCOM media pool will not be permitted into forward areas... [US Commanders] will exclude from the area of operation all unauthorized individuals... (Kelly, 1993: 146–7)

Kelly was to later break out of what he alluded to being an overly restrictive series of protocols and procedures, and reported the rest of his time in Iraq as a true freelance, with no military affiliations. Kelly (who lost his life in a 'friendly fire', or 'collateral damage' incident a decade later during the second Gulf War, when his car was hit by a missile fired from an American military helicopter) was by no means alone in wanting to break out from what is perceived widely as a censored, manipulated system that can become perilously close at times to propaganda. The question to ask is whether there is a great deal of difference between the films of Leni Riefenstahl which trumpeted the rise of Nazism in the Germany of the 1930s and the way that images of victorious western alliance troops in Iraq are pushed into the public consciousness.

Martin Bell – a correspondent who has covered wars on several continents during a career of over 30 years with the BBC, seems to have mixed feelings about the virtues and vices of the embedded system:

> Nothing was shown live on any channel except correspondents addressing cameras at a safe distance from the front line. I know that because I was actually on the front line, but able to broadcast only after a time delay for reasons of [military] operational security ... it's a trade off of freedom for access. I think it's OK so long as the intention of the military is to inform and not to deceive. But what's happening here [in the 1991 Gulf War] I think, is a different sort of embedding. The Alastair Campbell spin machine is being embedded into the Ministry of Defence. (Bell, 2003: 26–187)

It is unlikely that some of the greats of western writing who made at least some kind of living from writing about wars and their effects – the Churchills, Orwells, Gellhorns, Lees, Hemingways – would be completely at ease with the notion of embedded journalism. It is therefore no surprise to learn that Martin Bell, along with other colleagues such as John Simpson, Kate Adie and Jon Snow have also rarely appeared to show any true enthusiasm for the concept. At its best the embedding process subjects the journalist to an editing process headed by the local military command, which decides what can be seen and what cannot. At worst there is absolute censorship, again by the military whose agenda is rarely attuned to that of the journalist or indeed the viewer, listener or reader – the ultimate consumer of that journalistic product.

As was stated earlier in this book, the values applied by creators of news rely on factors including truth, validity, topicality and expectation, for their output to mean anything; the examples given above have the capacity to distort at least some of those criteria. When referring to the 1991 Gulf War Max Hastings makes mention of the need to attach 'health warnings' to coverage gained from embedded journalists so that readers of his newspaper could decide for themselves how much manipulation of events had been carried out early in the news gathering process (Hastings, 2002: 224).

It is such a cynical approach (a cynic being described as somebody 'who knows the price of everything and the value of nothing' – Oscar Wilde, *Lady Windermere's Fan*, and cynicism as 'an unpleasant way of telling the truth' – Lillian Hellman, *The Little Foxes*) that offers a chance for the future of news, and the application of the values to which we have referred. But such cynicism relies on two things; the first that incidences are flagged in some way, and the second that the consumers can actually be bothered to make the connection and exercise the requisite correctives. In other words, it requires an active, rather than passive, reader-, viewer-, listenership.

The final area suspected by some of corrupting the purity of news is the public relations industry. Grunig and Hunt define PR as 'the management of communication between an organisation and its publics' (1984: 6) but a more complex description is that established by Harlow who refers to it having: 'a distinctive management function which helps establish and maintain mutual lines of communication, understanding, acceptance and cooperation' (1976: 36). The key common term that must be borne in mind is management – which infers that anything that passes through the conduit of public relations has been managed, which some might interpret as massaged or manipulated but others will possibly consider to merely being made clear and unambiguous.

On any given day – Fridays and weekends included, for the industry pays little heed to notions of abstention from commerce on religious or other grounds – there are many thousands of news releases being delivered around the world. Press releases form the basis of a surprisingly high proportion of news items; journalism is a far more passive process than some might realise, with its practitioners becoming active only once an issue has been brought to their attention – and it is the PR industry that is the main driver of issues. Robert McChesney suggests that 'PR accounts for anywhere from 40 to 70 percent of what appears as news' (2004: 70) but fails to substantiate that claim; the reality is likely to be a lower overall figure, but still sufficiently high to have an impact on what the public gets to read, watch or listen to.

Typical examples of news items that have been driven by a press release can be easily found in just about any newspaper or broadcast news programme. For instance on 2 September 2006 the lead item in the *Daily Telegraph* was the headline **'Yard is watching thousands of terror suspects'**. At first glance this is a regular news story – but closer reading elicits that the news has emerged from an interview within a television documentary (*al-Qa'eda – time to talk?*) scheduled for broadcast the following day on BBC Two television. The item was publicised by the BBC in a press release issued on 1 September 2006, entitled: *Peter Clarke, Head of Scotland Yard's Anti-Terrorist Branch, talks to BBC Two*, and in that release were all the salient quotes used by the *Daily Telegraph*. Inside the same edition of the paper were other press release-led items, including one which related to research carried out into asthma and pregnancy by Aberdeen University and which ran under heading **'Asthma "linked to diet of mothers"'**, and another which related to child safety **'(Under 12s in your car must have safety seats)'** and which was based on a press release from the UK government's Department for Transport from 17 July, *Ladyman announces date for new child restraint and seat belt laws*. The delay in using this material, incidentally, was based on the need to balance the announcement date with the date on which the new rules were implemented, 18 September. A similar pattern of news items based on press releases is found throughout all newspapers and on most broadcast news programmes and bulletins.

A further item that appeared in that same day's edition of the *Daily Telegraph* also highlights another aspect of the collusion between PR and journalism, but with the addition of a third dimension, that of the newspaper's commercial department. The item in question related to the perceptions and recollections of the son of John Profumo, the disgraced English politician, with specific regard to the scandal that had brought about the demise of his father's political career. On reading the item '(**Son breaks family's 40-year silence on scandal of the Profumo Affair**)' it became apparent that the driver of the item was that David Profumo was about to publish his memoir. There is no surprise in this; the concept of a publication as inspiration for an editorial 'news' item is common practice. It is the third dimension that adds to the mix in such an interesting way; the paper had paid for the right to publish extracts from the new book, and so the news item was at least as much acting as a trailer for the serialised book as it was being a news item in its own right. Whilst it can be argued that there is a **topicality** (David Profumo's story is only now being made public) and that the piece is likely to be of direct and specific interest to *Daily Telegraph* readers (John Profumo had been a member of a Conservative government at the time of the scandal breaking – and the Conservative Party is the natural political allegiance of *Daily Telegraph* readers) meaning that it was also **worthy** because it casts new light on an event that fascinated the public in the 1960s, and as a consequence any reporting would be **expected** by that paper's readership. But there remains one question hanging in mid-air: are those values compromised by the commercial sub-plot to the item's appearance in the news section of the newspaper?

So far as the magazine industry is concerned, the reliance on press release-led, or PR engineered, source material is greater still. Most of the 'celebrity' items which form the mainstay of magazines such as *Hello*, for instance, are, as hinted at above, engineered to suit the requirements of the various publicity machines involved behind the individuals featured. Rarely, if ever, will film, television or stage actors make themselves available for interview, unless the interview can be attached to a film, a programme, a memoir or some other product. In the business-to-business press, most news items have their genesis in a press release issued on behalf of a company with a new product or service to promote.

In terms of news values, this means that the information has already been mediated before it reaches the publications or broadcasters, who then use it to suit the agenda of that organisation – the process known as remediation. Watson and-Hill describe mediation as 'shaping, selecting, editing, emphasising, de-emphasising – according to the perceptions, expectations and previous experience of those involved in the reporting of the event' (2006: 172) which is in itself problematic; any key facts have been altered to suit the expectations and requirements of the mediator, who acts on behalf of the commercial organisation. This means that the content is rarely critical, and any criticism can only come about by the diligence, perceptiveness and sheer doggedness of a journalist seeking to go beyond the declared content of the release. Tench and Yeomans suggest that this leaves scope for battles over the final outcome: 'This is the *media context* in which journalists and public relations practitioners engage in cooperative and conflictual relations and which structures the news that citizens/readers/listeners rely on in order to make sense of the world' (2006: 65) McChesney, for one, is unconvinced of the virtues of this kind of self-policing: 'Powerful corporate interests, wary of government regulation, spend a fortune to ensure that their version of science gets a wide play in the news as objective truth' (2004:71).

In reality, most journalists and public relations practitioners tend to be engaged in a symbiotic relationship in which power can shift from time to time, but in which the journalist tends to have the upper hand. This for no other reason that the journalistic side of the relationship controls the final output of content. Astute members of the public relations industry – which, it must be noted, in the UK now has a Chartered Institute (the CIPR), inferring a high degree of professionalism – will understand that those who routinely corrupt the essential truths of any situation they are handling will soon find themselves isolated from the media on which they rely to transfer their communications to the wider public. As one of the CIPR's own constitutional phrases has it, the Institute considers it vital: 'to promote public understanding of the contribution of effective public relations in encouraging ethical communication and in enhancing the efficiency and performance of all sectors of the economy.'

It is also by no means unusual for a high-profile interviewee to insist on the presence of a public relations practitioner during interviews. This is rarely the idea of the interviewee (though there are certain individuals with such an inflated sense of self-worth to demand such) but more often the organisation that has arranged the interview, often the film company, record company, book publishing house or whichever. The reason for this is much the same as that which occurs in the political world; to ensure that the subject of the interview remains 'on message'. It is also by no means unknown for 'celebrities' to demand final copy approval. Astute (or simply battle-hardened) journalists will make the requisite calming noises, and carry on regardless. In this respect broadcast journalists have a less difficult time than those who work in a print medium, as the 'press minders' will rarely, if ever, interrupt a recording, and furthermore can often fall back on standard industry practices of the media organisation to retain final control over content.

In conclusion, the landscape on which much news is crafted and honed into a suitable shape for its receivers is prone to becoming a battlefield. It remains the responsibility of the journalist to carve through the thickets of lies, misinformation and corrupted half-truths, and emerge as the victor on the far side.

Note

1 Later figures settled on a death count of 192 people.

Same Story, Different Media, Different Treatments

12

What can the Litvinenko Story Tell us about the Changing Media Landscape?

It had all the intrigue that any news editor could ever want; a retired Russian spymaster, hospitalised in London with suspected poisoning, and the finger of suspicion pointing at Moscow. With the Cold War still very much alive in the collective public memory – it was only a decade and a half since the 1989 fall of the Berlin Wall followed by a process of eastern bloc 'reunification' with the democractic west – there was the guarantee of an irresistible appeal to every journalist over the age of 35. Which means the majority of those who take editorial decisions throughout the world of media.

From the day the story of Alexander Litvinenko's serious, life-threatening condition first broke, on the BBC Russian edition of the World Service on 11 November 2006, it was almost inevitable that the story would be a major one – yet despite the intriguing content, it was almost a week before the mainstream media began to give it some serious levels of coverage. So from the student of media news value culture, the first questions should be: What changed? And how did the media react to the event?

The answer to the first question, What changed? is that the news wire services began to pick up on aspects of the story that had not previously been publicised; that rather than just being incapacitated by poison, Litvinenko had been the subject of a more serious crime; the poisoning had been intended to kill him, and his former paymasters in Russia's KGB secret services were the likely assassins. This was sufficient for journalists to begin drawing comparisons with the broadly similar characteristics of an earlier case, the death in 1978 of Bulgarian dissident Georgi Markov, who died after being injected with ricin poison administered, it is widely held, in London by an unnamed KGB agent using the tip of a specially-adapted umbrella.

Suddenly, the **unusualness** of the story moved up to a new level, one irresistible – and thus **worthy** – to news editors. Hence the answer to the second question is that the media reacted by springboarding the story to the very front of newspapers, internet newswires, and news broadcasts. It was *not* a **topical** story in the sense that it had been simmering on the BBC's World Service for more than a week, but it *was* new to the majority of readers, viewers and listeners. By Sunday 19 November it was the biggest story in the world, as a trawl of English language news organisations shows. In this sense it met both aspects and interpretations of the news value of **expectation**; the public expected to learn about the story, and they expected to learn about it through all media. It would also be a brave editor who chose not to follow the herd and run something on the story.

All of Britain's major news broadcast organisations led their Friday night and Saturday bulletins with the story – and the following morning it was a similar picture across the front pages of the nation's newspapers. The *Daily Telegraph* led with a major splash on the story, as did the *Times, Daily Mail, Daily Mirror, The Scotsman*, and other majors. But the story rippled out rapidly to other countries – many of which, at least initially, relied on material supplied by major press agencies; the Press Association, Reuters and Associated Press who splashed the story on their respective wire services. This was a classic case of a story that met standards of expectation throughout the British media, this being story of such an **unusual** nature (of the thousands who eat sushi in a day, no member of the general public would expect to contract radiation sickness from the experience...) and this was sufficient to ensure its roll-out through the rest of the English language media world.

Indicative of the international coverage was that it appeared under the banner '**British Look Into Suspected Poisoning of Ex-K.G.B. Agent**' in the

One story, rolling news: Alexander Litvinenko as treated by BBC Online

We are going to take a particularly close look at how the Litvinenko story was handled by BBC News Online. It is a hugely influential news source in its own right; but it also presents users with a chance to refer to other (past and present) elements of the story in a more readily accessible manner than most other media.

As with most other mainstream media, coverage started on the weekend of 18–19 November 2006. One of the early headlines was: 'Ex-KGB officer poisoning probed.' Among the firm elements of the story was the line: 'Clinical experts said he was poisoned with the highly-toxic metal thallium'. Reference was also made to coverage of the earlier stages of the story – before it reached the mainstream news outlets. The story highlighted the fact that Mr Litvinenko had been 'speaking to the BBC last week' about his poisoning; but without explaining why the story was deemed newsworthy that Sunday, but not the previous week. (Was it because his condition had worsened or because of a collective recognition that it should move from niche to mainstream media?) Other elements of the story were also highlighted: Alex Goldfarb's claim that '...this is the work of the Russian Secret Service'; and the approach of the Russian media. 'There has been no comment from the Kremlin and the Russian media is reportedly keeping quiet on the incident'. Links were also made to the death of Anna Politkovskaya, President Putin's clash with

New York Times of 19 November, and on that same day under the headline **'Kremlin in the dock over poisoned spy'** in *The Australian* of the following day. It also appeared on a wide range of websites: **'Condition of Poisoned Russian Ex-Spy Worsens'** on Foxnews.com; **'Poisoned ex-spy Litvinenko fights for life'** on *BreakingNews.ie*; **'Russian Spy Service Denies Litvinenko Poisoning Allegations'** on Mosnews.com and; **'Poisoned Russian spy condition worsens'** on Deutschewelle.com were just some of the headlines grabbed during the three days from the story's break. In the case of *Fox News* and *Deutsche Welle*, the story was also run on the broadcast news content of the parent businesses.

Back in Britain, by Sunday it was the dominant story – almost the only one in town – and news organisations were clamouring to find something to add to what was, in essence, a simple story of a man fighting for his life in a private room at University College Hospital in central London. Monday arrived, and the national daily papers and the London regionals carried the story as the main splash – and again it was the main lead on many broadcast news items, though some slipped it down the order, to give priority to other world events, particularly a resurgence of suicide bombings in Iraq. Coverage received a new approach on Tuesday when the previous day's supporting images – which had been mainly archive publicity shots of Litvinenko – were replaced by a dramatic image supplied (with approval from its subject) by his close friend Alex Goldfarb. This showed Litvinenko lying in his hospital bed, attached to sensors monitoring has condition, and having lost all of his hair as a consequence of the radioactive cocktail that he had ingested; that radioactivity, rather than the element thallium, which had initially been diagnosed as bringing about his illness.

The broadcast organisations went back into overdrive. CNN, for instance, ran the story as a package at the front of its hourly main news programmes,

---

Boris Berezovsky, and Litvinenko's book containing allegations about the 1999 apartment block bombings in Moscow, Buynakask and Volgodonsk (which were used as a reason for the new military campaign against Chechnya).

Links were provided to past Litvinenko stories: the reported seizure of his book in 2003, the suspended sentence imposed on him for 'abuse of office and stealing explosives' in 2002, and his flight to the UK in 2000. Shortly afterwards, in a classic journalistic move, a background piece entitled 'What is thallium?' appeared. The opening line read: 'Thallium, the substance which has poisoned ex-KGB agent Alexander Litvinenko in London, is a highly-toxic heavy metal.' (Note the absence of qualification: significant in view of later reporting). The reporting was straightforward in dealing with its properties and effects. The only potential link with the current story was the fact that: 'in 2004, at least 25 Russian soldiers were treated for thallium poisoning after finding a powdery substance in a can at a dump near their base in Khabarovsk.'

In another standard journalistic move, Alexander Litvinenko was profiled on the same day. As well as references to his closeness to Anna Politkovskaya and his book, we were reminded of the Berezovsky link (he 'first came to prominence by exposing an alleged plot to assassinate the then powerful tycoon Boris Berezovsky [in 1998]...'). We were also

(Continued)

which focused on whether it was thallium poisoning as originally claimed, or if Litvinenko had 'ingested a radioactive substance', and it was this which had led to the hair loss and jaundice from which the newly-available image showed him to be suffering. Sky News ran a very similar package (with similar claims) as second lead on its broadcasts, as did BBC 24, and even TV5 Monde Europe was seen to be running the story – although further down the running order. BBC News led on the story on that evening's 10 O'clock News flagship programme, a substantial package complete with (pointless) two-way with a reporter outside the hospital in which Litvinenko was being treated, footage of a press statement from Prof. John Henry, head of the medical team treating the victim recorded earlier in the day, footage of Litvinenko's associate Prof. Mario Scaramella, stock 'back-grounding' footage from Moscow, and shots of the Itsu sushi bar in London's Mayfair. Significantly, the story did not appear on the local BBC London regional summary having been relegated by other, more significant and newer items. The other major British news broadcaster, ITN, ran a similar package on its 10.30 p.m. show which again included input from the Prof. Henry press statement, and one of Scaramella denying any direct responsibility for the poisoning.

The story also ratcheted itself back up in importance on the following day's newspapers – though significantly, it did not gain much exposure in London's 'local' newspapers, possibly because the story had springboarded from being of local significance to international, and thus had gone beyond the *raison d'être* of such newspapers. As with all news stories it ebbed and flowed during the first few days, and by Wednesday 22 November it had been relegated to at best a news drop-in, and in many cases right out of the news. Litvinenko's condition had stabilised, it was reported, and other events (the flare-up of

reminded of his allegation that 'al-Qa'eda number two Ayman al-Zawahiri was trained by the FSB in Dagestan in the years before 9/11'.

While BBC television and radio news started to focus their resources on the story, on Sunday 19 November and Monday 20 November, feature journalists focused on fresh angles by the second day of mainstream coverage. The two main fresh lines on the Monday were the echoes of the Cold War, and the coverage (or absence of coverage) in the Russian media. The Cold War echoes were evoked by 'suspicions that this might be the work of his old Russian security service colleagues.' For the first time, the BBC invoked the shade of Georgi Markov 'who was murdered with an umbrella tipped with a ricin filled pellet.' Also summoned from the journalistic deep was what a recent *Economist* article had referred to as 'the f word'. According to the article cited, 'It is not there yet, but Russia sometimes seems to be heading towards fascism'. More detail was also provided on Alexander Litvinenko's movements between the apparent administration of the poison and the beginning of mainstream media reporting.

Meanwhile, attention soon focused on the Russian media's own response to the developments. Under the headline 'Russian media shun poisoning debate', it reported that '[t]he independent radio station Ekho Moskvy was the first broadcaster to break the story, quoting a report published on a Chechen rebel website.' However, 'Russia's three main trouble in Iraq, a revival of the prospect of peace between Israel and Lebanon) began to reclaim the headlines.

But then everything changed again on Thursday 23 November when Litvinenko's condition suddenly worsened, and he died; such was the significance of the news of his death that one major broadcast organisation, BBC Radio Two, took the very unusual step of interrupting an entertainment programme at 15.20 to announce his demise. By that evening it was back at the very top of the schedules throughout Britain, and was also back on the front page of the next morning's *New York Times, LA Times, Washington Post,* and *Sydney Morning Herald*, to name but a few major non-British newspapers.

'Russian Ex-Spy, A Putin Critic, Dies in London After Poisoning' was how the *Washington Post* headed their story – which incidentally was one of many that were published by that newspaper, both in its print and online editions – while the *Australian* used **'Poisoned Russian ex-spy dies'** as its headline. Virtually all English language newspapers throughout the world ran items on Litvinenko's demise – though interestingly (and perhaps in line with cultural expectations) the media in Russia worked hard to distance the country's leadership from claims of involvement; such **external influence** is only to be expected, as will be detailed.

But once he had died, there was an expectation that while it would continue to run, other angles would need to be followed, beyond simple reiteration of the unfortunate Russian's now-fixed situation.

So it was that the editorial focus shifted from Litvinenko himself to the risk to other members of the public; once it became apparent that he had been poisoned with some form of radioactive material, editors were provided with the excuse they needed to move from rehashing the existing facts and towards a fresh angle. And by Sunday – which, as we have noted

TV networks seem to have steered clear of the story ... press coverage, meanwhile, has been minimal, with most papers ignoring Mr Litvinenko's ordeal'.

Interestingly, in these early reports, Litvinenko was more often described as a 'dissident', 'former security officer' or 'former Russian agent'. The use of the word 'spy', which rapidly gained ground in other media reports, was largely absent from these early BBC Online reports. It was only later in the news cycle, as its use became widespread elsewhere, that it also became a regular feature of BBC Online reporting. The use of the term 'ex-spy' in a headline first surfaced on Monday 20 November. We were told: 'A former Russian KGB colonel ... poisoned by the toxic chemical thallium has returned to intensive care. ... Clinical toxicologist John Henry has said he was poisoned with a potentially lethal dose of the metal thallium'. A sizeable section of this report provided more information about thallium's availability, properties and dangers, on the basis of Prof. Henry's statement that there was 'no doubt' he had been poisoned by thallium. Other comments were quoted from 'Russian tycoon Boris Berezovsky', Oleg Gordievsky, 'another former KGB colonel', and 'friend' Alex Goldfarb.

The next major ingredient of the story was provided by the first Kremlin response. Allegations of its involvement in the 'poisoning by thallium' were dismissed by 'Kremlin spokesman Dmitry Peskov' as 'sheer nonsense'. (Textual purists were not to know at this

(Continued)

elsewhere, is a day when newspapers tend towards a more measured, and less hard news-led approach – the focus of British news organisations had again shifted in emphasis, towards speculation of precisely who had ordered the assassination. There was by no means consensus on this; while the majority tended to look towards Russia's political élite as being the ones pulling the strings (either positively or inadvertently) of those responsible for the assassination, at least one newspaper was promulgating the theory that the death was in fact self-inflicted. It stopped short of blame: 'Some reports in the Russian press have suggested that Mr Litvinenko's death could have been a "martyrdom operation", on the grounds that no state would want to attract the attention of a radioactive poison plot. But British officials warned against assuming that the spy staged his own dramatic demise. One senior source warned: "You have to remember this guy was on his guard 24 hours a day. Normal assassination methods may well not have worked."' (*Independent on Sunday*, 25 November 2006).

The *Sun*'s online edition of 24 November splashed with '**Death by Polonium-210**', 'stating that the 'former Russian spy' and 'former KGB Colonel' had made a dramatic claim that 'accused the Kremlin of plotting his demise just hours before he died'. The item continued with a direct quote 'just hours before he lost his fight for life'. 'The bastards got me. They won't get everybody', he said. He told his friend Andrei Nekrasov: 'I want to survive, just to show them'.

Interestingly, a brief diversion had blazed brightly and then disappeared, rather like a flare fired from a sinking ship, on Wednesday 22 November, when it was reported by a source within the hospital treating him that a scan of Litvinenko's torso produced images of shadows. These, however, proved to be nothing sinister:

stage that a denial couched in those terms would have been literally true!). This was supplemented by fresh police comments. Scotland Yard confirmed that it was treating the case as a suspected 'deliberate poisoning'. We were also given the news that: 'results of the [toxicology] tests would be available in days rather than weeks.' The implied uncertainty and explicit refusal to speculate further as to cause of death, though a standard police formula, clearly sat uneasily with the certainty both of the toxicologist and of the reporting itself.

On Tuesday 21 November Paul Reynolds' background feature on 'ghosts of the Cold War' was updated to include new information about Mr Litvinenko's movements prior to the story's emergence as a major mainstream media story. A reference was also inserted to the fact that Mr Litvinenko had been interviewed by the BBC Russian Service on 11 November – a week before that emergence. In this interview, he had said that he was 'in a state of being poisoned', and had provided details of his investigation into the death of Anna Politkovskaya. The absence of immediate follow-ups to this interview in the mainstream media tells us a lot about the operation of news values. The media 'herd instinct' often needs something quite specific to be triggered. A story with powerful journalistic elements may still not achieve that breakthrough even if it is run on an apparently high-profile outlet like BBC World Service because of a lack of specific details that may add to its attractiveness.

Despite previous reports that he had been poisoned with thallium, it emerged yesterday that his medical team had excluded it and said radiation poisoning was also unlikely. Three 'packages' found during X-rays of the patient's body – which raised the spectre of concealed spycraft – turned out to be routine shadows caused by the drugs used as part of his treatment.

Dr Geoff Bellingan, the director of critical care at the hospital, said: 'We are now convinced that shadowing on the X-ray was caused, as might be expected, by Prussian Blue – a non-toxic therapeutic agent which was administered as part of his treatment'. (*Scotsman*, 24 November 2006)

If nothing else, this indicates the desperation which was beginning to set in at that point in the story's life, when it was beginning to ebb; an un-named, unattributed source within the hospital had leaked that aspect of the story and it was leapt upon, despite there being no corroborative evidence.

As mentioned above, there exists the risk of political pressure being applied to any news story in which governments are involved, and so it is not unexpected that another approach entirely came from the Russian daily news source *Kommersant*, a news organisation that blends news and propaganda in equal measure:

Polonium-210 is accessible not only to terrorists and spies. Small quantities of the substance can be obtained for scientific purposes, among other ways, over the Internet from the American company United Nuclear of Sandia Park, New Mexico. That company will deliver polonium-210 in a hermetically-sealed capsule within 3 to 14 days for $69. The only condition for purchase is that it be shipped to an American address. The site indicates that the company does not ship abroad. (*Kommersant*, 2006)

That this is an attempt to deflect increasingly strident claims that Russian security agents, either legitimate or maverick, were to blame for the demise

For instance, are there particular UK-Russian tensions at the time? Is there specific information about the poison or the nature of its administration? Unquestionably, the fact that in 1978 Georgi Markov was poisoned specifically by an umbrella tip added to the journalistic potency of the story, and has accounted for its durability as a memory over several decades. Do the victim's own background and circumstances enhance the story's appeal to news organisations? These are all factors which may help to determine if and when a story is adopted. Once a critical mass of the mainstream media decides to run the story, however, such fine judgements are suspended, and the journalistic group psychology takes over.

Later on that Tuesday afternoon came the first crack in the wall of certainty as to the nature of the toxic material. In a story headlined 'Radioactive poison fear over spy', Prof. John Henry's latest reported statement contained the words: 'It's not 100% thallium'. The story then focused on the rest of his statement, to the effect that it could have been 'radioactive thallium, which would now be difficult to trace'. He also said: 'It may be too late. If it's a radioactive poison with a short half-life it may have gone'. Perhaps because of the note of doubt and caution this betokened, another medical expert was sought. For a while, medical diagnosis was back as the name of the journalistic game. Indeed, for the first time, reference was made to what was to become another central element of the

(Continued)

of Litvinenko (described by that publication as a dissident) is apparent; shift the blame, in traditional Cold War fashion, to the USA. This report came just two days after the 27 November report in the same newspaper that drew in turn on the *Times*'s claim that 'a former Russian consul in London who is in reality an intelligence agent and who was interested in him.' In that same report was the suggestion that the murder 'may be linked to events that took place in Dagestan in January 1996. Gusak said that, during the liquidation of Chechen militants who had captured the village of Pervomaiskoe, he asked Litvinenko to transport a wounded militant to a filtration point. "That evening, when I wanted to interrogate the Chechen, they told me that Litvinenko supposedly tortured him to death"', Gusak said, adding that the incident became "widely known." "The Chechens have blood vengeance"' (hommersant, 2006) (http://www.kommersant.com/p726072/Polonium-210/)

A further twist came eight days after the death of Litvinenko, when Italian academic Mario Scaramella was declared to be showing signs of poisoning with Polonium 210 'despite showing no signs of sickness' as BBC news phrased it. This, on top of the earlier news focus of the trio of quarantined British Airways aircraft (and up to 36,000 passengers who might have been exposed to polonium-210) indicates the way that news can continue to roll out, stretching the connection with the original story further and further, while still retaining a direct link. This, as we have observed elsewhere, is an institutionalised approach for rolling news stories. '**Britain Finds Second Case of Radiation Poisoning**' was how the *New York Times* of 1 December headed this latest development, while Canada's *Globe and Mail* used '**Polonium is costly, undetectable, trillion times more toxic than cyanide**'. Two days later in Britain The *Observer* splashed with '**Revealed: Litvinenko's Russian 'blackmail plot**' which built nicely on sister publication The *Guardian*'s story

story: radiation and radioactivity. Prof. David Coggon was quoted saying: 'In general, the chemical toxicity would be no different for radioactive as compared with non-radioactive thallium. The former will, however, also pose an additional hazard from its radioactivity'.

The next phase of the story opened on Wednesday, 22 November. Following on from the initial Kremlin denial came a more detailed denial of involvement from Russia's foreign intelligence service, SVR. This, incidentally, was described as 'one of the successor agencies to the KGB, which became world renowned during the days of concerted international espionage in the Cold War'. (At this stage of the story, no real explanation has been provided as to the respective roles and spheres of influence of the FSB and the SVR.) Also part of the same story is the first reference to the fact that Mr Litvinenko may not have been poisoned by thallium. 'The doctor treating the 43-year old said in the hospital's first official statement that the cause may never be found. Dr Amit Nathwani said it was possible he may not have been poisoned by thallium'.

A third new development was also referred to; the Rome press conference at which 'Italian Mario Scaramella' disclosed that he 'met Mr Litvinenko the day he fell ill and that both of them had received death threats.' The only additional information provided about Scaramella was that he was 'involved in an Italian parliamentary inquiry into KGB activity', and was 'sufficiently worried by the contents of an e-mail to ask for advice from Mr Litvinenko'.

of the previous day that 'Litvinenko laughed off my warning. He said it was like the plot of a film', which referred to a conversation that the dead man had apparently had with Mario Scaramella.

Yet not everybody bought wholesale into the Russophobia that had spun up around the Litvinenko saga:

> The horrific murder of Alexander Litvinenko, ex-KGB officer and minor conspiracy theorist, has unleashed a wave of Russophobia that is sweeping over the Western media with Katrina–like force – washing away reason, logic, and the natural curiosity that makes for good investigative journalism. In their rush to convict Russian President Vladimir Putin as the evil mastermind behind this grisly death, Western journalists don't seem to need all that many facts to condemn Putin as a murderous fiend. Litvinenko was a critic of Putin, he was subsequently poisoned in a horrible manner – and what more do we need to know? Apparently, nothing. (http://www.antiwar.com/justin/?articleid=10081)

This response was from an online news and opinion organisation, Antiwar, that was founded during the 1990s, and which describes its purpose as 'to fight for the case of non-intervention in the Balkans under the Clinton presidency and continued with the case against the campaigns in Haiti, Kosovo and the bombings of Sudan and Afghanistan' with the underlying agenda of avoiding the creeping 'state-ism' that can be insinuated into the social fabric during times of conflict. As a source, this is to be considered as reliable as the Russian organisation mentioned earlier; these are two organisations on different sides of the ideological divide, involved in propaganda and anti-propaganda. They might, however, be drawn into mainstream coverage of the story – particularly in this age of convergent media forms, and the resultant 'content stew' that can result, where the constituent parts are not always immediately identifiable.

This was the stage in the story cycle at which coverage had subsided considerably. It was relegated to News in brief status on many television bulletins, and copy-only updates on radio news. In hard journalistic terms, a major new development was needed to propel it back to the top of the news agenda. Clarification, further confusion, or some further compositional stimulus (new images, arresting audio, etc.) was needed just to maintain its daily presence in the news cycle. For television and newspapers (and, to a lesser extent, online journalism), this had been achieved by the release of the picture of Mr Litvinenko in his hospital bed – his baldness a graphic contrast with the healthy-looking images released earlier. In a story entitled 'Confusion over what poisoned spy', 23 November, we were given further information from Dr Nathwani, strengthening the line that it may not have been thallium, which went some way towards taking it on a further stage. However, a cautious medical bulletin, replete with qualifications and caveats, was not, perhaps, a strong enough line to do more than preserve the journalistic status quo. The views of a further pundit (Dr Andrea Sella, lecturer in chemistry at University College, London) were enlisted to provide further information on the possible administration of radiation, and even to speculate about motivation, 'My gut feeling …is that whoever did, this wanted not only to do him harm, but also to send a spectacular message to others mess with us and we make you die a lingering death'.

(Continued)

The same applies to bloggers – and as might be expected, this was a story with which conspiracy theorists (whose spiritual home has become the web) could stray as far as they liked from the *actualité*, whatever that might ultimately prove to be. For instance:

> With this extra piece of news today [that Thallium was not the poison used] it stuck me that it actually is from a spy novel. I just wish I could remember which one. For I have definitely read a novel where one of the characters is poisoned by the KGB. At first they don't know what it is, then they think thallium (aha!) and treat him with Prussian Blue, but the assassins were very sneaky and actually used radioactive thallium … it wasn't the thallium that was meant to kill him at all, it was the radioactivity. (http://timworstall.typepad.com/timworstall/2006/11/alexander_zlitvi_1.html)

or:

> Anyway, to the point: this wasn't simply an assassination. There are any number of poisons out there that would do the job painfully well but much more rapidly, and without the same scope for a diplomatic incident. Likewise, a bullet to the back of the head would have worked just as well (as witness the assassination of Anna Politkovskaya).
>
> What this is, is a warning: 'we have the capability to detonate a dirty bomb in central London any time we feel like it, so don't f**k with us'. (Just take Polonium and add a little TNT.)
>
> Who the warning is from, and who the intended recipient is, are another question entirely. I don't think it's any accident that the COBRA committee was convened the day after Litvinenko's death (on a Saturday, no less). And I don't think it's any accident that the British press have been very carefully pretending the phrase 'dirty bomb' is not part of their vocabulary for the past week. (http://delong.typepad.com/sdj/)

Later on Thursday 23 November, however, a series of developments began that were to propel the story back to the top of the news agenda, for the saddest of reasons. News emerged of a 'dramatic deterioration' in the condition of Mr Litvinenko. We heard for the first time from Geoff Bellingham, described as 'critical care head' at University College Hospital in London. As well as effectively dismissing the possibility of thallium poisoning, he also said he was 'concerned by speculation in the media by people who are not directly involved' in the care of Mr Litvinenko. Intriguingly, we were also informed that initial reports of poisoning 'with the heavy metal thallium', or 'some form of radioactive material', were both wrong: 'doctors are now dismissing both of these explanations'.

Thursday was also deemed a suitable day to take stock of the response of the Russian media once again: 'Russian media doubt ex-spy's tale'. By then, the case had 'drawn comment in the Russian media, which had largely ignored the story for days'. Brief extracts are given from three papers (Izvestiya, Moskovsky Komsomolets, and Komsomolskaya Pravda) largely exculpating the Russian authorities; and from the *Moscow Times* quoting another London-based ex-Soviet intelligence officer, Boris Volodarsky, as 'openly accusing the FSB of poisoning Mr Litvinenko'. A fifth publication, *Kommersant*, is cited as reviewing the arguments on both sides without taking a clear position, but as concluding that the net effect on perceptions of Russia will be negative.

Neither of these are what might be described as fair and balanced, nor are they of a standard that would be accepted as valid news by an editor; instead they are what they are supposed to be, independent and opinionated. And these are two rather mild examples of the many thousands of words that have been blogged about Litvinenko's story. They do perhaps serve as warnings against those who advocate free and unedited adoption of web-based material as news.

One aspect of the treatment that this news story has received is the impact it has had, throughout its duration, on many of the journalists who have written elements of it. What cannot be understated is the significance that to many British reporters, journalists, and their various editors the Cold War is a not-too-distant memory, and there remains, just beneath a surface veneer of 1990s-and-beyond *détente*, an innate suspicion of the old adversary Soviet Russia. It seems the paranoia that fuelled the 1963 Profumo affair, and also the Philby, Burgess, Maclean (and later Blunt) spying and defection situations of the previous decade, among other stories, easily breaks through to the consciousness of anybody over the age of 35. What this can do is combine with instinctive preconceptions – and even prejudices – to subvert (though not usually consciously) the true news value of a story. As one journalist points out, there is a problem when comment 'creeps in under cover of a paragraph' and 'has infiltrated before either the reader, and sometimes the writer, realises.' (Randall, 2000: 198).

The Litvinenko story has shown time and again that this can happen, as one extract from the *Daily Telegraph* article of 2 December 2006, which relates to a group identified as prime suspects in the murder of Litvinenko shows:

After these stories had been written and posted, events took a tragic turn, and Mr Litvinenko died on Thursday evening. Friday 24 November was naturally a day on which the news dominated most outlets (and later editions of newspapers). There were four major and distinct elements to the BBC Online news output that day. The death itself and reactions to it; Mr Litvinenko's deathbed statement accusing the Kremlin of poisoning him; the revelation that it was believed to be polonium-210 that was responsible for his death; and the first indications of traces of radiation in locations associated with Mr Litvinenko. Subsidiary lines were the responses of the Russian authorities and the Russian media to the death, and the early attempt to provide scientific background on polonium-210 and its properties. As polonium-210 made its early media appearances, thallium quietly returned to the journalistic obscurity from which it had seldom previously emerged.

One of the most visible manifestations of news values at work in BBC Online output is the positioning of stories. On several days of the story it commanded the prime position on the News Front Page – in effect, the splash story. Friday was naturally one of these days, as the implications of his death were assessed. The central line of the story, after the news of the death, was his deathbed accusation: 'Spy's death-bed Putin accusation' adjudged the finger pointed at the Kremlin by the dying man as the strongest line of the morning and afternoon.

(Continued)

In Russia, Dignity and Honour has a respectable front and a website, which names among its governors Evgeni Primakov, the former Russian prime minister, and former ambassadors to the US and UN.

Its ambitions are modest and include 'help to veterans' and 'help to needy children', as well as organising a prize in the name of 'legendary Soviet intelligence officer' Konon Molody, better known as Gordon Lonsdale, who ran the Portland Spy ring in the 1950s.

But the organisation also boasts a more shadowy role in the release of Arjan Erkel, the Dutch aid worker who was kidnapped in Dagestan in 2002 and held captive for 20 months. The organisation claims Erkel was a 'prisoner of war' and that they 'gathered information' before launching a 'joint operation with Russia's special services'.

Had it not been for the long-reaching memories of its writers (who in turn are aware of the pro-British establishment leanings of its core readership) this *Daily Telegraph* item would be unlikely to have made reference to an early Cold War incident immediately alongside a more recent – and to British readers culturally dissonant – event. And the language that is used – 'respectable front' 'shadowy' – underpins the sense of quiet outrage at the activities of such an organisation in England. Or this piece from The *Sun*, which is concerned with the fate of Mario Scaramella:

Detectives are convinced Mr Scaramella was 'nuked' as he breathed in particles coming from the former Russian spy's food at their sushi bar meeting. The news came as it was revealed Litvinenko's wife Marina, 44, also tested positive for the radioactive substance – on her slippers. The dose was said to be 'negligible' and she was not admitted to hospital.

Scaramella confidentially said he was 'clear on contamination' yesterday – then an hour later tested positive. A urine sample showed 'substantial' levels of polonium-210.

Yesterday lunchtime he was whisked to hospital from the hotel where Scotland Yard had hidden him away for questioning. Scotland Yard then asked him to return to Britain, where he is being treated as a witness.

Also making an early appearance, however, was what was to become one of the next phases of the story: the potential of a radiation risk to the public. As long as Mr Litvinenko was alive, the journalistic momentum was provided by updates on his condition and speculation as to the causes of it. With his passing, there is an almost subconscious pause while the journalistic community decided what would be the next major phase of the coverage. Would it be the formalities attendant upon a death? Not enough happening, and not quickly enough. What about the continuing debate over accusations of responsibility? Possible, but already extensively aired. Diplomatic and political consequences? Plausible, but a bit unreliable as a daily and even hourly source of news.

So, in what is likely to have been a combination of conscious decision and unconscious instinct, the journalistic focus shifts from the person of Alexander Litvinenko to the physical cause of his death. In common with many broadcast outlets, BBC Online News runs more on this than on other elements of the story throughout the remainder of Friday. '"No radiation risk" public told'; 'What is polonium-210?' and 'Radiation found after spy's death' were the three separate stories devoted to this during the later stages of Friday, the day after his death.

Some of the same methods previously applied to explaining the mysteries of thallium were now brought to bear on polonium-210. A suitably scientific-looking visual was

The terms 'nuked', and 'hidden away for questioning' again show a use of language that is totally in keeping with the *Sun*'s perspective of its readership.

What came next was a shift in emphasis – although Litvinenko has been referred to almost constantly in all media forms studied, he has become an abstract, and the focus of attention shifted to the risk of illness to which uninvolved members of the public are subjected. This again traded on **unusualness** – getting radiation sickness after a flight between London and Moscow is not what might be expected – and also gave a much broader public **relevance**; an individual or a small group of people (with whom the public is unlikely to consciously become involved with) who are likely to be harmed was one thing, but some malady which could affect up to 36,000 people is another matter entirely. As might have been expected this flared up and died within a relatively short period of time; the risk was only ever notional, and by the first days of December all three affected aircraft had been declared safe, being described as 'cleared by health officials on Thursday evening to fly again. The Health Protection Agency said passengers had not been at risk of radiation poisoning.' (Reuters, 1 December 2006).

Even so, one newspaper could not resist the opportunity to poke a little fun at members of the establishment; cabinet minister Tessa Jowell, and Lord (Seb) Coe, a former athlete who is now a senior member of the British House of Lords (and also chair of the 2012 Olympics organising committee) were each advised that they might need to take a radiation test, having been aboard one of the affected aircraft – though not on a London–Moscow flight. The *Sun* headlined the story '**Seb Glow**'.

Across the Atlantic, the *New York Times* of 3 December gave readers a classic example of the reflective account that is the province of Sunday newspapers. Under the headline '**Russian Ex-Spy Lived in a World of Deceptions**', the piece traced Litvinenko's life right back to the first time

---

produced to illustrate the respective penetrative powers of alpha, beta and gamma rays through paper, aluminium and lead. Also, the first reference was made to checks of associated buildings: 'The Metropolitan Police are said to be looking for any residual material at a number of locations where Mr Litvinenko has been, including [a] house in north London'.

A few hours later came first word of positive traces of 'above-normal levels of radiation at three locations in London'. We were once again given the penetrative rays visual; but added to it was a map of central London, highlighting the areas and buildings under investigation, and a timeline outlining developments since the date on which the poisoning was believed to have occurred.

A further new line was offered that evening by the first direct comment from President Putin himself: 'The death of a person is always a tragedy. And I convey my condolences to those close to Mr Litvinenko, to his family … ' were his first public words, spoken at a news conference. There was something of a dilemma for journalists as they assessed the new lines emerging after Litvinenko's death. For, as President Putin's first words were spoken, we also received initial words from the dead man's family. Which was the stronger line? For a medium like BBC Online News, it was not a case of 'either/or', since both could be easily accommodated within the normal confines of a story treatment. Following

(Continued)

he came into the pubic consciousness, in 1994. Extensive and wide-ranging – it drew on research from three members of staff operating in London, New York and Moscow – the article covered a lot of ground, including the telling paragraph: 'After Mr Litvinenko's death, sketchy facts and abundant speculation unfolded like some lost chapter of the Cold War. But unlike those days of East–West division and the half-light of shadowy, underground conflicts, this saga played out in the bright glare of newspaper headlines and 24-hour news channels'. British newspapers had already covered much of this ground – but the fact that it was being covered in such depth by a major American newspaper again indicates that the thaw after the Cold War is not yet complete.

Given the current state of American government – which has been accused in some quarters of stealthily returning to the McCarthy-era mindset of intense worry concerning anti-American activity[1] – could it be that this *New York Times* piece exemplifies some measure of **external influence**? This is unlikely; the *New York Times* has traditionally been critical of government regardless of its political base (on that same day as the Litvinenko piece was running, the lead op-ed column by Frank Rich – headlined '**Has He Started Talking to the Walls?**' was critical of the incumbent Bush government's grasp of political reality) and there is indication that this has changed. It is, however, always worth asking, when reading, viewing or listening to news whether there is undue influence being exerted by political pressure via the news organisation's management.

Alexander's own deathbed statement, his father, Walter spoke of his son's 'excruciating death', saying: 'Even before his death, in such a state, he never lost his human dignity'.

Meanwhile, the reactions of the Russian media were once again examined in light of the death. It is relatively rare for news media to comment directly on other outlets' news values and priorities as demonstrated by running orders, but the persistently down-bulletin appearance of the story on Russian media was pinpointed. In the story 'Russian media reticent on ex-spy', we were informed that 'The story figured low down the running orders of morning and lunchtime bulletins, as both channels [Channel One and Rossiya] focused on reports from the EU–Russia summit in Helsinki and the passage of the Russian budget through parliament'. By contrast, NTV 'which is owned by the state-controlled energy giant Gazprom, gave the story more prominence'. And, in a comment which also reflects on the UK and other worldwide media as well as the Russian outlets, we are told: 'The only high-profile outlet to lead consistently with Mr Litvinenko's death has been the independent radio station Ekho Moskvy, the first major Russian broadcaster to report the story on 11 November' (Earlier than in the UK domestic media, it may be noted!).

This brief overview of media was extended the next day in a slightly more detailed review of media comment: 'Litvinenko affair divides Russian press', Saturday 25 November. Interestingly, however, these press comments tend to highlight first-person commentaries rather than 'pure' news write-ups or editorials. It is difficult even for well-informed consumers of the news site to know how closely aligned these are with the papers' own editorial lines. However, the sample – representative or not – is more critical of the Russian authorities than the selection from earlier in the week. Also emerging on Saturday was the

Another example which might be worthy of closer interrogation is the coverage on Fox News in the USA on 2 December, concerned directly with the sickness of Mario Scaramella; this married together this story with another, the Bush government's apparent shift in emphasis regarding this policy concerning sanctions against Iran (one of the countries headlined in Bush's famous 'axis of Evil' speech of 2002) and included input from a leading American academic, Prof. Michael McFaul of the Hoover Institution at Stanford university – itself an institution with serious right-wing leanings. Given Fox's pro-conservative (for which some might read pro-Republican) stance it is no surprise to learn that the piece called for Putin's government to be brought to account. This is something that no leading American politician could be persuaded to go on record and say, but when a friendly media owner can be persuaded to ensure that his or her organisation or its invited pundit asks such questions or makes such statements ...

Back on the East side of the Atlantic, by Sunday 3 December there was another shift in emphasis; this time the claim that Britain's biggest security threat was proving to be Russia; older readers of the *Sunday Telegraph* could be forgiven for thinking that they had just time-travelled back to the 1960s. In addition to the main feature – which in common with earlier pieces in that newspaper was given a front cover plus several inner pages, and covered a broad range of aspects of the story – there was also a damning piece by editor Patience Wheatcroft: 'If the reports on Mr Litvinenko's ghastly death ... read more like the novels of John le Carré than accounts of what we expect to

first direct follow-up to the news of the possible radiation exposure. The Itsu sushi restaurant, and the Pine Bar of the Millennium Hotel made their journalistic bows and assumed centre stage: a position they would occupy for a while; even though, at this stage, details of individuals potentially affected or at risk were sketchy. Other new lines of the story, however, were hard to come by that weekend – as evidenced by the headlines of the other main stories: 'Russian mystery ignites message boards', 'Inquest due into ex-spy's death', and, on Monday morning, 'Date set for Litvinenko inquest'. The decision to run the inquest line as a 'later this week', and then as a 'this Thursday' story, illustrates the paucity of hard news. While the weekend papers felt at liberty to explore some of the wilder shores of speculation, BBC Online's self-imposed remit is to stick broadly to factual stories, and to mediate comment through the prism of reviews of other media. Meanwhile, the news that the Conservatives were first 'expected to', and then actually did, call for a Commons statement was reported but given relatively little prominence. This was perhaps as a result of its procedural predictability; and also because there had been little direct party political discourse or debate around the story, thus providing a slender context for the call.

An alternative to the Russian media reviews was provided by the story excerpting comments from the BBC's own 'Have Your Say' message boards. Tellingly, prominence is given to one which relates directly to the way audiences react to news media. Ivan Obzherin in Russia is quoted as saying: 'People accusing someone else without proof, trusting in everything that is written in newspapers – isn't that from Russian history, from the times of Stalin?' while Harry from Farnham asks: 'Is the media trying to stir up animosity towards Russia in the same way that it did during the Cold War?'.

(Continued)

happen in contemporary London, it is because President Putin's regime is still behaving as it did during the Cold War. Glasnost may have been celebrated but, as we report today, Russian spies are still alive and well and working in Britain'.

So by the weekend of 2–3 December, the story was beginning to dip again. Yet the story continued to command print headlines and to be reported on every major broadcast news service, although it was becoming apparent that new information has more or less been exhausted. In news terms the story was heading back to where it had been immediately before Mr Litvinenko's death had revived interest in the story. There is a likelihood that news editors across all media forms and platforms, while retaining an interest in the events as they continued to unfold, were hoping that another major story would break so that they could quietly let the story drop, without being the first to blink.

Note

1 The McCarthy era ran from the creation of the Tydings Committee, itself a sub-committee of the Senate Foreign Relations Committee established in February 1950 to conduct 'a full and complete study and investigation as to whether persons who are disloyal to the United States are, or have been, employed by the Department of State.' This was intended to be a wide-ranging investigation into 'anti-American activity' and was inspired by the fear of communism, subsequent to Stalin's change of side from ally to enemy in the closing stages of the Second World War. The prevalent fear at the time was the so-called Domino Theory, whereby if one of the Pacific Rim states fell to

The rest of the second week was dominated by the 'radiation trail'. 'Trio in clinic after spy's death' (27 November). 'Five sites tested in spy inquiry' (28 November), 'Eight tested over radiation alert' (28 November). 'New locations tested in spy probe' (29 November), BA passengers in radiation alert (29 November). 'Radiation "found at 12 locations"' (30 November). The other news lines followed were: 'BA passengers not getting help' (30 November), and 'Spy post mortem due to take place' (1 December). Journalistic 'quality checks' on the availability and usefulness of helpline information has become a common feature after major incidents. The reported shortcomings of the response after the Boxing Day tsunami of 2004 were still attracting journalistic attention two years later. In this instance, the refusal of the NHS Direct line to provide information to Britons ringing from abroad, and the paucity of information provided even to those ringing from within the UK, were the angles focused on.

As the 'radiation trail' angle played itself out, a brief lull in the perceived potency of the story was filled on the Friday 1 December by two tried-and-tested journalistic devices: 'Russian TV tracks radiation probe', and 'Q&A: Spy death investigation'. The questions posed were: Could it have been suicide? What is significant about the use of polonium-210? Is there still Russian spying activity going on in Britain? and, heralding the latest new line, Will Mario Scaramella … testing positive for polonium-210 help the investigation?

After the run of stories dealing with radiation alerts at specific locations, and a few specific write-ups about venues being given the all-clear, it was decided that the role and communism, they would all do so, leading to an absolute disruption of the still-fragile world peace. It was later to lead to the deployment of US military forces in Korea and Vietnam.

McCarthy, a member of the Tydings Committee, seized the moment, and began a campaign, hiding behind the authority vested in the committee, to winkle out every communist or communist sympathiser in the USA's administration. Freewheeling and fuelled by that most dangerous cocktail of paranoia, power and hatred of anything that could upset the capitalist system, he single-handedly destroyed a number of prominent careers. Once he started to investigate the US Army, though, it was realised that he was totally out of control, and by the time he moved on to elected members of government he was brought down. He became a discredited and disillusioned man, and died in 1957 of illness allegedly related to alcoholism. For an easily-digested, yet informed, insight into McCarthyism, it is worth watching the 2005 film *Good Night and Good Luck*, directed by George Clooney. Those interested in the genesis of Domino Theory might benefit from reading Graham Greene's *The Quiet American* (1955).

background of Mr Scaramella would hold the line, and provide fresh impetus. His health: 'Dead spy's contact "doing well"' and background 'Spyfinder Scaramella in spotlight' provided just enough to sustain a presence over the third weekend of sustained BBC Online coverage (2–3 December) while major new developments were awaited.

These were eventually to come in the form of UK police investigative activity – both domestic and in Russia itself, 'UK spy probe police go to Russia' (4 December) and 'Spy probe focuses on two capitals' (5 December) signalled both the continuing presence of the story (though no longer automatically in or near 'prime' position on the news site), and the opening of a distinct new phase of the journalistic operation. The remains of the previous lead lines (Scaramella and the radiation checks) continued to be included in the write-ups, but usually in the later paragraphs.

As the story entered its fourth week, and its third week in the mainstream media, it was entering that slightly ambiguous news territory where a story has clearly established itself as a near-automatic candidate for coverage, but where the pace of events does not always follow the demands of a 24-hour news cycle. A story that has had almost automatic entrée into the news agenda reaches a point where its very ubiquity can cause a backlash. The entry bar is placed much higher, and that automatic access is replaced by a higher-than-usual 'entry requirement'. Either by design or by a sort of institutional osmosis, a collective view emerges that a story has been 'done'; and only something very unusual can now justify its inclusion. That point had not yet been reached, but felt as if it may be near.

Conclusion

And finally... The case has been made
for a fresh approach to the news
value system

The case for a revised set of values has, we feel, been made; in the times when Galtung and Ruge were developing their theories there was no internet, no spin doctoring (although there were pubic relations activities in commerce which were geared to promote the interests of their employers at whatever cost might be applied to the public) and no rolling news. And the notion of citizen-journalism and its sibling user-generated content was still a couple of generations away.

Yet despite the Jeremiahs who might have us believe that we are all doomed, and that there will no longer be a place for professional journalists, the opposite holds true – there has never been a greater need for those who fully understand the nuanced nature of what the public expects as news. Yes, the public has an active role to play in the basic process of gathering news – but this is not something new, it was ever thus. It is simply that the blog and email have replaced traditional readers' letters as the mechanism for the public to inform editors of their feelings. And along with that role of public contribution comes the requirement that the content will be checked for validity and reliability, shaped, contextualised and eventually turned into something that is of value and significance to all who read or watch or listen to it. Otherwise it is not as valuable as the contributors might consider it to be.

But this revision of the news value system is concerned with more than just citizen journalism. The system of rolling news is here to stay – both in broadcast and online/print media – and this has brought with it its own problems. The need to constantly tweak and layer news stories can, as our analysis of the Litvinenko saga proves, lead to a dropping of standards, to the seizing on of rumour and suggestion and its metamorphosis into 'fact' – only for some of those 'facts' to be exposed as nothing of the sort shortly afterwards. This is a worrying trend, one which can lead to further erosion of the already-limited trust that some members of the public place in journalists; a 2005 Mori poll reported that: 'Just 16 per cent of British adults trust journalists to tell the truth ... the figure was even lower than the 20 per cent scored by politicians and left journalists at the bottom of the scale' (Dresser, 2006). Yet interestingly, more than 60 per cent of those polled said that they placed trust in news-readers to tell the truth. Which leads to the conclusion that the vast majority of the public do not realise that the words spoken by television news readers (and presumably the same level of trust applies to radio news broadcasters) have been gathered, verified, analysed, contextualised and ultimately written for them by journalists, and that the newsreaders themselves almost invari-ably contribute directly to that process.

What has emerged from our studies is that the majority of news is managed through a journalistic system which is essentially honest; any corruption comes from the impositions of a system that seems to chase viewer ratings and page impressions, rating the results of the daily, weekly, monthly or six-monthly figures higher than the content which leads to the reader–viewer attraction. At the risk of devolving into a rant about media ownership and hegemony, perhaps there is something in Noam Chomsky's perception that media systems are part of the corporate system and that: 'Corporations are basically tyrannies, hierarchic, controled [sic] from above. If you don't like what they are doing you get out. The major media are just part of that system' (Chomsky, 1997). Or is there less to such a conspiracy theory than meets the eye? It could just as easily be that, in a quest to ensure that nobody misses out on the big story that everybody else has, no journalist can appear to be less on top of the 'facts' than anybody else.

Clearly, many other factors in the news landscape are changing rapidly and continually. The relationship between news providers and news receivers – between journalists and audiences – is much more complex and polyvalent than before. Indeed, as has been argued, it is our belief that much of contem-porary journalism is geared towards reinterpreting that relationship *to the audience itself*. The discussion of User Generated Content and/or Citizen Journalism is predicated on the basis that the activity is as much about per-suading the audience of that change as it is about changing the nature of jour-nalism itself.

And are we still dealing with News in the accepted sense? Or should we redefine the very name of the commodity itself? Robert Cauthorn, CEO of City Tools, says:

> We need to forget news, we have to get away from the idea of news and get back to stories.
>
> Our readers think of stories; news is an alien concept, stories are interesting. News is a terrible fate for a story to fall into. (Journalism.co.uk, 9 November 2006)

It may not be necessary to subscribe fully to Cauthorn's thesis. It is certainly true, however, that many broadcast journalists are being encouraged to envisage themselves more as narrators than as news breakers. Some see this as a corollary of a move towards 'human interest' agendas as against the automatic reporting of the activities of power elites. It is unnecessary to equate this with what is often called 'dumbing down' or infotainment. It is, however, a significant reconfiguration of what makes news and how news professionals work.

Much of this is beginning to be widely discussed and appreciated. Perhaps less so is the 21st Century version of what Galtung and Ruge referred to as 'Composition'. Part of the purpose of this book has been to attempt to unravel some of the conscious and unconscious motivations which may be at work in the formulation of news output. Positioning, inclusion or exclusion, and juxtapositions are all filtered through aesthetic criteria to an extent greater than is widely appreciated. Journalists have always been wary of theoretical models which seek to account for these decisions and processes and frankly, there is still relatively little discussion of such factors in newsroom environments. Despite the proliferation of media and journalism courses, awareness (or memory) of such theoretical models seemingly remains low. Perhaps understandably, journalists also remain resistant to the notion – implied if not stated by some academic writers on the subject – that they are pawns on the chessboard of a clash of ideologies or power structures of which they are only dimly aware. Even the more benign versions – that they are routinised or socialised into an unconscious perpetuation of the status quo, or of global market capitalism, or of the self-selecting power elites and over-represented voices – is regarded as patronising and inaccurate by the more reflective practitioners.

What we have attempted to do is to bridge at least part of that gap: and to do so by close individual output analysis. This is almost more important than our attempt to update and reconfigure Galtung and Ruge's criteria for the 21st Century. Anyone who studies journalism needs an awareness of the pressures, motivations and compromises that operate in the construction of news output. And, for those who aspire to make the leap from student to practitioner, it is helpful to realise that the approaches taken in academic study are not there simply to be discarded as soon as the move is made from student to professional.

What remains is our appreciation that a theoretical framework for the analysis of news may have little direct application in the heat of a newsroom; it is a system which helps explain what makes news newsworthy for the benefit of students and analysts of all media forms. In the hourly battle to make sense of events, to check, contextualise and explain them – regardless of deadlines – the journalist will still be working mostly by instinct. Reiterating what has been said to both authors on countless occasions during the research process of this book, the response to the question 'why is this news?' may well remain: 'It just is!'.

References

Adie, K. (2002) *The Kindness of Strangers*. London: Headline.

Alden, C. (ed.) (2006) *Media Directory 2006*. London: MediaGuardian.

Allan, S. (2004) *News Culture*. Maidenhead: Oxford University Press.

Allan, S. (ed.) (2005) *Journalism: Critical Issues*. Maidenhead: Oxford University Press.

Anderson, B. A. (2004) *Newsflash*. San Francisco: Jossey Bass.

Arthur, C. (2006) News is personal in a connected world, Media Guardian, 19 June.

Associated, Press Reporter (2006) *Bloggers to join the Mainstream* Wired, 10 April.

Auletta, K. (2004) *Media Man: Ted Turners Improbable Empire*. New York: WW Norton.

Bale, P. (2006) Personalisation of the newspaper: good or bad? Editors Weblog, 9 May, www.editorsweblog.org.

Bell, A. (1991) *The Language of News Media*. Oxford: Blackwell.

Bell, M. (2004) *Through Gates of Fire: A Journey Through World Disorder*. London: Phoenix.

Benn, T. (1981) *Arguments for Democracy*. London: Jonathan Cape.

Bourdieu, P. (1998) *On Television and Journalism*. London: Pluto.

Bowen, J. (2006) *War Stories*. London: Simon and Schuster.

Buerk, M. (2004) *The Road Taken*. London: Arrow.

Burke, E. (1769) *Observations on the present state of the nation,* in E. Kramnick (1999) *The Portable Edmund Burke*. Harmondsworth: Penguin.

Burton, G. (2005) *Media and Society: Critical Perspectives*. Maidenhead: Oxford University Press.

Carlyle, T. (1841) On Heroes and Hero Worship and the Heroic in History (1997 e-version, New York: Gutenburg Project).

Celant, G. (1994) *The Italian Metamorphosis, 1943–1968*. New York: Guggenheim Museum Publications

Chabanenko, S. (2006) *Isotope that Killed Litvinenko Sold Freely in U.S.* Kommersant 30 November 2006.

Chartered Institute of Public Relations: www.cipr.co.uk

Chomsky, N. (1997) What makes mainstream media mainstream? From a talk at Z Media Institute, New York: http://www.zmag.org/zmag/articles/chomoct97.htm

Clifford, M. and Levin, A. (2005) *Max Clifford: Read All About It*. London: Virgin Books.

Cohen, S. and Young, J. (eds) (1981) *The Manufacture of News: Deviance, Social Problems and the Mass Media* (2nd edn). London: Constable. pp. 69–90.

Cornwell, C. (2006) *BBC regional TV news network to benefit local press, says chief*. The Scotsman 7 November 2006.

Cottle, S. (ed) (2003) *News, Public Relations and Power*. London: Sage

Davies, H. (1998) *Born 1900: A Human History of the 20th Century – For Everyone Who was There*. London: Little, Brow.

Day, R. (1989) *Grand Inquisitor*. London: Pan.

Dresser, G. (2006) Polls fuel debate over trust in the media, Reuters, 27 April.

Dyke, G. (2004) *Inside Story*. London: Harper Collins.

Columbia Journalism Review Editorial. All that glitters: how years of monopoly undermined newspapers, March/April.

Economist Media Pack – available on request from the publishers via www.economist.com

Este, J. and Sainsbury M. (2006) Web before print for Guardian, *The Australian*, 15 June.

Fleming, C, Moore G. and Welford D. (2006) *An Introduction to Journalism*. London: Sage.

Fletcher, K. (2006) On the press: the web trail, MediaGuardian, 12 June.

Fowler, R. (1991) *Language in the News.* London: Routledge.

Frankel, G. (2004) Full exposure: PR king spins news for cash to brit tabloids, Washington Post, 21 May.

Freedland, J. (2003) *Can a Newspaper Make Peace? The role of the press in ending conflict* Hetherington Memorial Lecture, University of Stirling, 22 October 2003.

Friedman, T. (2006) *The World is Flat* (2nd edn). Harmondsworth: Penguin.

Galtung, J. and Ruge, M. (1965) Structuring and selecting news, in S. Cohen, and J. Young (eds) (1973) *The Manufacture of News: Deviance, Social problems and the Mass Media* Communication and Society Series, 4th Edn. London: Constable. pp. 52–64.

Gamble, A. (2005) The right to return to life: www. citized.info/pdf/commarticles/James _ Shoesmith.pdf.

Gans, H. J. (1979) *Deciding What's News,* Evanston, I'll: Northwestern University Press.

Gans, H. J. (2004) *Deciding What's News: A Study of CBS Evening News, NBC Nightly News, Newsweek, and Time*. Evanson, IL: Northwestern University Press.

Gardham, D. (2006) *Man who leads group accused of killing ex-spy* Daily Telegraph 2 December 2006

Gillmor, D. (2006) *We the Media: Grassroots Journalism by the People, for the people*. Sebastopol: O'Reilly.

Gillmor, D (2006–2) http://citmedia.org/blog/2006/04/02/straw-men-versus-citizen-journalists/

Goodchild, S. and Elliott, F. (2006) *Litvinenko: police probe claims he may have killed himself* Independent on Sunday 26 November 2006.

Greenslade, R. (2003) *Press Gang: How Newspapers Make Profits from Propaganda*. London: Macmillan.

Grossman, L. (1995) *What's news?*: web.mit.edu/cms/reconstructions/interpretations/

Grunig, J. and Hunt, T. (1984) *Managing Public Relations*. New York: Holt, Rinehart & Winston.

Hachten W. A. and Scotton, J. F. (2007) *The World News Prism*. Oxford: Blackwell.

Hall, S. (1981) The determination of news photographs, in S. Cohen and J. Young (eds) *The Manufacture of News: Deviance, Social Problems and the Mass Media* (2nd edn). London: Constable. pp. 226–43.

Hall, S., Chritcher, C., Jefferson, T., Clarke, J. and Robects, B. (1981) The social production of news, in S. Cohen and J. Young (eds) *The Manufacture of News: Deviance, Social Problems and the Mass Media* (2nd edn). London: Constable. pp. 33–63.

Hamilton, M. (2006) Debating that deadline: www.tamark.ca/students/?p=2391

Harcup, T. (2004) *Journalism: Principles and Practice*. London: Sage.

Harcup, T. (2007) *The Ethical Journalist*. London: Sage.

Harcup, T. and O'Neill, D. (2001) What is News? Galtung and Ruge Revisited. *Journalism Studies*, 2 (2): 261–280.

Hargreaves, I. (2003) *Journalism: Truth or Dare*. Oxford: Oxford University Press.

Harlow, R. (1976) Building a definition of public relations, *Public Relations Review*, 2 (4): xx

Harrison, J. (2000) *Terrestrial TV News in Britain.* Manchester: Manchester University Press.

Harrison, J. (2006) *News*. Abingdon: Routledge.

Hartley, J, (1982) *Understanding News*. London: Methuen.

Hastings, M. (2002) *Editor: An Inside Story of Newspapers*. London: Macmillan.

Hayes, W. (1990) *Henry: A Life of Henry Ford II*. London: Weidenfeld & Nicholson.

Hellman, L. (1978) *Six Plays* New York: Random House.

Hetherington, A. (1985) *News, Newspapers and Television*. London: Macmillan.

Hewitt, G. (2005) *A Soul on Ice*. London: Macmillan.

Heyward, A. (2006) *Is the rôle of editors more or less important in the digital age?:* www.edit; crosweblog 17 March.

Horrie, C. (2003) *Tabloid Nation: From the Birth of the Daily Mirror to the Death of the Tabloid*. London: Andre Deutsch.

Jardin, X. (nd) http://www.artfutura.org/02/A_Xeni.html.

Jenkins, R. (2001) *Churchill*. London: Macmillan.

Jowell, T. (2006) *A public service for all: the BBC in the digital age*. London: HMSO.

Karim, K. H. (2000) *Islamic Peril: Media and Global Violence* Montreal: Rowman and Littlefield.

Keane, F. (2005) *All Of These People: A Memoir*. London: HarperCollins

Kelly, M. (1993) *Martyrs' Day: Chronicle of Small War*. New York: Random House; (London: Picador.

Kelner, S. (2006) statement, *Independent Media Pack*.

Kommersant (2006) URL laddress from p. 216

Krull, S. (2006) http://news.bbc.co.uk/l/hi/world/europe/4566826.stm

Lacey, R. (1986) *Ford*. London: Heinemann.

di Lampedusa, G. (1960) *The Leopard* (Colquhoun translation). New York: Pantheon.

Land Mobile Media Pack – available on request from the publishers via www.landmobile. co.uk/advertisers/media-pack

Lee, L. (1975) Writing autobiography, in L. bee, *I Can't Stay Long*. Harmondsworth: Penguin.

Lemann, N. (2006) Amateur Hour: Journalism without journalists, *The New Yorker,* 7 & 14 August: pp. 44–49.

Liebling, A. J. (1956) *A Talkative Something or Other*. The New Yorker 7 April 1956.

Lu Stout, K. (2006) Korean bloggers making a difference, 31 March: www.edition. cnn.com

Luft, O. (2006) US experiment in citizen journalism offers alternative model for local news reporting, 6 July: www.journalism.co.uk.

Luft, O. (2006–2) The philosophy behind the integrated newsroom, 6 October: www.journalism.co.uk

Luft, O. (2006–3) Internet-first publishing does not mean the death of newspapers, 19 June: www.journalism.co.uk.

Luft, O. (2006–4) Newspapers need to 'forget about news', 9 November: www.journalism.co.uk 9

Lule, J. (2001) *Daily News, Eternal Stories: The Mythological rôle of Journalism*. New York: Guilford Press.

Macmillan, A. (2006) It really was 'the Sun wot won it' for Tories, *Scotland on Sunday*, 21 January.

MacShane, D. (1979) *Using the Media*. London: Pluto Press.

Marr, A. (2004) *My Trade: A Short History of British Journalism*. London: Macmillan.

Marrin, M. (1993) *No to Feather Dusters* Sunday Telegraph 2 May 1993.

Marx, K. and Engels, F. (1987 edn) *The Communist Manifesto*. London: Pathfinder.

Matheson, D. (2004) Weblogs and the epistemology of the news: some trends in online journalism, *New Media and Society*, (6): 440–68.

Mayes, I. (2006) *Open door* The *Guardian*, 25 March.

McChesney, R. (1999) *Rich media, Poor Democracy: Communication Politics in Dubious Times*. New York: New Press.

McChesney, R. (2004) *The Problem of the Media: US communication politics in the 21st Century*. New York: Monthly Review Press.

McGinty, S. (2006) *Former Russian spy dies in hospital as mystery over 'poisoning' deepens* The Scotsman 24 November 2006.

McIntosh, N. (2006) Have I Got News For You, *MediaGuardian*, 20 March.

McIntyre, I. (2006) Bloggers Beware The *Star*, 2 August.

Morgan, P. (2005) *The Insider: The Private Diaries of a Scandalous Decade*. London: Ebury.

Mould, D. and Schuster, E. (1999) Central Asia: ethics – a western luxury?, In M. Kunczik (ed.) *Ethics In Journalism: A Reader on Their Perception in the Third World*. Bonn: Friedrich-Ebert-Stiftung.

Newspaper Society www.newspapersoc.org.uk/Default.aspx?page=1920.

O'Brien, J. (2006) Why blogs need a health warning MediaGuardian, 24 April.

O'Hagan, A. (2005) MediaGuardian, 17 September.

Orwell, G. (1946) *Why I Write*. Harmondsworth: Penguin.

Page, B. (2003) *The Murdoch Archipelago*. London: Simon & Schuster.

Page, N. (2005) 'Reality television' and the American reality that produces it: http://www.wsws.org/articles/2005/mar2005/real-m31.shtml

Palser, B. (2005) Journalism's back seat drivers *American Journalism Review*, August–September 27 (4): 42.

Paxman, J. (2002) *The Political Animal*. Harmondsworth: Penguin.

Payack, P. (2005) Unprecedented global media outpouring in coverage of Pope John Paul II's passing *Global Language Monitor*, 14 April.

Pearson, K. (2006) Citizen journalists are among those targeted as press freedoms erode around the globe *Online Journalism Review*, 8 December.

Preston, J. (2005) *Max Clifford exposed!* Sunday Telegraph Review 25 September 2005.

Price, L. (2005) *The Spin Doctor's Diary: Inside Number 10 with New Labour*. London: Hodder & Stoughton.

Radcliffe, S. (ed.) (2000) *The Oxford Dictionary of Thematic Quotations*. Oxford: Oxford University Press.

Randall, D. (2000) *The Universal Journalist* (2nd edn). London: Pluto.

Raynsford, J. (2003) http://www.journalism.co.uk/features/story604.shtml

Reevell, P. (2006) Keeping television local, *Television*, March, 43 (3): xx.

Roshco, B. (1975) *Newsmaking*. Chicago: University of Chicago Press.

Sandman, P. (1993) *Responding to Community Outrage*. Fairfax: American Industrial Hygiene Association.

Schlesinger, P. (1978) *Putting 'Reality' Together*. London: Constable.

Schlosser, E. (2001) Fast *Food Nation: Tlie Dark Side of the All-American Meal*. New York: Houghton Mifflin.

Schudson, M. (2003) *The Sociology of News*. New York: W H Norton.

Scott, C. P. (1921) Leader, *Manchester Guardian*, 5 May.

Silver, J. (2005) Max Clifford: the dirt-disher comes clean The *Independent,* 15 August.

Simpson, J. (1998) *Strange Places, Questionable People*. London: Pan.

Simpson, J. (2000) *A Mad World, My Masters: Tales From a Traveller's Life*. London: Pan.

Simpson, J. (2002) *News From No Man's Land: Reporting the World* London: Macmillan.

Smolkin, R. (2006) Too transparent?, *American Journalism Review,* April/May:. xx

Snow, J. (2004) *Shooting History: A Personal Journey.* London: Harper Collins.

Stabe, M. (2006a) Public input will 'liberate journalism' predicts Snow, *UK Press Gazette*, 30 March.

Stabe, M. (2006b) User content key for Trinity Mirror's regionals says multimedia chief *UK Press Gazette*, 17 August.

Stanshall, V. (1978) *Sir Henry at Rawlinson End* London: Charisma audio CD.

Stewart, G. (2005) *The History of The Times, Volume VII: The Murdoch Years*. London: Harper Collins.

Storey, G. (1951) *Reuters' Century*. London: Max Parrish.

Tench, R. and Yeomans, L. (2006) *Exploring Public Relations* London: Prentice Hall.

Thompson, M. (2006a) BBC Statements of Programme Policy 2006–7 London: BBC.

Thompson, M. (2006b) *BBC 2.0: why on demand changes everything* Royal Television Society Baird Lecture, Birmingham University 22 March 2006.

Tuchman, G. (1978) *Making News: A Study in the Construction of Reality*. New York: The Free Press.

Tunstall, J. (1971) *Journalists at Work*. London: Constable.

Venables, J. (2005) *Making Headlines*. Huntingdon: Elm.

Watson, J. and Hill, A. (2006) *Dictionary of Media and Communication Studies* (7th edn). London: Hodder Arnold.

Whaley, D. (2001) Reality television, *Education Age*, 15 August.

Wilde, O. (1998) *The Importance of Being Earnest and other plays*. Oxford: Oxford Paperbacks.

Woodward, S. (2005) Annual Programme Statement 2005 and Programme Review 2004. Manchester: ITV Publications

Wyatt, W. (1997) in B. Page (2003) *The Murdoch Archipelago*. London: Simon & Schuster p. 425.

Young, J. (1981) Beyond the consensual paradigm: a critique of left functionalism, in B. Cohen and J. Young (eds) *The Manufacture of News: Deviance, Social Problems and the Mass Media* (2nd edn). London: Constable. pp. 393–421.

www.bbc.co.uk/news/editors blogs.

www.editorsweblog.org/analysis//2006/12/cooperation_between_newspapers_and_blogs.php.

www.fabian-society.org.uk/documents/ViewADocument.asp?ID=117&CatID=52

www.newspapersoc.org.uk/Default.aspx?page=777#electronic

Index